Critical Acclaim for
PORTRAIT OF A MONSTER

"This well-detailed book is disturbing and haunting in its revelations of a self-centered cad with a dark side."
—*Publishers Weekly*

"Journalists Pulitzer and Thompson zero in on Joran van der Sloot, a wealthy young man suspected of killing two young women within five years to the day of each other. . . . This true-crime account delivers excellent and gripping reporting of the crimes and the manhunt." —*Booklist*

"A thorough, journalistic recounting of two crimes, five years apart, linked by the same alleged perpetrator. . . . A worthwhile read for true-crime fans and followers of the case." —*Kirkus Reviews*

"Chilling. Disturbing. Captivating . . . *Portrait of a Monster* is a fantastic read." —*True Crime Book Reviews*

Also by Lisa Pulitzer

Stolen Innocence (with Elissa Wall)
The Daughters of Juárez
(with Teresa Rodriguez and Diana Montané)
Murder in Paradise
Fatal Romance
A Woman Scorned
Crossing the Line (with Joan Swirsky)
Crime on Deadline (with foreword by Edna Buchanan)

Also by Cole Thompson

A Deadly Game (with Catherine Crier)
Final Analysis (with Catherine Crier)

PORTRAIT OF A MONSTER

Jordan van der Sloot, a Murder in Peru,
and the Natalee Holloway Mystery

Lisa Pulitzer and Cole Thompson

St. Martin's Paperbacks

PORTRAIT OF A MONSTER

Copyright © 2011 by Lisa Pulitzer and Cole Thompson.

For information address St. Martin's Press, 175 Fifth Avenue, New York, NY 10010.

ISBN: 978-1-250-01185-5

Printed in the United States of America

St. Martin's Press edition / July 2011
St. Martin's Paperbacks edition / February 2012

St. Martin's Paperbacks are published by St. Martin's Press, 175 Fifth Avenue, New York, NY 10010.

10 9 8 7 6 5 4 3 2 1

A NOTE ON SOURCES

This book is based on scores of interviews and several thousand pages of police reports. We traveled in Aruba and Peru. We interviewed police, attorneys, witnesses, family members, scientific experts, and others tied to the story. We also made use of newspaper articles, television reports, and books written about the case. There are no fictional or "composite characters." Certain events, sequences, and conversations were reconstructed from a synthesis of all the evidence, including the confessions, police reports, witness statements, interviews with participants, and other information.

PROLOGUE

The frantic call came in just before midnight to the front desk of Lima's Hotel Tac, a budget lodging on the edge of the city's tourist district of Miraflores.

That night, nineteen-year-old receptionist Adeli Marchena picked up the line.

"Mr. Van der Sloot, Room 309, please," the caller said.

Adeli checked the computer to confirm that the man was still registered, as she did with all inbound calls, and then transferred the line to his room. About a minute passed when the call bounced back to the receptionist.

"I'm sorry, there's no answer," Adeli told the female caller.

Glancing at the room keys hanging on hooks behind her station, she noticed the one for Room 309 was missing. Since all guests were encouraged to leave their room keys at the reception desk when leaving the hotel and collect them upon their return, she assumed Mr. Van der Sloot must be upstairs resting. He'd been at the hotel for more than two weeks, and she'd become familiar with his comings and goings. She'd been the one to check him in when he arrived at the hotel early on the morning of May 14, carrying a duffel bag and several other items. He was one of just five guests to check in that day, and the only foreigner.

Although the Hotel Tac catered mainly to Peruvians, tourists from Spain, Portugal, Colombia, Brazil, Ecuador, and even Switzerland lodged at the establishment during the first half of May. Many of the city's visitors were merely transients passing through Lima on their way to Cuzco and the lost Incan city of Machu Picchu, discovered on a mountain ridge some eight thousand feet above sea level. Most travelers opted for the convenience of staying in the commercial district close to the casinos and shopping malls, but budget-conscious visitors chose more affordable lodgings such as the Hotel Tac, located on the outskirts of the main tourist area of Miraflores.

Tourism was the lifeblood of the area and every measure was taken to keep the out-of-towners safe. The eighty-room Hotel Tac had security cameras in the lobby and strategically positioned on each of its seven floors. The reception area was manned twenty-four hours a day.

Adeli worked six nights a week. Her shifts began at 8:00 P.M. and ended at eight the following morning. Over the past two weeks, she'd seen more of Joran van der Sloot than she had of any of the other guests at the hotel. The Dutchman kept strange hours, typically leaving the hotel near midnight and returning some time around dawn. Standing six feet four, with a pale complexion, angular features, and piercing brown eyes, the twenty-two-year-old cut a striking image. Adeli remembered him well. Peruvians tend to have black hair, olive skin, and, for the most part, rarely break the six-foot mark. This foreigner was the polar opposite.

After he handed her a Dutch passport, Adeli copied the young man's name and particulars into the guest book and into the hotel's computer, Joran Andreas Petrus van der Sloot, born August 6, 1987, passport number NWJ77F425.

Chain-smoking, unshaven, and quiet, the brown-haired guest in Room 309 was a night owl and a loner. Although tourists traveling alone were the exception, those who did tended to enjoy chatting with the women behind the desk, practicing their broken Spanish, and inquiring about the historical and cultural sites to explore outside the confines of the hotel. Questions such as "Are you from Lima? . . . Have you ever been to Cuzco? . . . Are there any cool bars nearby?" were happily addressed by the hotel staff. The young man in Room 309, however, was all business. Other than the occasional thank you or hello, he hadn't once engaged Adeli in small talk during his two-week stay.

Mr. Van der Sloot had opted for the cheapest rate, fifty nuevos soles for a small, third-floor accommodation with a TV and private bath and sporadic chambermaid service. That's the equivalent of about eighteen U.S. dollars. Unlike most tourists, he paid in cash for the first night, and came back to her several times to settle his bill—also using cash.

Adeli told the caller she imagined the guest in Room 309 must be sleeping—it was past midnight, after all. But the caller persisted. She wanted to know when the receptionist had last seen him. Thinking back, Adeli realized it had been several days since he had returned to the hotel, most recently in the company of a young Peruvian woman. It was after 5:00 A.M. when the two had gone upstairs together, but their behavior did not seem indicative of a lovers' tryst. Mr. Van der Sloot was leading and the young woman followed several steps behind him as they started for the staircase. Working in a small hotel was a bit like watching one of her *novelas* (soap operas) on television. There was little that escaped the clerk's inquisitive eye.

Adeli had seen the Dutchman a second time that same morning when she was on her way home from her shift. It was just after 8:00 A.M. when the two crossed paths on the sidewalk a half block from the hotel. He was carrying what looked like two paper cups of coffee, and nodded a hello as she passed in the company of her coworker Juan. She realized it had been three days since their sidewalk encounter and she hadn't seen him again since that morning.

Feeling uneasy, Adeli hung up the phone and returned to her computer registry. It was then that she noticed that

Mr. Van der Sloot was two days behind on his hotel bill. Though it was already past midnight, she couldn't let this slide. She'd only been working at the hotel for a short time, and didn't want to jeopardize her meager $280 a month salary. A hotel job in Miraflores was certainly better than any job she'd find in her own neighborhood of Chorillos, where she'd grown up in the shadow of the Santa Monica Penitentiary for Women.

At 12:30 A.M., Adeli headed up the stairs to Room 309 to ask Mr. Van der Sloot to settle the bill. She knocked several times. There was no answer. Standing in the hallway, she could hear that a TV or radio was on inside the room, but when no one came to the door she decided not to disturb the guest further. Returning to the first floor, she found Iris, the night manager, and explained the situation.

"Take a copy of the room key and go back upstairs and open the door," Iris instructed.

Adeli was a bit apprehensive as she slid the key into the lock, and slowly opened the door. She was worried about intruding on a guest. A foul smell overwhelmed her as she stepped across the threshold. She noticed that the TV on the table directly in front of her had been left on. Empty soda bottles, cigarette butts, and coffee cups covered the tabletop. It was the beginning of the Peruvian winter and the room felt cold. A window across the room had been left open and a nylon curtain swayed in the breeze. The queen-size bed was in disarray; the mattress was askew revealing the wooden slats of the bed frame. The sheets were balled up in a heap on the floor between the mattress and the TV table, and clothing, a tennis racket, and a pair of sneakers were mixed in with the bed linens. The room was in shambles, but at least it appeared the hotel guest hadn't skipped out without paying the bill.

As Adeli stood in the doorway scanning the room and wondering what had happened to Mr. Van der Sloot, she felt an eerie presence. Turning to her right, she caught sight of a person sprawled out on the floor. She gasped, and with her heart racing, she stepped farther into the room to get a better look. She assumed it was the Dutchman. But getting closer, she saw that the person had long, black, wavy hair and was drenched in blood. This was a woman. And she was dead.

The body was bloated and badly disfigured. There was what appeared to be dried blood around the woman's nose. Whoever this was, she had clearly met a violent death. The corpse looked posed in an almost sexual manner; the legs were bent at the knee and apart, exposing red panties. The upper torso was dressed in a dark-colored T-shirt and partially covered with a white jacket that, like the body, was soaked in dried blood. The grisly sight was too much for the young receptionist to process. Confused and overwhelmed, Adeli backed away from the corpse, paused to switch off the television, and ran screaming into the hall.

The ghastly scene that Adeli uncovered would not only launch a murder investigation, but spark an international manhunt for a manipulative and callous fugitive connected to a tragic event on a small Caribbean island exactly five years earlier.

At the center of it all was a young man with a promising future, whose charm and manipulation helped him elude detention for years—until his spree came to an abrupt halt on June 3, 2010. Night receptionists, cabdrivers, security guards working double shifts—all found themselves in the spotlight due to their chance encounters with the Dutch national.

The criminal case against Joran, whose arrogance had captivated the media for years, would span four continents and involve law enforcement agencies around the globe, ultimately climaxing in Room 309 of a low-end Peruvian hotel.

ONE

MAY 30, 2010
LIMA, PERU

Ricardo Flores was an early riser, even on Sundays. Cracking open the door to his daughter's bedroom, he saw that she hadn't come home from her night out with friends. Her bed was still made and arranged with the stuffed teddy bears she loved and collected.

The fifty-eight-year-old remembered his youth when kids still had curfews. These days, the parties continued well past dawn. He only had a few ground rules with Stephany but checking in was one of them. She hadn't even left a message about her whereabouts. She was going to get an earful when she did report in.

The last time Ricardo had spoken to his daughter was the previous evening. He'd reached her on her cell just before 10 P.M. to invite her to an impromptu family dinner at a grill not far from the Floreses' home in Santiago de Surco. Stephany told her father she was hanging out with friends in Larcomar, a three-level mall of boutiques, eateries, and movie theaters carved into the cliff at the edge of Miraflores, overlooking the Pacific Ocean.

By day, Miraflores was a bustling place full of foreigners eager to see the sights. A half-hour drive from Jorge Chávez International Airport, Miraflores catered to both well-heeled travelers residing in four-star hotels on the cliffs overlooking the Pacific Ocean and backpackers flopping in cheap hostels. Special tourist police and English-friendly information booths sought to give the place a feeling of calm and safety amid the polluted chaos that was greater metropolitan Lima.

In the district's central square, Parque Kennedy, olive-skinned women in colorful Indian garb sold traditional indigenous paintings, tapestries, and other knickknacks. "Hey Mee-stir" or "Hey Lay-dee," they would call out, employing the little English they knew. Camera-toting travelers from all points of the globe would stand in line, tickets in hand, for seats on the red double-decker Mirabuses to explore a myriad of museums, pre-Incan ruins, and even catacombs buried deep beneath an ancient Spanish monastery farther downtown. At lunchtime, barkers with broad friendly smiles would stand on the sidewalks corralling hungry foreigners into relatively inexpensive cafés to feast on enormous plates of ceviche, *pinchos,* and Chifa, a wild fusion of traditional Peruvian and Chinese cuisine. Restaurants were equipped with special hooks on the underside of tables to keep purses, knapsacks, and cameras away from street thieves.

The intoxicating smells of lunchtime, the biggest meal of the day, almost masked the thick odor of exhaust that hovered over the city; trapped between the cool winds of the Pacific and the foothills of the Andes on the other side of town, the sickening, damp, polluted air had no place to go. To say the air quality was poor was an understatement. From June through December, a thick, gray fog, known as "*la garúa,*" hung over the city, obscuring what would otherwise be spectacular views of the Pacific coastline.

By night, Miraflores was another place entirely. Cars would race by at breakneck speeds, making the simple act of crossing the street a dangerous endeavor. Neon signs advertised McDonald's, Burger King, and Starbucks and might seem out of place, but the American fast-food establishments were always packed with budget travelers and locals. The action started late and typically began with a round of pisco sours, Peru's national cocktail made from brandy, lemon juice, and sugar, topped with frothy egg whites and a drop of Angostura bitters. The drink, surprisingly strong, tasted a bit like margaritas and fueled the laughter, loud conversations, and occasional bar fights. Nightclubs and casinos sprang to life when the sun went down.

After dusk, the district of Miraflores was party central and the revelry often spilled into the streets as bleary-eyed packs of tourists stumbled from bar to bar. Patrols of heavily armed police officers in black flak jackets kept a careful watch over the foreigners, wobbly from the excesses of the evening and vulnerable to petty crime.

Ricardo was aware of Miraflores's wild nightlife, and although he worried about his daughter's absence that morning, he also realized she was twenty-one and an adult.

Annoyed that she hadn't touched base with the family, Ricardo dialed her cell phone. It rang a few times and then went to voice mail. Clearly the phone was on, but she wasn't answering.

Ricardo had always been a little overprotective of Stephany. The father of five children, he only had one daughter, his baby girl. As Stephany was growing up, he was rarely seen without his little *nenita* in tow.

When Stephany was two years old, the family owned a circus. It was a good, old-fashioned tent circus, complete with trapeze acts and a menagerie of exotic animals. Stephany loved to be around the elephants, bears, and tigers. Because her mother, Mariaelena, was the manager, she was able to spend her days hanging out with carnival workers who shared their strange and curious world with the tiny brown-eyed brunette. The performers loved Stephany and saw her as a kindred spirit. Like them, she was a bit mischievous and utterly fearless.

One day, Ricardo received a call from his wife asking him to head over to the main tent. When he arrived, there was a rehearsal in progress. He nearly passed out when he saw his two-year-old dressed in a frilly, pink tutu seated atop an elephant making its way into the arena. It was an unforgettable moment. Ricardo felt pride tinged with horror as he admired his tiny daughter's courage. She was all smiles balanced atop the giant pachyderm. It turned out she'd been practicing for weeks without his knowledge under the direction of the circus's veteran animal trainer. And his wife was a co-conspirator.

Years later, Stephany would be involved in another daredevil stunt, this time with her father. The two of them decided to keep Mariaelena in the dark. Ricardo was a well-known race-car driver, a good-looking older man with thick jet-black hair, deeply tanned skin, and a cleft chin, and his televised skills on the rally racing circuit had earned him near-celebrity status in Peru. His team's name was Riflo, a contraction of his first and last names. The team had won the internationally famous Caminos del Inca Peru Rally in 1991, a 2,700-kilometer (1,680-mile) circuit divided into five grueling stages. The race placed tremendous pressure on both the car and driver. The Andean leg took drivers and their vehicles to altitudes of 15,000 feet, about 4,500 meters, and required that participants carry oxygen on board. Speeding up and down steep mountain roads, past high cliff walls lacking any safety rails, an unlucky driver could easily slide off a crumbling embankment into the abyss. Certain death lay below. The danger, the speed, the steely grins of the racers who had survived the sometimes deadly course generated female groupies. These men were superstars in their own right.

In the years following his victory, Riflo enjoyed this celebrity status. He also served two terms as president of the Peruvian Automobile Club. Off the track he wore tailor-made suits that hung gracefully from his lean, well-toned body. His look was classy and successful but he had a gangster's edge and carried himself with a confidence that would serve him well from the racetrack to the boardroom.

Rally drivers were always accompanied by a navigator

whose job was to shout out the unseen course in front of them. The navigator had to know the route and read from written notes as he simultaneously watched for the dips and turns in the road ahead. He had to know every curve and elevation change. It was a position with no margin for error. The slightest miscalculation could send a driver over the edge of a high cliff wall before he even realized he'd reached it. The driver and navigator had to be in sync and must have complete faith and trust in one another. On and off the racecourse, Ricardo Flores loved being behind the wheel and insisted on being in the driver's seat. Even when he was out with his family he did all the driving. He selected a navigator with great care.

Stephany was in her teens when she first expressed an interest in racing, and she and her father hatched a plan to get her into the navigator's seat for a real race. Normally, Team Riflo wore red fireproof racing suits, red being the team color. But Ricardo had two blue uniforms custom-made for him and Stephany. They would also register using pseudonyms.

In a sport dominated by men, it would be unheard of for a driver to use his sixteen-year-old daughter as a navigator. And he was sure his wife would object. The plan went awry when Mariaelena caught the two sneaking the suits out of the house. Admitting everything, Ricardo pleaded with his wife to let him take Stephany. He promised to keep his daughter safe.

Ultimately, Mariaelena acquiesced. She trusted her husband. When Stephany was a baby, the family had nicknamed him *"Papá Gallina,"* or Father Hen, because of the way he guarded over her. She accepted that he would not recklessly endanger their daughter's life. Their shared passion for racing trumped the risk.

Now, standing in the hallway outside of Stephany's bedroom, Ricardo felt his daughter slipping away. There was more to his concern than her failure to check in that evening. She had been spending a lot of nights out on the town. He'd recently discovered she was frequenting the casinos of

Miraflores, and had gotten herself in over her head. He'd even bailed her out earlier in the year, buying her a new car after he learned that she'd sold her Mitsubishi in an online auction for the equivalent of U.S.$12,000 to cover her gambling debts. Ricardo was upset when he found out what she had done, and he settled the obligation, warning his daughter that owing money was both reckless and dangerous. He didn't know for sure, but he suspected his daughter was still gambling.

Gambling in the Flores household was something of a family pastime. It was done for recreation, just like Americans might bet on the Superbowl or basketball's March Madness with friends. Sometimes the buy-in was U.S.$100, which might seem steep, even obscene, in a country as poor as Peru, but in the Floreses' minds dinner out and a night on the town would be just as expensive.

The senior Flores had been a gambler, and knew it had a darker side. Ricardo's game had been baccarat. But at home the family played poker. And Stephany was good. She even told friends and family that she dreamed of becoming a professional poker player. She excelled at everything she did, and hated to lose. While she shared her mother's light complexion and soft facial features, she had definitely inherited her thick, dark hair and competitive nature from her father.

Ricardo had hoped his daughter had learned her lesson after hocking her car, but just a few days earlier she'd hit him up for the equivalent of U.S.$1,000, claiming she needed a new laptop for school. As far as he knew, she hadn't yet purchased one. He hoped she wasn't gambling again.

Stephany's mother, Mariaelena, a striking blonde who was stylish and chic, was equally concerned when she learned their daughter had not contacted them. She and her husband had both checked their cell phones; neither had a message. When she dialed Stephany's number, the Nextel phone she carried appeared to be on, but it just rang several times before going to voice mail. This was odd.

When Stephany had stayed out all night in the past, she was good about letting her parents know her whereabouts.

In fact, she was usually the one keeping tabs on her father, who, like Stephany, was a free spirit.

The Floreses' home was in the quiet neighborhood of Chacarilla, an affluent oasis within the district of Surco, fifteen minutes from Miraflores. Surco itself ran the gamut of economic conditions, from rich to poor. Chacarilla was a work of gentrification in progress. The blocks of beautiful, expensive homes and classy shopping malls that made up its core deteriorated rapidly at the periphery. Almost from one block to another, the upscale areas changed to cinder-block storefronts and half-built dwellings that formed the backdrop of an impoverished district. Street children juggled plastic balls at stoplights for coins and women sold fruit from push-carts as groups of men stood in small clusters drinking beer on the corners. Where rich and poor collided, the affluent tended to be on edge.

Armed paramilitary patrols would attempt to keep these affluent transplants safe as they relocated to the neighbor-hood, attracted by low real estate prices and the illusion of finding safety in numbers. Many of the homes on Ricardo's block were new and a few were still under construction.

Ricardo had been able to keep his family protected within the sanctuary of their new home. To prevent would-be home invaders from gaining easy access, he had built a twelve-foot concrete wall surrounding his house. Many of the city's residents installed an additional layer of razor wire or electrified fencing to fend off the home invaders and burglars that plagued Lima. But Ricardo had forgone this additional precaution. The private security booth, manned twenty-four hours a day, was next door.

With all these safety measures, he was only able to provide protection for his wife and the couple's three children—Stephany, a second son he also named Ricardo, and Bobby—when they were at home. Outside one needed street smarts and luck. Stephany had neither.

Ricardo was a relatively lenient disciplinarian. He gave his children a certain amount of freedom and believed that kids learned best by making their own mistakes. Still, it wasn't like Stephany to be out of touch for more than a few hours.

Ricardo's mind cycled through the possibilities. Repeated calls to Stephany's cell phone went unanswered. By late morning, he and his wife were frantically calling anyone who may have seen her, including her two older brothers, Ricardo Jr. and Enrique. The two were Ricardo's adult sons from his first marriage, but they were very close to their half sister.

Ricardo Jr., nicknamed Richie, was fourteen when Stephany was born. He had been the one to choose her name and its unusual spelling. Now thirty-five and a single dad, he cut a larger-than-life figure in the bars and restaurants of Miraflores. He stood well over six feet tall with thick curly hair, long sideburns, and a broad and expressive smile, which made him one of the most eligible bachelors in the neighborhood. As a younger man working for a catering company in northern California, he'd developed a taste for good food and was both fond and proud of Lima's nouvelle cuisine. He was treated like a VIP by the chefs and maître d's and was always the one to suggest the hot new restaurant when meeting his father and the rest of the family for impromptu get-togethers.

The day before, Saturday, he had invited the family to lunch to celebrate his son, Sebastian's, first birthday and was disappointed that his kid sister hadn't been able to join them. Stephany had told the family she had to sit for an exam and wouldn't be finished in time. Richie had recently gone back to school himself, studying for a Master's in business administration, and understood the pressures of academic life. He had just settled in on the couch and was watching cartoons with Sebastian when his phone rang.

"We can't find Stephany. She never came home last night. Have you heard from her?" His father sounded nervous and worried.

"No, Dad, I have no idea where she is."

"We've been calling her cell phone and she's not picking up. I'm worried something's happened to her."

Richie had never heard his father so rattled and did his

best to calm him down. "I'll call Enrique and see if he's heard anything."

Enrique was the younger of the two and had recently married. His bride, Carolina Jorge, was a stunning brunette from a small town in the tropical Amazon basin of south-eastern Peru who quickly became like a second daughter to Ricardo and Mariaelena. A call to Enrique's home yielded no further clues. It wasn't unusual that Stephany's two older brothers had not heard from their baby sister; they were grown and no longer lived at home. But they were protective of Stephany, whom they affectionately called "Booboo," and immediately offered to help their father with the search.

By evening, the Flores family still hadn't been able to get in touch with Stephany or her friends. The truth was they didn't even know many of them. Stephany was a college se-nior and rarely brought her friends home like she had done when she was a child.

Panic was beginning to set in. Ricardo and Mariaelena were making no progress. Their daughter had vanished. Hours had passed and there was still no word. Ricardo was com-pelled to call the police.

"You have to wait for the ransom call," an officer from the kidnapping squad of the Division of Criminal Investigations of the Peruvian National Police instructed.

Like every wealthy or well-known businessman in Lima, Ricardo Flores was acutely aware of the dangers faced by high-profile individuals and their families. Residential bur-glaries, street crimes, and carjackers were an ever-present reality in Lima. Gangs of young street toughs, known as "piranhas," operated in packs, typically swarming their vic-tims in broad daylight, quickly stripping them of anything of value.

Kidnappings were also a dangerous possibility. Although not as rampant as in the past, abductions were still common in Latin America and Lima, Peru, was no exception. The ab-ductions usually fell into one of two scenarios, the "kidnap express" and the "kidnap and ransom."

The kidnap express was quick and dirty. Kidnappers usually snatched their victims off the street around 11:00 P.M., drove them to an ATM machine, and ordered them to use their bank cards and passwords to withdraw the daily maximum, about $500. Typically, the victims were held until just after midnight, when they were instructed to again withdraw the daily limit, another $500.

Odd as it may sound, these kidnappings normally ended without violence. The victim was returned traumatized but otherwise unharmed, so long as the withdrawals were made. From a detached perspective, these were merely business transactions.

The second, less frequent type of abduction was the traditional kidnap and ransom. The stakes and demands were much higher, the negotiations could be prolonged and any number of things could go wrong during the victim-for-cash exchange. This was an urgent, grave business that was as likely to end in death as release.

Luckily, Ricardo Flores had not been a target as yet. But he wondered if Stephany could have fallen victim to a kidnap and ransom scheme. With his now-distraught wife sobbing in the background, he began blaming himself for not teaching his children about the evils of the world. He had given all five of them expensive private school educations, vacations at the family's seaside beach house and trips to the United States. He had given Stephany money whenever she asked for it. He now found himself second-guessing the freedom he had afforded his daughter.

By Monday, dark and terrible thoughts of what might have happened flashed through his mind. Each time the phone rang Ricardo anxiously answered it. But it was never Stephany, only family members and concerned friends checking in. It was just before 1:00 P.M. when the family finally received some news.

A member of the Peruvian police force was on the phone and believed he had located Stephany's Jeep. Minutes earlier, officers responding to a suspicious vehicle call had run the plates, discovering it was registered to Stephany Flores. The truck with the tinted windows was found unlocked and abandoned in front of 154 Jorge Chávez Pasaje in the district of Surco Viejo, an impoverished, crime-plagued neighborhood. The officer described the vehicle as a black Jeep Compass 4 × 4, license plate number A1B-333. It had to be Stephany's. She had purchased the car after selling the Mitsubishi in the Internet auction.

Ricardo jumped into his Mercedes and sped to the location. The four-lane, palm-lined boulevard to Surco Viejo ended in a dusty warren of one-way streets blocked by construction, detours, and police checkpoints. The sad empty eyes of poverty seemed to be the distinguishing feature of the people in the streets.

Cursing to himself, Ricardo watched as the neighborhood grew worse and worse. Two- and three-story apartment buildings painted in drab shades of brown, yellow, and cream sat abandoned, under construction, or in varying states of disrepair, many with exposed steel rebar jutting from the upper unfinished floors. Heavy metal grates protected first-floor windows and doors. Clothes hung limply on makeshift lines on rooftops alongside a tangle of electrical wires that illegally siphoned electricity from the nearby grid. Elderly women in housecoats stood in doorways, and children in well-worn clothes and bare feet played soccer in the street. Ricardo knew the area was a *zona roja,* a red zone, with a reputation for drug activity and violence.

Pressing gently on the brakes, he looked left and right as the boulevard dead-ended at Las Palmas Air Force Base, where a young officer in combat boots and paramilitary garb stood guarding the entrance; a tank painted in white-and-green camouflage was parked just inside the perimeter. Looking out the passenger-side window he immediately spotted police vehicles and knew this was the place.

His daughter's Jeep was parked nose in amid a row of late-model cars and taxis. A rusted-out red VW Bug sat just to its left. Above her vehicle, the words *"Sí a la Vida, No a las Drogas"* (Yes to Life, No to Drugs) were spray-painted in bold blue letters on the twelve-foot brick wall that surrounded the military base.

Ricardo was met by uniformed officers and briefed on what they had been able to piece together so far. They told him his daughter's truck had been found about an hour earlier after a neighbor called in to report that an unfamiliar vehicle had been parked on the street for much of the weekend. The Jeep was brand new, and had seemed out of place on this impoverished block. Witnesses thought the vehicle might have belonged to someone from the air force base, which sat on the other side of the wall. They worried that its owner might have been the victim of foul play. Their hunch was half right.

Police criminalist José Sandoval Reyna had already begun his inspection of the Jeep. Sandoval had sprayed a reactive agent on all of the flat surfaces of the exterior and interior. His tests yielded fifty-four adhesive tapes containing partial fingerprint impressions lifted from the vehicle, along with samples of all the liquids found in the soda bottles and other containers collected from inside the car. He would soon send them to the lab for analysis.

The vehicle was messy, strewn with plastic bottles of Inca Cola, assorted fast-food wrappers, and dirty clothes, but it didn't appear as if it had been the scene of a violent struggle.

Sandoval now needed to know if Ricardo knew the vehicle well enough to know if anything was missing.

"That's Stephany's, and so is that," Ricardo told police as they held up various items found in the Jeep.

Ricardo recognized his daughter's belongings, a jean jacket from the Hard Rock Café, a yellow Hollister sweatshirt, and a gym bag.

"She had a gaming system. I believe it was a Wii," Ricardo said. "She had it with her on Saturday, but I don't see it in the car."

Investigators also found a blister pack for medicine, open and empty, on the passenger-side floor, a finding that fueled early reports in the press that Stephany may have been drugged by her assailant.

With Stephany's Jeep located, police began working with the premise that the young woman had been abducted. Standing in the street next to Stephany's car, officers from the kidnapping division asked Ricardo for his help in reconstructing his daughter's movements over the past few days. The local media had already picked up the story, and there were conflicting reports in the press about Stephany's whereabouts in the hours before her disappearance.

Neighborhood witnesses were sure that Stephany's black Jeep had been parked on their block since as early as Friday. But from what Ricardo had told the officers, these witness reports didn't seem possible. Ricardo was equally certain he had seen Stephany on Saturday morning. Confused, he called his wife to help construct a reliable time line. Mariaelena confirmed that Stephany had been home that Saturday morning, and that her daughter had returned to the house in her Jeep around 4:00 P.M. that same afternoon before heading out with friends for the evening.

Believing Stephany may have been abducted, police began tracking down informants and looking into criminal enterprises that specialize in kidnappings. But this line of inquiry went nowhere. Information was currency in Lima, but there was none of the usual chatter on the street level; none of their sources knew anything. There was also another concern. In their experience, a demand for money should have come by now. That no ransom call was received was very troubling.

Desperate for answers, Ricardo began to do some digging of his own. He started with his daughter's phone service provider, Nextel. For nearly three hours, he pleaded with phone company operators and their managers, explaining that his daughter had been kidnapped and he needed their help. The distraught father was convinced they could use her GPS-enabled phone to pinpoint her exact location. Nextel was only able to provide Flores with a list of the most recent outgoing calls made from Stephany's phone.

Information on the incoming calls, he was told, would take fifteen days to process.

Ricardo was furious. He was sure the technology existed to pinpoint his daughter's exact location and couldn't believe the phone company hadn't been more helpful, given that this appeared to be a kidnapping.

Taking a deep breath, he began dialing the numbers the company had provided. There had been six calls between Friday, May 29, and Saturday, May 30, when she went missing. Two of them were to a medical insurance company, Pacifico Vida, probably about claims related to Stephany's asthma treatments. Two others were to a fried chicken restaurant. Dialing the next number, Ricardo finally reached someone helpful, one of the girls Stephany had been out with on the night she disappeared.

Carola Sanguinetti was Stephany's friend from the University of Lima. The two women had met during Stephany's freshman year in 2006 and were teammates on the school's *futsal* team, a fast-paced cousin to soccer that is played indoors. Carola, a well-toned and physically fit brunette with shoulder-length hair she wore tucked behind her ears, was seven years older than Stephany and had already graduated from the university, where Stephany was now a senior and poised to receive a diploma in business administration in the fall. Despite the age difference, the two shared many of the same interests and had been spending a good deal of time together of late.

With Carola's help, Stephany's father was able to flesh out a time line.

What he learned was that she, too, was worried about Stephany and had been trying to get in touch with his daughter since Sunday morning. The two had spent much of Saturday together, laughing and swapping gossip over lunch at Polleria Mediterraneo, an inexpensive grill near the Floreses' home that specialized in *pollo a la brasa,* a Peruvian staple of salted chicken cooked over charcoal and typically served with French fries. It was a laid-back Saturday afternoon and they were dressed casually in jeans and sneakers.

"She seemed happy. She was in a great mood," Carola told Mr. Flores.

She had been pleased to see Stephany so upbeat. Stephany tended to despair about her weight, unable to restore the thin figure of her youth. She had the family curse, her father and two older brothers being large men. Coping with the unwanted weight gain as a young woman, however, was causing her considerable stress.

While a fierce athlete, Stephany had a soft, self-deprecating side. If she took any offense to her friend calling her by the pet name "*Gordita,*" Little Pig, she didn't show it. In turn, Stephany playfully referred to Carola as "*Chinita,*" an endearing term in Peru that literally translates to "little Asian girl," or a girl who looks like she is mixed with more than one race.

The two women loved playing video games, and after lunch they set off in Stephany's Jeep to Polvos Rosados, a market known for pirated DVDs, video games, and assorted black market electronics. There, they bought a movie and several games for Stephany's Wii gaming system. Stephany had the system with her in the car, and was planning to rent a room at a hotel in town so she and Carola could play.

In Lima, as is true in most of Latin America, adult children typically lived at home with their parents until they were married. For privacy, they often rented hotel rooms, sometimes by the hour. While it sounds odd, Stephany's older brother, Richie, said it wasn't unusual for his sister to spend a few hours partying at a hotel, watching movies and socializing with friends.

On their way to the hotel, they drove past the Markham College, and discovered the school was hosting a carnival. It looked like fun and they decided to stop. The Markham College was a private preparatory academy where Lima's elite sent their children to study. Stephany's younger brothers had both attended. Having grown up in a circus environment, Stephany grew nostalgic at the sight of the festival. There were clowns with painted faces, food vendors, and games of chance.

Stephany parked the Jeep at the school and grabbed her wallet out of the truck's glove compartment. To Carola's astonishment, Stephany pulled out a thick wad of crisp, high-denomination Peruvian currency while the two stood on the sidewalk, a calliope chiming a carnival tune in the background.

"Can you hold on to these?" she asked. "I don't want to leave them in the truck," Stephany said, explaining she had won the money at a casino five days earlier.

Carola was stunned. Stephany was driving around with the equivalent of thousands of U.S. dollars in her glove compartment. If she had won the cash five days earlier, why hadn't she put it in the bank or at least in a safe place in her home?

Carola was one of the few friends who knew Stephany liked to gamble. During a phone call that past Monday, Stephany had boasted of winning 7,000 nuevos soles, about U.S.$2,500, in a poker tournament. Carola had been skeptical about the amount of money her friend claimed to have won. She had heard these big-fish stories before. As was true with most gamblers, Stephany tended to inflate the sum of her winnings and minimize the sum of her losses. Sometimes she would even offer proof. "Take a look at this," she would say, opening her wallet to reveal thick wads of cash.

Carola found this side of Stephany's personality disturbing. People were killed in Lima for smaller sums all the time. It seemed dangerous to be walking around the city carrying so much cash. Yet, Stephany didn't appear at all concerned.

Not wanting to spoil her friend's good time, Carola agreed to hold the money while they walked around the carnival. She told Ricardo that Stephany was particularly jovial as they strolled the school grounds, at one point declaring that she was having the time of her life. She loved their spontaneous decision to enjoy something different.

After several hours of eating cotton candy and playing *tombola,* a game similar to bingo, the two headed to the El Pacifico Hotel, a moderately priced hotel in the Jesus Maria district, not far from Miraflores. There, they rented a room so they could try out the video games and enjoy a few hours of privacy.

At around 11:30 P.M., Stephany and Carola rendezvoused with another friend, Carolina Gallo, in the hotel lobby. Gallo was a slender brunette with brilliant white teeth. She had also attended the University of Lima with them and was on their *futsal* team. The three women had plans to go to the Pub del Gringo in Barranco, a lively Bohemian district south of Miraflores that was popular with Lima's young hipster set. The neighborhood, built on cliffs overlooking the Pacific, had a rich colonial history evidenced by the stunning homes built by German and British immigrants dating back to the 1800s.

Unfortunately, Barranco, the once beautiful seaside resort, had fallen on hard times and had been plagued by drugs and crime for decades. Now it was in a renaissance, with trendy new bars and art galleries opening on an almost daily basis. It was the hot place to be seen and party.

At 2:00 A.M. the three called it a night. Carolina was tired and had to get up early for work. Stephany agreed to drop her off at her boyfriend's house in Miraflores. From there, she drove Carola to the Phillips Company on Avenida Paseo de la República in San Isidro, where she worked in tech support earning the equivalent of about U.S.$1,000 a month. Carola planned to sleep on the couch in the small sixth-floor staff room before reporting for her shift at 7:00 A.M. rather than go home.

"I'll call you as soon as I get home," Stephany said. She then waited at the curb to make sure that Carola made it safely past the doorman and into the building before pulling away. It was 2:54 A.M. when she sent her friend a text, "I love you. I need to pee, did they open the door?"

"Yes, my love," Carola replied at 2:58 A.M. "Did you arrive?"

Eight minutes passed before Carola received a reply. "I'm going up right now, I'll call you."

Carola was relieved thinking that her friend had arrived safely at her destination and fell asleep believing that Stephany was on her way upstairs to her bedroom. But it simply wasn't true.

After dropping Carola at her office, Stephany had other plans. She drove straight to the Atlantic City Casino, one of the swankiest and most visually striking casinos in Miraflores. Sitting at the crossroads of the main drags of Alfredo Benavides and Larco avenues, the glow of the Atlantic City was visible from blocks away. Thousands of brilliant light-bulbs illuminated the mirrored gold surface of the building creating an almost supernova-like effect on an otherwise dark and uninteresting block populated by Internet cafés and office buildings. Valets in coats with long red tails and top hats looked like they'd stepped out of Victorian England standing beneath the curving red and gold marquis to greet gamblers at the enormous entryway framed by forty-foot waterfalls. The marble floors and colossal gold chandeliers were as glitzy as anything found in Vegas.

The Atlantic City Casino was a modern and full-service establishment and was open twenty-four hours a day. In addition to five hundred slot machines and gaming tables on the main level, there were also private poker suites and a karaoke lounge upstairs, as well the five-star restaurant, Eliazar, and the more casual Lulo's Ice Cream Shop.

Stephany was already at a gaming table in one of the upstairs poker suites when she sent a text message to Carola saying she had arrived home safely. Her parents and friends had no way of knowing that her secret visits to the casinos of Miraflores were becoming more frequent, the stakes increasingly high.

It was just before 3:00 A.M. when casino surveillance cameras captured her taking a seat alongside a young Dutchman named Joran van der Sloot. Seen on video, the encounter seemed friendly and random. The two shook hands. For a minute Stephany appeared unsure about taking either of the two vacant chairs next to the lanky, dark-haired foreigner with the thin mustache and closely cropped beard. The fair-skinned young man was dressed casually in a long-sleeved collared shirt that hung loosely from his athletic frame. His well-worn blue jeans had holes in both knees. Cameras caught Stephany considering an empty chair at another table before she settled into a chair to the man's left side, leaving the seat between them empty.

Pulling her hair back nervously with her fingers, she seemed on edge, perhaps simply the result of the rush of adrenaline that went along with sitting down at the gaming table.

Joran watched as she pulled a small wallet with peace symbols and the words "peace," "love me," and "flower power" in purple and blue lettering from the pocket of her jeans, unzipped it, and tossed a wad of bills onto the table in front of the dealer. In a city where pickpockets and purse snatchings were part of the norm, many Peruvians kept their money in a simple billfold in their front pockets. And Stephany was carrying a lot of cash. Her wallet was stuffed with 100 and 50 nuevos soles bills.

For the next two hours, Stephany sipped wine while Van der Sloot downed the complimentary whiskey and colas and smoked countless cigarettes doled out one by one, courtesy of the house, by cocktail waitresses dressed in revealing black-and-white uniforms. He had entered the casino an hour earlier than Stephany, most likely anticipating her arrival.

The two had been introduced at the tables earlier in the week by a thirty-five-year-old Uruguayan poker player named Elton García, who was in Lima to participate in the Latin American Poker Tour, scheduled to begin at the Atlantic City Casino in a few days. García, like Joran, was a guest at the Hotel Tac, and the two men had struck up a casual friendship.

Joran had also wanted to be a competitor in the four-day poker tournament. Although he wasn't a registered player like García, he had come to Peru with $25,000 and had hoped he would be able to buy his way in at the last minute. But the last two weeks had been a bust. He'd lost almost all his cash and barely had enough money to pay his hotel bill.

Joran was a well-known figure in the poker world, though more for his media notoriety than his poker skills, and had a reputation for being a "railbird." Railbirds, in pokerspeak, were gamblers who watched from the sidelines. They got their name because as observers not placing bets, they must stand behind a rail. True railbirds would often scam or hustle to get back into the action.

Joran couldn't pinpoint when his gambling became an addiction, but it had taken over his entire life. His world revolved around cards and jackpots, his next fix. All his actions were a means to that end.

Since his childhood back on the Caribbean island of Aruba, he had wanted to be a "player." Now at twenty-two his life was in shambles. His mother wanted to have him committed to a psychiatric hospital, he had no real friends to speak of, and he suspected that the FBI was after him for an unsolved disappearance of a young woman in Aruba. All that remained from his once-promising former life was an all-consuming desire to gamble. Gambling was an expensive addiction to feed. With the Latin American Poker Tour just three days away, he needed cash desperately. The buy-in for the tournament was U.S.$2,700, and he would need additional money for betting.

Stephany Flores was oblivious to all of this as she sat next to the dangerous and desperate man. She had played cards with him earlier in the week, and he seemed like a nice, friendly Dutch tourist. During Joran's stay in Peru, Stephany had been a regular at the Atlantic City Casino and there was a buzz about her recent winning streak. He knew she'd scored U.S.$10,000 at the baccarat tables that past Monday and had been winning ever since. The staff at the casino fawned over her, treating her like a VIP. Casinos didn't do this for just anybody.

Since being introduced to her by Elton García earlier in the week, he and Stephany had played poker together several times, including an hour the night before. Joran had been quick to size her up. He learned that her father was a big shot and that she came from money.

It was 5:00 A.M. when videotape from a camera trained on the casino floor captured Stephany cashing in her chips.

Another in the establishment's parking lot recorded her driving into the night with Joran, known internationally as a suspect in an unsolved murder. What ruse he used to lure the young woman out of the casino would prove one of the greatest mysteries surrounding the case.

Stephany appeared nervous on the tape, as though her instincts were telling her to walk away. But the Dutchman's charm was almost hypnotic.

TWO

Five years before Stephany Flores's fateful meeting with Joran van der Sloot, the Dutchman was captured on security video inside another casino some 1,800 miles to the north of Lima on the Caribbean island of Aruba, a constituent country of the Kingdom of the Netherlands. This time, he was at the blackjack tables of the Excelsior, the oldest casino and poker room on the island. He had joined up with a group of college-bound girls from Alabama. The young women had no way of knowing that this brief encounter would irrevocably change their lives or that one of them would never return home to Alabama.

Joran, though only seventeen, was in the throes of a downward spiral. In the past couple of years, he'd been in trouble constantly. Despite having a monthly allowance of $160, he'd stolen money from his parents—fifty euros, about sixty-five dollars, from his father, and additional cash from his mother. Anita and Paulus had also caught their son in countless lies. Although he'd been a sweet child, he had become increasingly aggressive toward his siblings. During a family trip to Miami, he roughed up his middle brother, Valentijn, and had also been accused of attacking others outside the home. He had used his brother's mobile phone without permission, and then broke the phone's chip. Concerned, his parents sent him to a psychologist.

Anita and Paulus van der Sloot had hoped that the changes their eldest son was going through could be attributed to the fact that he'd entered puberty at an unusually young age. Early-onset puberty, or precocious puberty, could sometimes lead to aggressive conduct in boys who mature sexually before their peers.

Desperate to find a way for Joran to channel his emotions, his mother had pushed him to participate in yoga classes. She was convinced relaxation and meditation would improve his sense of well-being. But Joran was almost eighteen and the problems just seemed to be multiplying.

Unbeknownst to his parents, his drinking had become problematic. Joran was fifteen when he first tasted liquor, and while he assured his mother he was not drinking, on most nights he was out with his friends getting drunk on free cocktails at the casinos before hitting the clubs.

While he considered himself a social drinker, he had a high tolerance for alcohol and preferred the extra kick of whiskey and Coca-Cola to beer. He once bragged that he had to drink a case of beer before he began to feel tipsy or twenty to thirty glasses of whiskey or rum to get drunk. Physically, he was much bigger than his high school classmates. He was a muscular guy, standing six feet four, slender and athletic. His friends and family called him a "sporter," a jock.

He was a star tennis player at the Aruba Racquet Club, where he and his father competed in regular doubles tournaments. He was also a standout soccer player and was recognized for his aggressive style at the private school he attended. When Joran channeled his anger, especially in athletics, he was capable of remarkable achievement, but his darker side was always circling just beneath the surface.

His friends knew that he was prone to aggression when

intoxicated. They'd been out with him and seen him drinking. A few months earlier, while partying at the annual Mardi Gras celebration in the capital city of Oranjestad, Joran got into a confrontation with a homeless man. At first, Joran had sought the help of a policeman, who sent the homeless man away. However, when the homeless man returned, the situation escalated and Joran, somewhat intoxicated, snapped and threw the man off a bridge and into the water. His friends found his actions somewhat amusing, and excused him. After all, he had been provoked.

In recent months, friends said he had pushed a classmate through a glass display case while waiting to see a movie at the local cinema. Joran later minimized the event, saying the other person had accidentally fallen into the case. Both sets of parents intervened to help their sons reach an acceptable resolution.

While these incidents might have landed most juveniles in jail, or at least in trouble with the police, Joran had a way of explaining his way into and out of any and all situations. His impassive brown eyes could be so utterly sincere that it was almost impossible to believe he was not telling the truth. This skill of "believability" would serve him well when on the prowl for the young female tourists who frequented the island.

Joran and his friends had nicknames for each other. His was "Jojo." When cruising the town, they jokingly referred to each other as "pimp" and their circle of male friends as the "Pimpology Crew." They had a system for picking up girls, their targets often being American tourists like the teens from Alabama who had just joined Joran at the blackjack table. He thought American girls were the "loosest of the lot," followed by the local girls, and then the Dutch girls. The Americans, he thought, tended to overindulge in alcohol, probably because the drinking age in the States was twenty-one. On Aruba, the legal age was eighteen, and even then it was not carefully enforced.

Located in the southern Caribbean Sea, below the hurricane belt and seventeen miles north of Venezuela, Aruba was a rum-soaked oasis of powder-fine sand beaches, calm turquoise waters, and raucous bars and beachside tiki huts. Its sultry temperatures were cooled by signature trade winds that permanently bent the island's divi-divi trees toward the sea. It was a place to lose oneself, if only for a long weekend.

The perfect weather, the rhythm of steel drum bands, the cool, crisp Balashi beer, and the whir of blenders mixing daiquiris and piña coladas fueled a party atmosphere that began early in the morning and continued well into the night. For American tourists, Aruba was a place of escape, a tropical retreat where they could forget about work and school, cast their inhibitions aside, and for the length of their vacation lead lives of unrestrained debauchery.

But despite its motto "One Happy Island," there was another side to Aruba that most tourists never saw. As on any other Caribbean islands, crime and drug trafficking were serious problems. Because of its close proximity to Venezuela, drug traffickers used Aruba as a way station to move heroin, cocaine, ecstasy, and other narcotics from South America to the U.S. and Europe, sometimes recruiting cruise ship employees as couriers.

The U.S. Drug Enforcement Agency kept a close eye on Aruba. But nobody was keeping an eye on the teenage population of Aruba. Many of Joran's friends were locals whose parents worked in the service industry. The long and often late hours of hotel and restaurant jobs left them little time to devote to parental supervision and their children tended to run wild. While Joran's parents were professionals and preferred the company of their insular circle of Dutch ex-pats, Joran wanted nothing to do with the stuffy transplants from his native Holland. He had moved to Aruba with his family when he was four and considered himself an island boy.

Joran's parents were inclined to keep their eldest son on a tight leash, but the call of the island nightlife was just too strong. Despite juggling at least two girlfriends, Joran had an insatiable sexual appetite and was often out on the prowl. He'd lost his virginity at fourteen, and devoted much of his free time to trawling downtown bars such as Carlos'n

Charlie's, Choose-A-Name, Tantra, and Club Báhia, hoping to hook up with tourist girls. That he was tall and physically developed made him appear older than he actually was.

Joran was also becoming a familiar face at the casinos along the Palm Beach strip. The beachfront resort area was on the leeward side of the island and boasted full-service, brand-name hotels, including the Marriott, the Wyndham, the Hyatt Regency, and the Holiday Inn. Of the dozen gaming establishments on Aruba, all but one were located on Palm Beach.

The Excelsior Casino inside the Holiday Inn was Joran's favorite. It was shabby compared to the other casinos on the strip but still saw plenty of action. Despite having the character of an Elk's Club lounge with its black metal chairs upholstered in fake blue leather and drab gunnel-green carpeting with bright orange swirls, it was a favorite among the island's locals. In fact, Caribbean stud poker was born there in 1988.

Its location on the second floor of the Holiday Inn made it convenient for tourists, especially guests of the oceanfront resort, but American gamblers sometimes found playing in the Excelsior a frustrating experience. English was the official language at the tables, but after a hand was played, many players reverted to Papiamento, their native language.

Papiamento is a patois of Spanish, Portuguese, Dutch, English, French, a smattering of African languages, and Arawak, the language spoken by the indigenous population before European conquest. It was the preferred language of the locals, and was widely spoken on the neighboring islands of Bonaire and Curaçao.

To the untrained ear, Papiamento sounds much like Spanish, and many of the islanders who spoke the language could also speak Dutch, Spanish, and English. American gamblers didn't understand the Creole, and believed the Papiamento-speaking players, in concert with the dealers, used the language to dupe them.

Joran's native language was Dutch, but he was fluent in Papiamento. He had been a regular at the Excelsior for more than a year. He'd been honing his skills at regular Sunday and Monday night poker games, developing a deep understanding of the game. He was good with math, and had an uncanny ability to size up the vulnerabilities of those around him.

At seventeen, he was a juvenile who was technically not allowed in the casinos. But his father held a prominent government post on Aruba and no one raised any objections when he brought his son to the tables.

His parents might not have recognized that poker was fast becoming an obsession for Joran. The shuffling of the cards, the clank of the chips, the luxurious feel of the felt on the table in front of him, Joran loved it all. He felt like an adult, an important person, when he was gambling. The complimentary cocktails didn't hurt either. Joran usually ignored the plastic cups of cold Balashi beer, a locally brewed pilsner, preferring whiskey or rum.

This particular Sunday, he was in a losing streak. He'd been in the Excelsior since four o'clock, participating in a Texas hold 'em tournament with his father, Paulus. Joran, although several inches taller, bore a striking resemblance to his father. The elder Van der Sloot was tall and handsome, and at fifty-three had a receding hairline and metal-framed glasses, but there was no mistaking that the two were father and son.

While Paulus's game was baccarat, Joran was developing a passion for poker and had actually taught his father and several of his own friends how to play. The Texas hold 'em tournament at the Excelsior was a "free" tournament, meaning there was no entry fee and each player was given $500 worth of play money, like Monopoly money. The players were dealt seven cards and used their five best cards to form combinations. Gamblers were eliminated from the competition when the play money ran out. Real cash prizes were awarded to the winners.

Joran and his father had begun playing in the tournament at 4:00 P.M. But after two hours, Joran was forced to fold and gave up his seat to walk around and watch others play. He knew that so much could be learned simply by observing.

During a break in the action, Paulus located Joran and told him he was going home. His wife, Anita, was in Holland for her grandmother's ninetieth birthday celebration, and he was in charge of their three sons. Joran's ten-year-old brother Sebastian was at a friend's house and due to be dropped off shortly, and fourteen-year-old Valentjin was either already home or on his way. Paulus needed to feed the boys and get them to bed early because it was a school night. Joran also had school in the morning. Because it was final exam week, his schedule was light and varied from day to day.

Not wanting to spoil his son's fun, Paulus told him he could stay longer and take his seat at the poker table. While his wife would never have allowed this, Paulus was proud of Joran. He had been accepted to six schools, including Saint Leo University, in Saint Leo, Florida, a Catholic school about thirty-five miles north of Tampa. The college was his son's first choice, and he had been awarded a full scholarship.

Joran's mother had taken him to the States to visit several of the schools that had accepted him. Anita was pleased that Joran had chosen Saint Leo's. A small Catholic college would provide a structure similar to the one she tried to create in the Van der Sloot household. The psychologist Anita had forced Joran to visit at least once every three weeks agreed. Although she had only seen him five times, she also liked the structure and supervision that Saint Leo's could most certainly provide.

This night, however, had Anita been home, she would never have permitted her son to stay out sipping cocktails and gambling when he should have been at home studying. She was the disciplinarian in the household and a strict one at that.

Joran loved his mother, but he found her smothering and at times overbearing. At seventeen, he wanted her to give him a little more space. But she had been unwilling to give him much freedom, especially in light of recent incidents.

What Anita didn't know wouldn't hurt her, Paulus reasoned.

"Call me when you're ready to come home," he told his

son in Dutch upon leaving the casino that night. "I'll come pick you up."

After only thirty minutes at the poker table, Joran again ran out of play money and went to find a cocktail waitress. After four hours in the casino, he wasn't quite ready to call it a night and once again checked out the action from the sidelines before taking a seat at a nearby blackjack table. He was there only five minutes when the Alabama teens settled in next to him.

The four teens looked like cheerleaders, two blondes, two brunettes, all young and pretty. Joran could tell by their blue plastic wristbands that they were staying at the Holiday Inn SunSpree Resort and were guests with the all-inclusive package.

Located near the end of a strip of high-rise hotels on J. E. Irausquin Boulevard, the boxy, yellow six-story structure wasn't the nicest hotel on the island. Not by a long shot. But it was directly on the beach and surrounded by palm trees with fun island-themed décor. The all-inclusive plan, with no additional fee for meals and soft drinks, was particularly attractive to groups and budget-minded travelers. The blue plastic bracelets issued at check-in identified these guests, who were then entitled to unlimited food and sodas at the resort's four restaurants and three bars.

The young ladies explained that they were on holiday with 124 members of their senior class to celebrate their graduation from Mountain Brook High School, located in suburban Birmingham. The four, Natalee Holloway, Ruth McVay, Lee Broughton, and Katherine "Madison" Whatley, were all good friends and had elected to share a room. They had been assigned a ground-floor room with two double beds, a patio, and a partial view of the ocean.

Seven chaperones had accompanied the group, but supervision had been loose. Many of the students were already eighteen, the legal drinking age in Aruba, so the chaperones had been permissive when it came to their alcohol consumption. Basically, as long as everybody checked in once a day, the adults didn't ask any questions.

Many of the teens were really enjoying their five days of tropical freedom. They had been drinking booze literally by the "yard," bar slang for the tall yard glasses typically used in British pubs for drinking ale. A true yard glass, fluted at the top with a round bulb at the bottom, held two and a half pints of beer. Some of the students were also gambling in a casino for the first time, including Natalee Holloway and her three roommates.

Natalee's roommate, Ruth McVay, had been more curious about gambling than Natalee and the other girls. Over the course of several nights, Ruth had lost some money at the blackjack tables and wanted to win it back.

Sliding into an empty seat next to Joran, Ruth quickly fell deeper into the hole as her friends watched over her shoulders. Down nearly U.S.$30, she turned to the young man in the blue-and-white-striped polo shirt, his brown hair close cropped like a young Marine's, and half-jokingly asked if he could help her win her money back.

Van der Sloot chuckled but agreed to assist. "I'll do what I can," he said. "My name is Joran." He was more than happy to gamble with someone else's money. Besides, the girls were cute.

Ruth and the three other teens introduced themselves. Though the same age as her friends, Ruth looked like the youngest of the bunch. She had a sweet Southern voice and shoulder-length brown hair with long bangs, and wore a turquoise tank top that showed off her light, even tan.

Standing behind Ruth, her three friends watched as Van der Sloot schooled their friend in blackjack 101, telling her when to hit and when to pass. He looked like a nice guy, tall, good-looking, athletic, and fluent in English. He wasn't aggressive or flirtatious like so many of the men the girls had met on the island who just wanted to get them into bed. He was focused on his hand, and looked serious about the game. He seemed like a normal teenager, one of them.

But it was all an act, one he had nearly perfected. Joran had spent much of the past year in the casinos learning how to deceive his opponents at the gaming tables. It was a sim-

ple system. When dealt a bad hand, he knew it was important to disguise his emotions, so he would visualize a winning
hand and his facial expressions would fall in accordingly. To
be believed, he had to convince himself that the lie was the
truth. The strategy also doubled as a foolproof way to pick
up tourist girls.

Joran and his Aruban friends were aware that young
women on vacation seemed to have a certain distrust of the
locals, so it was best to pretend to be a fellow traveler, one of
them. That way they wouldn't suspect he was a beach bum
looking for a one-night stand.

Joran told the four friends he was a Dutch tourist visiting
Aruba from Holland, and like them, was staying at the Holiday Inn. It was the first of many lies he would spin that night
in his attempt to become more appealing to the young women.
He knew they were leaving the following day, so he was just
looking to hook up. He needed to act fast.

While he tried not to show it, Joran was attracted to the
shapely blonde in the white tank top and floral-print skirt
standing between Ruth and him. She told him her name was
Katherine, but her friends called her by her middle name,
Madison. Madison was definitely Joran's type; she was petite and bubbly with naturally highlighted hair.

Leaning in close, Joran quietly inhaled the faint blend of
coconut oil and sea salt that lingered from a day in the surf
as Madison quizzed him about his background in her soft
Alabama drawl.

"How old are you?" she asked.

"Nineteen," Joran lied. He didn't want to seem like a kid.

There was another blonde at the table who was thinner
than Madison and didn't seem to care about gambling at all.
"My name is Natalee," she said, tilting her head back and
smiling.

In between hands, Ruth told Joran this was her last chance
to gamble on the island and she didn't want to end on a losing
note. She and her friends were catching a morning flight
back to the U.S.

Lee Broughton, who was standing just behind Ruth,

jumped in on the conversation. The statuesque brunette stood a head taller than her three friends, and spoke excitedly about their plans to spend their last night partying at Carlos'n Charlie's, a lively bar and nightclub.

Carlos'n Charlie's had become an instant favorite with the Mountain Brook seniors. The club was part of an international chain with outposts in Acapulco, Cancún, Cozumel, and other Mexican tourist spots. There were even two in the U.S., in Austin, Texas, and Lake Mary, Florida. The bar in Aruba catered to thirsty tourists stepping off the cruise ships that docked just steps away in the busy harbor. On weekends, the place pulsated with teenage testosterone, catering to scantily clad kids and serving supersize drinks with names like the "Poison Kiss," the "Guava Colada," and the "Ticket to Fly." The Mountain Brook students had been going there since discovering it their first night on the island.

After learning where the visitors were from, the house DJ had started playing Lynyrd Skynyrd's "Sweet Home Alabama" whenever they showed up at the bar. Hearing the opening guitar chords blasting though the bar's state-of-the-art sound system, the kids would go crazy. "Turn it up," they screamed in unison as the Southern rock anthem reverberated through the bar, across the beer-soaked dance floor.

"Carlos'n Charlie's sucks on Sunday nights," Joran said.

While the girls didn't pick up on it, he was speaking from experience. Joran was no tourist visiting the island from Holland. He was an island boy and he and his friends were regulars at Carlos'n Charlie's. Joran explained that the bars and nightclubs downtown tended to be more crowded on the weekends when the cruise ships were in. Sunday nights, however, were a bust.

But the plans were already set. The teens were meeting at least sixty of their classmates at the bar for one last party.

Joran's gambling strategy seemed effective. Soon, Ruth was up $100 and Joran told her she should walk away. She was reluctant. She was riding high on her victory and wanted to press her luck. But her friends convinced her she should heed his advice and cash out. While he'd done well for Ruth, Joran's game was off. The girls noticed that he'd lost U.S.$250 at the table. Parting ways, they invited him to join them at Carlos'n Charlie's.

"I'll do my best to come," he said.

Not long after leaving the casino, Joran bumped into the Alabama teens at the sports bar inside the Holiday Inn. The young women were sitting on barstools, drinking and laughing, so he walked over to say hello.

"You'd better come tonight," they teased, giving him a gentle ribbing.

Joran smiled. In his mind, he was already there; he just needed to line up a ride to get downtown. He was happy to share the wealth with anyone who gave him a ride. It didn't really matter who drove him, there were plenty of girls to go around.

It was nearing 10:00 P.M. when Joran left the sports bar on foot and made his way to the McDonald's on the corner of Palm Beach Road. The fast-food restaurant was the halfway point between the hotels of Palm Beach and his family's home in Noord. It normally took him about twenty-five minutes to walk home. But his father had promised to pick him up when he was done at the casino, so he called to let him know he was ready.

"I'll be there in fifteen minutes," Paulus told his son.

Strolling past the shops and sidewalk vendors along J. E. Irausquin Boulevard selling merchandise only a tourist would buy—shot glasses, wind chimes, hammocks, and T-shirts—Joran punched the number of his friend Jaime into his cell phone. He had a group of guys he hung around with, and Jaime "Beto" Carrasquilla Caceres was part of the gang. Even though he attended an expensive private school, Joran considered himself an islander. Most of Joran's friends were locals who attended the public schools; many were older than Joran. His friend Jaime was from Colombia and lived with his parents in Alta Vista, a small village in the northeastern hills overlooking the blue-green waters of the Caribbean Sea.

While Joran's parents hoped he'd make friends with the children of the other ex-pats living on Aruba, Joran and Jaime were part of a group of local guys who liked to prowl the beaches and hotel pools along the Palm Beach strip, hoping to hook up with tourist girls. Of the group, Joran's English was the best so he usually did most of the talking. It was a numbers game. With so many hotels lining the beach, their choices were limitless. If rebuffed by one of the dozens of bikini-clad teens sunning on hotel lounge chairs, they could just walk farther down the white sand of the "turquoise coast" and try again.

Joran told Jaime that he'd just met a group of American girls at the casino inside the Holiday Inn and they had invited him to go out. "Would you like to come along?" he asked, knowing his friend was usually good for a ride. Jaime wanted to join them, but he wasn't sure he could make it. He had to work at a restaurant that night and said he would get back to him.

"Okay, I'll call Deepak," Joran said before hanging up. Scrolling through his contacts, he dialed his Surinamese friend. It was an imperfect plan. Deepak wasn't exactly a ladies' man. With dark skin, a square chin and chiseled features, he was not a bad-looking guy but he was awkward around females, preferring the anonymity of online chatting to real-life interactions. It didn't much matter to Joran. The simple reality was that the driving age on Aruba was eighteen, and while Joran's father permitted him to drive, he didn't have a car or a license. But his friend Deepak Kalpoe did.

Deepak was twenty-one, and had a tricked-out gray Honda Civic with tinted windows, custom wheels and tires, and a body kit to make the car look more aerodynamic. The vehicle was about six years old, but he took care of it as if it were brand new. According to Joran, Deepak treated the four-door sedan like a girlfriend. He wouldn't drive it on unpaved roads and washed it regularly, at least once a week.

He'd installed two TV screens hooked up to a DVD player, all tied into an expensive sound system. Joran described it as a "unique" car, and said the mufflers made a lot of noise. Initially, Joran's parents were curious as to how the youth was able to afford such an expensive car. After all, he worked at a cyber café. The dark-skinned teen told them it was a used car that he'd customized himself, buying parts cheaply.

Joran had known Deepak for about five months. Deepak's younger brother, Satish, had introduced them. Satish was eighteen, and attended Colegio Arubano, the same public school as some of Joran's other friends.

Since meeting Deepak the past January, the Kalpoe brothers and Joran had been hanging out on weekends, going to bars, casinos, and movies. Joran admitted that he and his friends sometimes used Deepak for a ride. He had a really cool car, and was the only one of the group with a full-time job, which meant he could buy rounds of drinks at the bars. Mixed drinks on the island were cheap, costing not much more than a beer.

Deepak was just getting off his shift at the Cyberzone Internet Café in Oranjestad and didn't have to be back at work until the following afternoon. "I'm going home to take a shower and I'll come pick you up," the twenty-one-year-old said.

Arriving at McDonald's, Joran stepped into the air-conditioning and ordered a McFlurry milk shake, and then settled into an empty booth to wait. His father would be there soon.

His living arrangements at home afforded him a certain amount of personal freedom that even his mother was not aware of, and that most teenage boys could only dream of. His parents had given him the private apartment located between the garage and the swimming pool. It was completely detached from the main house, and had its own private entrance, which allowed Joran to discreetly come and go as he pleased. A line of trees obscured Joran's apartment from the main house, making it easy for him to slip in and out without his parents knowing.

The apartment was added some time after the family bought the house in the early nineties, as was the garage, two bedrooms in the main house, and the swimming pool. For a time, a Jamaican housekeeper resided in the apartment, and kept watch over the Van der Sloots' three sons while their parents were at work. As the boys grew older, and needed less supervision, the family released the housekeeper and rented the apartment. But after a bad tenant stiffed them on a rent payment, the apartment went to Joran.

Joran knew his father wouldn't go to sleep until he knew his son was in for the night. He accompanied his dad to the main house where he worked on an English paper on the computer in the living room. He was writing an essay about *The Life of Pi,* a novel by Yann Martel.

As soon as his father went to bed, Joran dialed Deepak to make sure he was still planning to pick him up. It was just before midnight.

"I'm in your room," Deepak informed him.

Joran was busy printing his school assignment in the living room, and told his friend he'd be right there. His father was fast asleep when he quietly walked across the backyard to his apartment where he found Deepak and his younger brother, Satish.

Satish had been the one to pick up his brother at work earlier in the evening, as he did most nights. Because Deepak had pimped out the Honda, he didn't like to park it downtown for fear it might be scratched so he had Satish shuttling him to and from work. Like always, the Kalpoe brothers had parked Deepak's four-door Civic on the dirt road a half block away from the Van der Sloots' orange stucco home, so the loud rumble from the car's customized exhaust system wouldn't wake up Joran's parents.

Climbing into Deepak's car, the group set off for town.

Like Joran, Satish also had school in the morning. He was three years younger than his brother, and a senior at the Colegio Arubano, a public junior and senior high school with two campuses on the island. The boys' mother would have been furious if she knew that Satish was going out with Joran and Deepak to party. But she was not home that night.

The Kalpoe brothers lived with their mother, stepfather,

and younger sister in Hooiberg, a town named after Mount Hooiberg, or "haystack" as it translates in English. At 541 feet, Mount Hooiberg was a well-known landmark and the highest point on the island; on a clear day, Venezuela could be seen from its summit. The surrounding community of single-family homes was located at the center of the island, far removed from the tourist district and inhabited mainly by working-class locals.

Their mother worked in a steakhouse at an island resort. She and her husband were still at work and unaware of the two boys' whereabouts.

It wasn't unusual for Deepak and Satish to go with Joran to Carlos'n Charlie's to hook up with a fresh batch of tourists. Joran or one of their other friends, Freddy, often made the first move.

Like wolves, they hunted in a pack and Joran, with the best English of the group, was the alpha male. Joran and his friends admired the older island's "players," who often bragged about their sexual escapades, and they aspired to be like them. Aruba's nightclubs throbbed with sexual energy and Joran and his Pimpology Crew were fast learners. If they struck out, which they often did, they were relentless. With an everchanging cast of young women on the island, their efforts would eventually pay off. Sometimes, these encounters would go no further than kissing on the dance floor of Carlos'n Charlie's, but on lucky nights, they'd drive their conquests back to their hotels where they'd have sex.

Joran was always quick to share the lurid details of his latest exploit, once bragging that he was given a blow job by an American girl on the balcony of a rented hotel room while Deepak was in the bathroom with another tourist girl, and a third friend was in the main room with another. If all went well, they'd have stories to share about the girls from Alabama in the morning.

Last call was less than an hour away when Joran flashed his VIP pass to the bouncer at Carlos'n Charlie's and ushered his two friends into the noisy nightclub. The place closed at

2:00 A.M. on weekends, but it was Sunday and that meant the doors would shut promptly at 1:00 A.M.

Music was blaring. About sixty people, mostly young Americans, were dancing and drinking outlandish alcoholic concoctions from plastic neon-colored, yard-long glasses.

Making their way to the bar, the three ordered a round of whiskey and Cokes and a couple of shots of Bacardi 151. As they stood downing their cocktails, Joran noticed Natalee, the quiet blonde who had stayed at the blackjack table only a few minutes before wandering off to socialize with friends. She was dancing on the stage near the front entrance, wearing the same outfit she'd had on earlier in the evening, a short denim skirt and a cute bandana-style halter top. Her long blond hair was pulled to one side in a barrette. She was full of energy, and had the rhythm and moves of a professional dancer.

Joran grabbed his drink and worked his way through the crowd to get a better look. Natalee's friend, Lee, the tall brunette, was on the raised dance floor with her. Lee had been doing body shots at the bar. Typically, a woman lay across the bar, stomach exposed, as a man stood over her and sucked a shot of alcohol, usually tequila, from her navel.

"I'm going to the bar to do another shot," Lee yelled over the music.

Natalee nodded and smiled. When Lee looked back from the bar, she noticed Joran, the Dutch tourist from the casino, standing by the stage steps watching Natalee dance. Lee and Natalee had bumped into Joran earlier as the two were walking out of the bathroom. Joran had nodded to them, but Natalee had not even said hello.

Sometime after midnight, two of Natalee's roommates, Ruth and Madison, decided to call it a night. Madison went outside with two of her classmates to look for a taxi while Ruth went to find Natalee to make sure she understood they were leaving.

Across the crowd, Ruth spotted her friend standing at the bar with Joran, the young Dutchman who had helped her win back her money at the casino. The two were talking and Ruth jumped and gestured, trying to get her attention.

"We're leaving," she mouthed over the classic rock blasting from the speakers.

Natalee, like most of the Mountain Brook teens, had been drinking but seemed sober and in control. "Okay," Natalee mouthed back, smiling.

Ruth waved, and Natalee waved back. If she had thought for a moment that Joran posed any danger to her friend she would have pulled Natalee from the bar. There were plenty of other people still milling about, and they knew Lee, their other roommate, had also stayed and figured that the two would return to the hotel together. Besides, Joran seemed harmless. That night as they pulled away from Carlos'n Charlie's in the taxi, the teens from Alabama, filled as they were with such glee, could never have imagined that this would be the last time they would see Natalee alive.

THREE

Unable to sit idly, Ricardo Flores started working his contacts. More than twenty-four hours had elapsed since he'd heard from his daughter. A call to his decades-old friend Rafael Rey, the head of Peru's Ministry of Defense, resulted in a personal visit from the government official. Flores had dabbled in politics a decade earlier and Rey, a former political crony, would become a constant presence at the Floreses' home, sitting vigil into the early morning hours. But there were very few leads. Both were operating under the assumption that Stephany's disappearance was a kidnapping. Under these circumstances, the best course of action for the family was to sit by the phone and wait for the ransom call. But the call was not coming.

By Tuesday, the Flores family feared the worst. In addition to Rey, there were police officers in the house. If this wasn't a kidnapping, there must be some other explanation. Police began questioning Ricardo about his relationship with his daughter. Had he and Stephany been fighting? Could she have simply run away?

"Perhaps she left home?" the investigators suggested.

"We have a solid friendship," Ricardo told them. "We fight like anybody fights."

Ricardo Flores was a realist. He understood that the questions, while uncomfortable, were necessary. However, he thought that the officers were running down a blind alley. Stephany had no reason to run away. *She has a good life here,* Ricardo thought. He was getting nowhere sitting by the phone. He needed to get personally involved.

He knew from friends that Stephany had been frequenting the casinos of Miraflores lately, and he thought they were as good a place as any to start. Perhaps she'd gotten caught up in the hype surrounding the Latin American Poker Tour going on at the Atlantic City Casino? This was the first time the tour had hosted a tournament in Peru and it was getting lots of publicity in the local press. The tour's previously scheduled stop in Viña del Mar, Chile, had been canceled after a devastating earthquake shook the country in March and Lima had been substituted as a replacement city. In the days leading up to the event in Lima, players had been arriving from around the world. The players were "poker-world" celebrities in their own right and it stood to reason that Stephany would want to meet them.

The Atlantic City Casino was the largest of the eight casinos in Miraflores and a favorite of the Flores family because they were friends of the owner. This was a logical place for the desperate father to start his search.

Darkness had already arrived when Ricardo and his two adult sons, Ricardo Jr. and Enrique, and Enrique's young bride, Carolina, pulled into the parking garage of the Atlantic City Casino. They were hoping to find Stephany sitting at a gaming table. People were known to lose track of time in the artificial perpetual daylight of a windowless casino. Like most casinos there were no clocks on the walls that might remind gamblers when it was time to call it a night. However, forty-eight hours had passed since they'd last heard from her.

Striding into the Atlantic City's ornate marble lobby, the

three men were instantly recognized by casino staff. Ricardo Flores and casino owner Omar Macchi were close friends. Ricardo had known Omar's father for decades. When the elder Macchi died eight years earlier, Ricardo stayed in close touch with Omar, the heir and new proprietor of the casino. Omar and Riflo were both popular figures in Lima's tabloid press. The flamboyant young casino owner was often photographed on the town, decked out in gold lamé designer shirts, with a supermodel on each arm. The moment Omar learned that Ricardo Flores was downstairs asking about his daughter, he dropped everything to offer his support. Omar had essentially grown up with Stephany and thought of her as family.

The distraught father wanted to review the casino's surveillance tapes, hoping to find an image of his missing daughter. Normally, Macchi would not entertain such a request without a court order, but this was a friend. There would be no objections, no red tape.

"Anything you need, my friend," Omar said, putting his arm around Ricardo. "Don't worry, we'll find her."

Omar immediately directed members of his staff to begin reviewing the casino's video footage, beginning early Sunday morning when Stephany's trail went cold. Despite playing host to the Latin American Poker Tour, Omar excused himself from the excitement and sat with the Flores family screening the tapes. Two hours passed before they spotted an image of Stephany's black Jeep pulling into space number four of the casino's parking lot.

"Freeze the frame," Omar directed, noting the time and date stamp in the lower right hand corner. It was 2:54 A.M. on Sunday, May 30. Having isolated a time, Macchi instructed a member of his staff to cut to the camera covering the casino entrance for that same time period. Seconds later, Stephany's image appeared on the screen. From there it was simply a matter of following her movements from camera to camera as she walked through the casino. It was 2:57 A.M. when Stephany was seen heading for the poker tables, taking a seat next to Joran van der Sloot.

For Ricardo Flores, the experience of watching his daughter sitting at a poker table at three in the morning with a stranger was distressing. However, the young man did not appear to be a threat. He looked like a tourist, a gringo on vacation. As the sequence of videotapes progressed, Ricardo viewed his daughter calling it quits around 5:00 A.M. and heading to the cashier's window to cash in her remaining poker chips. Another video clip showed her leaving the casino parking lot with the young stranger in Stephany's Jeep around 5:15 A.M., turning left onto Avenida Benavides, and driving off in a southerly direction.

In a tragic irony, at that moment, Ricardo also worried about the stranger, thinking that they both had been abducted. His daughter's companion was someone's child, and Ricardo hoped that both children could be rescued unharmed and returned to their panicked families. He wondered if anyone even realized that the young foreigner was missing.

Video footage before Stephany's arrival that night revealed Van der Sloot arriving at 2:06 A.M., less than an hour before Stephany, wearing a beige long-sleeved shirt and a pair of blue jeans. Further review of video recordings from earlier in the week showed that the two had met before. Ricardo Flores observed his daughter with this same man at another gaming table that past Friday. That was the same night he had given Stephany U.S.$1,000—supposedly to buy a laptop computer.

Stephany's friend Carola Sanguinetti would later tell police that Stephany told her that she'd spent about an hour that Friday evening playing poker with a Dutchman at the Atlantic City Casino before coming to meet her for a night out.

Because the two arrived at the casino within an hour of one another, Ricardo speculated that perhaps their meeting had been prearranged and that Stephany had intended to go to the casino after dropping off her friends early Sunday morning.

Omar provided his friend with a still image of the unidentified male that Ricardo planned on distributing to the media. It was around 11:00 P.M. when he was ready to head home. Standing in the parking garage, Ricardo realized he had left his cell phone upstairs in the casino and went to retrieve it.

Once upstairs, he was approached by a hostess with more information that Omar had been able to garner. "We have the guy's name and passport number," the young woman said.

Every night the casino sponsored a raffle, which was open to gamblers who'd won even small amounts of money at slot machines and gaming tables. Sometimes the prizes were large sums of cash or even cars.

A casino employee remembered that the man in the video had won a small prize and was quick to find his winning ticket. Joran van der Sloot had put his name and passport number on the prize receipt.

Now Ricardo Flores and police had an identity to go with the photographic image. One of the hostesses remembered seeing Van der Sloot with Ricardo's daughter days before, and said they had been conversing in English. It didn't surprise Flores. Stephany had studied English and knew it well. "Yeah, Stephany was with this guy," one of the casino employees confirmed. "He seemed nice. He looked like Brad Pitt."

Those poor kids, Ricardo thought, looking down at the picture.

With a name and photograph, Ricardo sped home to tell the family he now had a lead. But his sense of excitement was soon replaced with a sense of horror.

Curious about the unidentified stranger, and knowing the resources of the Internet, Carolina, the wife of Ricardo's son Enrique, went upstairs to Stephany's room and powered up her computer. She had been with Ricardo at the casino and wanted to see if there was any information on Joran van der Sloot online. Specifically, she was thinking there might be a posting about him being a missing person.

For a moment Stephany's sister-in-law sat stunned as the search engine turned up page after page of links to news articles connecting Van der Sloot to a possible murder of another young woman, also someone he had met in a casino, five years earlier. There had been security footage of the two sitting at a blackjack table, Carolina read, as she thought about the video Omar had just shown them.

The rest of the Flores family was downstairs when they heard Carolina's anguished screams. Racing up to Stephany's room, they found their relative seated in front of the monitor, trembling.

Soon, all their eyes were transfixed in horror on the computer screen, tears streaming down their cheeks. They scrolled through article after article detailing the Dutch national's suspected involvement in the disappearance of Natalee Holloway, an eighteen-year-old teen from Alabama vacationing on an island named Aruba. Because Holloway's body had never been found, no charges had been filed and the suspected murderer had been able to travel the world, legally and unrestricted.

"I can't believe it," Enrique wailed. "How could she be with that guy?"

As members of the Flores family struggled to come to terms with the sickening discovery, a similar scene was playing out at the headquarters of the Dirección de Investigación Criminal, Division of Criminal Investigations (DIRINCRI), a monolithic concrete structure at 323 Avenida España in Lima's gritty downtown.

Because of his connection to the Ministry of Defense, Ricardo Flores had the full attention of the Peruvian police department. Investigators from the kidnapping division had Googled Van der Sloot's name, as well. Their search produced a five-page news article titled "El Caso Natalee Holloway." The article, written by Dutch journalist Willemien Groot in 2008 and translated into Spanish, included a comprehensive chronology that began with Holloway's disappearance on May 30, 2005, while on holiday in Aruba, and detailed numerous failed attempts to bring her suspected abductor, Joran van der Sloot, to justice. Soon detectives added other key words to the mix, including "Aruba," *"asesinato,"* "*desaparición*," "Natalee Holloway," and "Van der Sloot." The officers were stunned. How had this supposed killer entered Peru unnoticed? Surely he must have been flagged by Interpol.

Given this new discovery, the theory that Stephany's disappearance was a ransom-driven abduction seemed less likely. The possibility of homicide could not be denied.

While Natalee's disappearance had been front-page news in the U.S. and for a time in Holland, the story had not generated any media interest in Peru. At this point, Peruvian officers had never heard of the Alabama teen or her alleged killer, Joran van der Sloot. But it was becoming increasingly apparent that they were now in the middle of a case with international implications. Officers who had been working the case for two solid days were now working overtime, quickly fanning out across Lima, checking hotels, casinos, airports, any place Van der Sloot might be seeking shelter or escape.

Officers stationed at the Floreses' home braced the family for the worst.

"There is very little hope," they told Ricardo and Mariaelena.

FOUR

Ruth McVay woke up with a start. It was just after 8:00 A.M. and departure day, and she needed to be sure she was packed and in the lobby by 10:00 A.M. All the classmates were gathering there before the trip home to Alabama. The groups were split into two separate flights, and Ruth and her roommates were booked on the second, scheduled to take off at 3:00 P.M.

Ruth pushed off the blue-and-yellow patchwork comforter, and sat up in bed. "Hey, where's Hootie?" she asked Lee, who was just waking up in the double bed next to her. Hootie was Natalee Holloway's nickname. When she first moved to Birmingham in the eighth grade and discovered that most of the kids had nicknames for each other, she told everyone that her friends back in Mississippi had called her "Hootie Hoo Holloway." She'd made up the name just to fit in, and it had stuck.

"She probably didn't want to wake us, so she slept in another room," Lee suggested. Climbing out of bed, she pulled back the yellow, floor-length curtains of the sliding glass doors, letting in the morning sun. The girls' room was right on the beach and had a small patio with a few chairs.

Ruth smiled. "You're probably right." Over the course of their vacation, she had become accustomed to waking up next to her good friend. For the past three days, Natalee had been the first one up, and was usually the one to rally the group. But she had definitely not slept on her side of the bed last night. The bedding was tucked in tight.

The living arrangements in Room 7114 had been loose, flexible at best. Madison would often stay with a friend in another room, and other classmates would take naps, or even stay the night in her vacant spot. Natalee, Ruth, and Lee, however, had steadfastly maintained their occupancy in Room 7114.

During their four days on the island, Natalee and Lee had slipped into a daily routine. They'd wake up, have a morning cocktail and then hit the beach around 10:00 A.M. to swim and lay in the sun. If they weren't taking an afternoon trip, they'd lunch at the pool. At 5:00 P.M., they would return to the room to nap for an hour before getting ready to go out to eat. After dinner, the bar hopping began.

At five feet four, and weighing 110 pounds, Natalee didn't have the same tolerance for alcohol that some of the other teens did. That Saturday, Lee had become concerned when the petite blonde had had one too many and asked another Mountain Brook teen to escort her back to the room to sleep it off. But despite this embarrassing incident, Natalee was drinking Red Fires, an over-proof Cuba libre made with Bacardi 151 and Diet Coke, at dinner that Sunday night. Again, she had seemed unsteady and friends told her to slow down. She ordered several more cocktails at Carlos'n Charlie's. But Ruth thought that she had looked sober and in control when she saw her standing at the bar talking to Joran.

Natalee was most likely grabbing breakfast and would be back soon to pack up her suitcase. She was an amazingly responsible friend.

Lately, she had been telling Ruth about her dream of becoming a doctor. Most of the other gals in the graduating class seemed preoccupied with which sorority they would pledge. The last few evenings, she'd stayed up late talking with Ruth about how excited she was to be going to the University of Alabama.

Natalee's family had been elated when they learned she had received a full academic scholarship to the university, where she was planning to enroll in the pre-med program in the fall. She had made plans to share a dorm room at the Tuscaloosa campus with another Mountain Brook classmate. She promised Ruth she would visit her at her college.

Ruth and Lee showered and finished packing, but by 9:00 A.M. there was still no sign of Natalee. When Madison returned from her friend's room, they told her they had not seen Natalee since the night before at the bar. Did she know where she was?

Madison had left Carlos'n Charlie's with Ruth and hadn't seen Natalee since. Pulling their friend's purple duffel bag from the closet, Madison and another friend, Holly Brown, who was staying in an adjoining room, packed up Natalee's belongings so that she would be ready when she returned for her bag. If she missed her flight, her mother was going to be mad, the friends joked. They could only imagine Natalee's mother's reaction if her daughter missed her flight because she was still basking on the sun-soaked Palm Beach on Aruba.

The first group of students was catching a 1:00 P.M. flight back to the U.S. and was already gathering in the lobby for the bus to the airport.

"Where in the world could she be?" Ruth asked. "This is so unlike Natalee."

Convinced she had spent the night with some of their friends on the trip, Lee and Ruth began calling other rooms before walking around the hotel knocking on the doors of their fellow students. No one had seen Natalee since the night before at Carlos'n Charlie's.

Lee began to panic and she started to cry. The last time she had seen her friend, they had shared the dance floor at Carlos'n Charlie's eight hours earlier. The two had gone crazy, rocking out to the eighties classics. Whenever the DJ played a song by Lynyrd Skynyrd, Natalee's favorite band, she would go berserk. "Sweet Home Alabama" was the DJ's top pick of the night.

Natalee was a particularly talented jazz dancer. Her natural, graceful moves often attracted the attention of the opposite sex. She was a member of her high school dance team, the Dorians. The previous night, the two friends danced their hearts out for an hour before Lee finally left her to return to the bar for another round.

When the bar had closed at 1:00 A.M., Lee looked around for Natalee but couldn't find her. She filtered outside with about sixty other Mountain Brook teens, where taxis were lining the street to provide rides back to the Holiday Inn. With so many people spilling out at once, no one was specifically looking out for Natalee. A general presumption prevailed that everyone was looking out for everyone.

Still, Lee wanted to be sure Natalee was safe. She walked around the corner to another bar, Choose-A-Name, to see if Natalee might be there. Her instincts told her that Natalee had not been in the crowd outside Carlos'n Charlie's. She would have called her on her cell phone, but the teens were in the unusual and frustrating position of having no cell service on the island. However, looking in the karaoke bar, Lee didn't find Natalee there either and she returned to Carlos'n Charlie's to take a cab back to Palm Beach.

At 3:00 A.M., Natalee still hadn't returned to the room. However, she could easily have been in the company of scores of other Mountain Brook seniors still outside partying by the pool. She assumed that Natalee was pulling a last hurrah all-nighter.

Now, however, having fruitlessly searched the hotel, Lee felt sick at the thought that something might have happened. Overcome with nausea and panic, she ran to find a chaperone.

Bob Plummer, a teacher and golf coach at Mountain Brook Junior High School, was outside in the hotel parking lot. He had just completed a final head count and passport check of the students on the first bus when Lee, Ruth, and several other girls came running out of the hotel. They looked distraught, and one of them was crying.

"We can't find Natalee," Lee blurted out between sobs. "Nobody's seen her since last night." Plummer walked with the girls back into the lobby where the other adults were busy assembling the second busload of students, checking their tickets and passports.

"Has anybody seen Natalee this morning?" Plummer yelled out to the teens who were gathered near the wicker couches, seated on suitcases, listening to iPods.

"Yes," one of the guys said. "I saw her leave Carlos'n Charlie's last night with some guys in a silver car."

Several of the classmates claimed to have seen Natalee in the backseat of the vehicle next to a tall white guy. Two dark-skinned locals were with them in the front seats. Natalee did not seem to be held against her will. They speculated that maybe Natalee thought she was getting into a cab with the guy since many of the taxis on the island are unmarked. When the car passed, Natalee rolled down the rear window and yelled out to her classmates standing on the curb. "I'm going to ride back to the Holiday Inn," she shouted. "Aruba!"

It sounded to Lee like Natalee had gotten into a car with the Dutch tourist from the casino. She'd seen him at Carlos'n Charlie's, standing by the front stage watching her dance. Her hunch was confirmed when one of her classmates said he'd recognized the guy from the Excelsior.

Lee was trying hard to control her emotions. This was not like Natalee. Something was terribly wrong. She would never get into a car by herself with strangers. It didn't make any sense.

Plummer noticed Lee trembling. She was having a hard time catching her breath. Putting his arm around her, he tried to soothe her. "She probably just lost track of time," he told the terror-struck friend. "She'll show up. Let's just go to your room and see if maybe she's come back."

Room 7114 was empty. Except for the purple duffel bag, there was no sign of Natalee. Plummer found her passport and a few dollars in one of the pockets of her luggage. Natalee, like most of the other kids on the trip, had left her cell phone in the room because her phone lacked an international calling plan, which rendered it useless on the island. Not wanting to leave Natalee's belongings unattended, he picked up her bag and the two vacated the room and returned to the lobby.

The young women stayed with Plummer as he reported their missing classmate to the security officers at the Holiday Inn. Lee watched through her tears as one of the uniformed men scribbled something on his clipboard. He didn't seem particularly concerned, and said little to comfort her.

The first bus was already on its way to Aruba's Queen Beatrix International Airport and Plummer told Ruth and Lee that they needed to be on the second bus or they would miss their flight. The friends didn't want to go; the thought of leaving Natalee behind was almost unbearable.

Chaperone Paul Lilly volunteered to stay at the hotel. He promised that everything would be all right. "I'm not going anywhere," Lilly reassured Lee and Ruth. "I'll be right here in the lobby waiting for her. Now go catch your flight."

While her daughter and her friends were celebrating their high school graduation in Aruba, Natalee Holloway's mother, Beth Twitty, had taken a vacation of her own. The month of May had been an exhausting blur of activity with Natalee's prom, graduation, and the preparation for her big senior trip to Aruba. Beth had relished every moment of it. She loved her daughter, but she was worn out and looking forward to a few days of down time with friends.

Beth, a willowy Southern woman in her early forties, was a speech pathologist who worked with special needs children. She had arranged to spend Memorial Day weekend at her family's lake house in Hot Springs, Arkansas, and had invited two friends, Linda and Marilyn, to join her. The family lake house was just a thirty-minute drive from Pine Bluff, where Beth grew up, and she held fond memories of her childhood days splashing about in Lake Hamilton.

She and her girlfriends had set off for the lake house the same day that Natalee left for Aruba. It was a relaxing time, and a chance to unwind. Everyone asked about Natalee's graduation ceremony, and Beth promised she would send some pictures when she returned to Birmingham. After several days in Hot Springs, Beth and her friends decided to spend Sunday night in Memphis, Tennessee, rather than attempt the nine-hour drive home in one day.

Beth was excited when she woke up on Monday morning knowing she'd be seeing her daughter later that evening. Natalee was scheduled to arrive in Birmingham at 10:30 P.M. and Beth had made plans to pick her up at the airport. She couldn't wait to see her daughter's expression when she gave her the *Wizard of Oz* figurines she'd bought for her at a gift shop in Hot Springs. Natalee had become captivated with the film during grade school, and it was an infatuation she never outgrew. Her friends found it amusing when Beth had surprised her daughter with a *Wizard of Oz* birthday cake that past October when she turned eighteen. It was classic Beth.

Beth was happy to stretch out in the backseat while her girlfriends sat up front. The group had just left Memphis and was driving south on Highway 78 when Beth received the call that every mother dreads.

Blakye Bearman, one of Natalee's classmates, was on the line. She sounded scared and was stammering. "My mom wants to talk to you," she said.

Blakye's mother, Jodi, was the travel agent who had arranged the students' senior trip. She and her mom were supposed to be in Aruba with the group but had to cancel at the last minute when Blakye came down with appendicitis.

"What's the matter, Jodi?" Beth demanded, sensing something was wrong.

"Natalee didn't show up this morning to get on the plane." Jodi's words hit Beth like a cold slap.

"What do you mean she didn't get on the plane?"

Jodi related what the chaperones down on Aruba had told her. Natalee hadn't returned to her hotel room after a night out at a bar. Her three roommates were frantic. Natalee was missing.

"Pull over!" Beth directed. She needed to call Jug. George "Jug" Twitty was Beth's second husband, and Natalee's stepfather. The couple had married in 2000, when Natalee was in the eighth grade.

Twitty was a large, rugged man with bushy salt-and-pepper hair and a cleft chin who looked like he could have played college football in his youth. He was the manager of an Alabama metals company that distributed steel and other materials used in construction, and had invited his pretty strawberry-blond bride and her two children, Natalee and Matt, to move in with him after the wedding.

Jug had two children of his own, George Jr. and Megan, who were several years older than Natalee and her brother. The four children got along well, and there was plenty of room for everyone in his stately red brick Mountain Brook home. While Jug was a successful businessman, his home was modest compared to some of his neighbors.

The nearly all-white bedroom community was a maze of streets lined with grand homes and carefully manicured lawns. People who lived outside the wealthy enclave jokingly referred to it as "the tiny kingdom" because of the disparity of wealth between Mountain Brook and the rest of Birmingham.

"Jug, something's happened to Natalee. I need your help," Beth pleaded. She told her husband she wanted to get down to Aruba immediately and asked if he could arrange a charter flight.

At first, Jug thought his wife was overreacting, just being a nervous mother. "She probably just missed the flight," he told her.

But Beth was insistent. "You know Natalee, she's never been late for anything. Something's wrong."

"I'll see what I can do."

Hanging up with Jug, Beth and her two friends dialed anyone they could think of who might have access to a plane. But it was Monday of Memorial Day weekend and many of the private pilots had already had a few beers at backyard barbecues, rendering them unable to fly. As the women made their calls, Linda continued to drive but was so upset that her driving was becoming erratic.

"Let me take the wheel!" Beth insisted. Ignoring the posted speed limits, Natalee's mother raced toward Birmingham. The crumbling red soil of cotton and soybean fields filled the side windows, the few trees along the shoulder a tangle of green, strangled by kudzu, an invasive Asian vine. Steering wheel in one hand, cell phone in the other, Beth fielded calls from Natalee's friends who were at the airport and about to board their flight. She learned that her daughter was last seen at a bar called Carlos'n Charlie's.

Hearing that, Beth grew even more alarmed. She had spoken to Natalee about this very place in the days before her departure. Beth had been told by one of the Mountain Brook students who had been on a previous trip to Aruba of local men who trawled the bar, targeting tourist girls and luring them out of the nightspot.

Beth listened in horror as one of the students told her that Natalee had climbed into a silver or gray Honda with a person from Holland whom she had met at a casino. It was almost too much to process. She needed to get to that island. Pressing harder on the gas pedal, Beth gunned the engine. Not wanting to endanger anyone else on the road, she dialed 911 and asked for a police escort. "I'm doing a hundred and twenty miles an hour in the left lane," she said, reading out her location to the dispatcher.

Natalee's brother, Matt, had received the news as well. Convinced that something horrible had happened to his big sister, he called his mother and advised her to call the FBI, feeding her telephone numbers for the various offices as she raced down the highway.

Dialing number after number, Beth couldn't get anybody on the line who seemed to be in a position to help. It was Memorial Day weekend and all the agents were home celebrating with their families. Beth's cell phone continued to ring with calls from the Mountain Brook students relating what little information they had.

One of them was Jug's nephew, Thomas, also a senior at Mountain Brook and on the class trip. He had actually seen the guy who had left with Natalee from Carlos'n Charlie's. He shared a poker table with him at the Excelsior Casino during the trip. The young man told Thomas he was from Holland and staying at the Holiday Inn. Thomas also remembered his first name. "It's Gerran or Juran or something like that. I don't think he would hurt Natalee. He seemed like a regular guy, like me."

The private jet carrying Beth and Jug Twitty hit the tarmac of Aruba's Queen Beatrix International Airport at 10:00 P.M. on Monday, May 31. Also on board were Madison Whatley's father, Matt, and Ruffner Page Jr., the owner of the jet. Ruffner's daughter had also been on the trip. Beth's friend, Jodi Bearman, the travel agent who had booked the travel for all 124 students and seven chaperones, was also on the flight.

Ruffner had arranged for private handlers to meet the party at the airstrip to assist with customs, ground transportation, and anything else they might need. The two local men were waiting at the airport as promised, and quickly ushered everyone into a white van.

The group's first stop was the Holiday Inn SunSpree Resort, where Natalee and her friends had spent their holiday. Hurrying into the hotel lobby, the Twittys spotted Paul Lilly, the Mountain Brook chaperone who had stayed behind in case Natalee returned to the hotel. He was seated uncomfortably on a wicker couch to the left of the reception desk talking with a dark-skinned American man.

Amid a lobby abuzz with laughing tourists sipping piña coladas, the grim-faced gym teacher looked Beth straight in the eyes and sadly shook his head. The look said it all. He had no news about Natalee. Striding over, Beth immediately noticed her daughter's purple duffel bag on the table next to him.

Seeing the bag, Beth's mind flashed back to Thursday morning when Natalee had carried it out of the house just after 3:00 A.M. to catch her flight. She had been so excited. The farthest from home Natalee had been before the Aruban adventure was to Austria with her mother. But this would be her first time out of the country without a parent to accompany her. Natalee's mother had set aside money so that her daughter could attend. She felt Natalee had worked hard in school and deserved the trip.

Her stepson, George, had gone on the senior trip to Aruba two years earlier. Natalee's stepcousins, twins named Thomas and Hunter, were joining her on this celebratory Caribbean getaway.

In the weeks leading up to the trip, Beth had attended meetings at which the role of the chaperones had been discussed. She'd even sat her daughter down and warned her to be careful, that there were predators out there, men who might try to pick her up or try to slip drugs into her drink.

With 124 students going on the trip, Beth had assumed there would be safety in numbers. Now standing in the lobby of the Holiday Inn, she realized she'd been wrong. Natalee was out there somewhere, alone and frightened, or worse.

The Mountain Brook chaperone explained that earlier in the day he'd reported her daughter's disappearance to members of the Visibility Team, who were stationed at various locations around the resort.

Judging by their official-looking uniforms, he assumed he was dealing with law enforcement. For years, drug dealing and petty crime plagued the tourist zones, threatening the tranquil image of "One Happy Island" promoted by the tourism industry. In response, with funding from the private sector, a high-profile Visibility Team was created in 2002 to patrol the beaches along the high-rise strip, as well as other parts of the island.

Dressed in either white or baby-blue shirts and dark-colored shorts or slacks, team members wore baseball caps with the word "Police" written on them in large white lettering. Members of the Visibility Team, which included both police officers and private security guards, were hard to miss as they cruised the Palm Beach area atop blue four-wheel all-terrain dune buggies, walkie-talkies in hand. The Noord Police Station's district commander was the Visibility Team's supervisor.

In spite of the team's exaggerated visibility, Lilly still described frustration at the procedure for reporting a missing person. No one seemed to know the chain of command. Finally, by accident, Lilly encountered Eric Williams, on vacation himself in Aruba, and now seated beside him. Williams said he was an agent with the U.S. Drug Enforcement Administration (DEA) and offered Lilly his assistance.

Beth was relieved to hear he was from a U.S. federal agency, and promptly shared everything she had learned from Natalee's friends. Williams made a few calls to police on the island and was told that on Aruba, just as in the United States, an adult must be missing for twenty-four hours before an official report can be filed. Natalee was eighteen and an adult in the eyes of the law.

It had been twenty-two hours since Natalee's friends had last seen her hanging out the window of a car in the company of three young men, yelling the word "Aruba" back to her puzzled classmates standing outside of Carlos'n Charlie's. Beth was beside herself. Time was of the essence.

Marching to the reception desk, the distraught mother approached the night manager, Brenda, with questions about her missing daughter and a possible companion. Did she know a hotel guest named Joran?

Brenda knew instantly who she was talking about. The young man was a regular at the hotel casino upstairs, and he liked to pick up young female tourists, especially blondes.

Furthermore, he wasn't a hotel guest; he was an islander and lived year-round on Aruba.

"He is a tall, good-looking boy," Brenda volunteered. "Like a Dutch Marine."

Beth's apprehension was turning to fear. Nothing she had heard about this stranger appeared to be the truth.

FIVE

Anita van der Sloot was worried about her seventeen-year-old son. Often, she felt like she was dealing with two different people with completely separate personalities. The transformation had been gradual but was now impossible to ignore.

At home, Joran had become difficult. The lies and inappropriate behavior had begun years before, but his mother hoped he would outgrow it as he matured. But puberty had brought on a new set of challenges that Anita could never have anticipated.

Almost overnight, Joran shot up physically, and became increasingly argumentative and aggressive. His younger brothers were fearful of him. Anita suspected her introverted husband was, as well, but he did his best to keep his distance. Paulus was not one for confrontation and tended to retreat to his work and let his wife handle the discipline.

However, the power shift in the Van der Sloots' household was undeniable. With any reproach or criticism, Joran became so brooding and irritated that the family shrank away from him, terrorized by a young man they couldn't comprehend.

A year earlier, when Joran brought home a new girlfriend, Melody Granadillo, his mother had been ecstatic. She was a dark-skinned beauty with curly black hair and a long, delicate neck. They had met at a birthday party in October 2003 and for a spell, Joran seemed truly happy. It was a typical teenage courtship. The two went to movies and concerts on the beach.

Anita loved seeing her eldest son so infatuated. He had been giddy with excitement the day he told her about taking his new girlfriend to the Japanese steakhouse Benihana's for her birthday.

"I gave her a vase full of red Skittles," he said, explaining that Skittles were Melody's favorite candy. He'd purchased several bags of the multicolored candies and he picked out the red ones. "She was so surprised."

In turn, Melody gave Joran a two-month-old boxer/Great Dane mix for Valentine's Day. He named the puppy "Charro," slang for "street person." Charro joined Silly, a black-and-brown mutt that Anita had rescued from the streets.

Joran had had other girlfriends. When he was fourteen, he briefly dated an American girl whose father was in Aruba on business. He had enrolled his teenage daughter at Joran's school, the International School of Aruba. Joran once confided to his mother that this girlfriend thought he was too sweet, and not strong enough for her liking. After she moved back to the United States with her family, Joran became involved with a local girl named Carmen. That relationship was short-lived. His parents had never witnessed Joran so in love as he was with Melody.

However, after seven months the relationship was over. Melody discovered that the boy she so endearingly called "Chi Chi" or "Mr. Wiggles" was unfaithful. She had ignored her friends' previous warnings about his lothario ways, but when she discovered he was having an affair with a classmate of hers, she dumped him over the phone.

His obsession with gambling was also highly disagreeable. He was known to incorporate gambling metaphors into love poems he wrote to her.

"You are my very own seventeen, the best hand ever dealt," he opened one tender ballad saved in her blue scrapbook.

Most problematic of all were his relentless, fantastic, pathological lies. He lied about everything and then lied about lying, a perplexing and unacceptable situation to Melody.

For the narcissistic young teen, the alpha male of his Pimpology Crew, the breakup was devastating. Still, Melody remained an important person to Joran and they continued to stay in touch. Joran knew that his lies and cheating ways had been the reason for their breakup but he just couldn't seem to help himself.

By May 2005, he was again juggling two different girlfriends and constantly seeking meaningless hookups on the side. Other boys at the Aruba Racquet Club, where his family actively enjoyed the facilities, saw Joran for what he was—a playboy and a bully. They couldn't believe how popular he was with the ladies. Perhaps they were attracted to his bad-boy image.

On the court, Joran exhibited all the sportsmanship of an uglier version of a young John McEnroe, cursing, throwing his racquet and menacing other players. He was a regular at the club's gym, where he worked out obsessively in the afternoons after his private tennis lessons, trying to sweat out the booze from the night before. But the late nights of partying were taking their toll. When Joran looked in the mirror, he saw the beginnings of a double chin. He'd been chubby as a child, and was terribly self-conscious about his weight. He wanted to be strong and sexually attractive.

Joran had been a quiet child, almost shy. However, because he was the oldest, he felt the need to be the little man of the house, especially when his father worked such long days, sometimes weeks away from the home.

Now, Anita found herself missing her little man. He had helped her when she was lonely. He had always listened to her and followed the rules she laid down. Even now, she held on to the belief that her son's short temper, his rebelliousness, and his lies were all part of a misguided teenage attempt to exert his independence. He just needed to find his way.

Joran van der Sloot was born on August 6, 1987, in the city of Arnhem in the eastern part of the Netherlands, less than an hour's drive from the German border on the banks of the Rhine River, and one of the few Dutch cities with hills. Located about sixty miles southeast of Amsterdam, Arnhem was the site of a famous World War II battle. Much of the city center had been rebuilt after it was nearly destroyed in the Battle of Arnhem, and as a result it was missing much of the Old World charm found in other Dutch towns. Only Rotterdam had sustained more damage. *A Bridge Too Far,* the World War II movie classic, was set in Arnhem. Today, an ever-dwindling group of veterans makes the pilgrimage back to Arnhem to see the famous John Frost Bridge, named for Britain's legendary airborne officer.

Paulus and Anita van der Sloot were not married when Joran was born, believing they didn't need a court document to honor their commitment. The couple met in Arnhem when Paulus moved to the city in the late 1970s to accept a job after graduating from Tilburg University, one of Europe's most prestigious law schools. Instead of taking a government post, Paulus chose to join a private practice representing citizens who had conflicts with the government.

Anita, a gregarious and free-spirited young redhead who was fascinated by Eastern religions and philosophies, was completing her undergraduate studies in art education at Hogeschool voor de Kunsten, a fine arts academy in Arnhem. She found work at Lorentz College, teaching art to middle- and high school students while earning a master's degree.

Paulus, on the other hand, was more reserved. He was four years older and stood nearly a foot taller than Anita, and was an introverted bookworm who was passionate about the law. He believed everyone should be afforded due process and was uncompromising in his principles. But he did have a lighter side. He played in a local brass band and shared Anita's passion for traveling. The couple took a relaxed approach to having children, choosing to travel and see the world before facing the commitments of family life.

Anita was thirty when Joran was born, and later told her son that he had been conceived during a trip to Ecuador. She and Paulus had also visited Egypt during her pregnancy. Valentijn was born two years later in 1989.

By then, Anita had completed her master's work, and was supplementing the family's income tutoring art students in her home.

Paulus had earned a reputation as a serious lawyer and he fought hard for his clients. His stubborn nature didn't win him many friends and there were some in his hometown of Boxtel who considered him a troublemaker.

During the 1980s, his personal and professional life collided when the Van der Sloots' ancestral home was embroiled in a government land-grab dispute. The quaint town center had been laid out in an era before commercial truck traffic. Most people in town walked or rode bikes wherever they went. The red brick homes with sloping tile roofs were built right up to the curb of the narrow cobblestone streets. This made a dangerous situation for pedestrians, especially children, forced to share the road with vehicular traffic.

The Dutch government had wanted to seize a slice of scenic and valuable property owned by Paulus and his brother Peter to build a proper motorway. Paulus and a local group of affected landowners, who called themselves BEL (Bewonders van de Eindhovenseweg en Liempdseweg, or Dwellers of the Eindhoven and Liemds Roads), protested the project. Paulus was adamant that his opposition to the plan was not personal, that the plans were flawed and would mar the beauty of a scenic and historic area and didn't fully address safety concerns.

But the town council had already invested money in the planning stages. They were unswerving in their devotion to the project and wanted to see it through to its fruition. During the protracted court battle, there were several more fatalities and local residents accused Van der Sloot of being indirectly complicit. He became a pariah. He was deeply hurt by the accusations and felt that his neighbors' anger was misdirected. The battle raged for nearly two decades, from 1973 to 1993, when a more suitable route for the bypass road was approved. By then, Paulus had already moved his family to Aruba.

In 1991, Paulus van der Sloot was ready for a drastic change and began searching for a new job. He was offered a position as an attorney for the Aruban government, and eagerly signed a five-year contract. It was a chance to move his wife and children to an exotic locale. He hoped that in the small island setting his legal skills would quickly gain notice. Paulus and Anita were seasoned travelers and researched the local customs and culture. While it was perfectly acceptable, and in fact common, to have children out of wedlock in Holland, those Dutch sensibilities were not shared by the more conservative-minded citizens of Aruba. Paulus and Anita married in a civil service before bringing the family overseas.

For four-year-old Joran, the balmy tropical island was a strange and wonderful place to spend a childhood. The Van der Sloots were well-off by Aruban standards, but by no means affluent. When the couple arrived with their two young sons, they spent their first months living in a hotel, The Mill, a small resort on Palm Beach.

Palm Beach was a beautiful spit of blinding white sand lined with the highest concentration of high-rise hotels on Aruba. Though smaller low-rise and bungalow-style hotels dotted its seventy-five square miles, Palm Beach was the most commercial and, for many, the most desirable spot on the island. Unlike other parts where the currents could be rough, the waters surrounding Palm Beach were ideal for swimming, windsurfing, and catching a sunset.

Ironically, there was nothing natural about the "natural" beauty of Aruba's Palm Beach. Its willowy palms were transplants and maintained for the benefit of the tourism industry. In its natural state, Aruba was a desertlike environment where aloe, prickly pear, and Turk's cap cactus dotted the barren landscape. In the last thirty years, however, the growth of "landscaped" palms had charted the growth of tourist dollars. The eastern side of the island remained relatively undeveloped and looked very much like the desert areas surrounding Tucson, Arizona. Goats wandered down unpaved roads and roamed the cactus scrub, where hawks, bats, and lizards made their homes.

After three months of hotel living, the Van der Sloots bought a house in Noord, a few miles inland on the island's desirable north side, not far from the California Lighthouse, a major tourist attraction. The house was small and off a dirt road in a community of locals and foreigners of modest means.

The family's first years on Aruba were difficult. Paulus and Anita were homesick for their native Holland. Joran's father immersed himself in his new government post while Anita stayed home to care for their young sons.

For Joran, however, this was a magical time, with endless days of sunshine and freedom. He and his brother, Valentijn, loved exploring the empty lots and junkyards of Noord. Every day brought new potential for adventure. When Joran was eight, his brother Sebastian was born, and Sebastian became the baby of the Van der Sloot clan and a "true islander," as Joran referred to him.

With no relatives on Aruba, the family made an effort to travel to their homeland at least once every two years to visit Anita's mother.

Joran appreciated his mother's efforts to keep their Dutch traditions alive, but grew to despise their family trips to Holland. He was isolated there, and he missed the sunshine of his Caribbean home, where he could run around barefoot, swim, windsurf, and hang out with his friends. Joran felt like an outsider in the Netherlands. In his opinion, the people there were uptight. He longed for the unhurried pace of island life.

In reality, Joran's lifestyle was not typical for an island

boy. His father's high-placed government post afforded the family a certain amount of clout and standing. The family belonged to a country club, and Joran and his brothers attended the International School of Aruba, a small, private English-language school where their mother, Anita, taught art, as she had back in Holland. The school was expensive, about U.S.$8,000 a year, but faculty family members paid a discounted tuition.

Having his mother at the school had its perks and its disadvantages. The Van der Sloot boys didn't have to endure the long ride on the school bus on the days she was teaching. However, if Joran committed any infractions, be it bad grades, fights, or cutting classes, his mother found out immediately. There were also the awkward moments when his mother doubled as his art teacher.

While all the other kids referred to her as Miss Van der Sloot, Joran addressed her as "Mam." Some of his classmates teased him, saying the only reason he received good grades in art was because his mother was the teacher. But by all accounts Joran excelled academically in all his subjects.

He studied government, economics, and calculus, which was his most difficult subject, was enrolled in an English advanced placement program, and had a gift for languages. In addition to speaking his native Dutch and English, he was also fluent in Papiamento.

Joran was introduced to Papiamento in nursery school. He was three when his parents enrolled him at a local preschool where it was the only language spoken.

Joran attended this nursery school for only a short time before his parents moved him to another program, where he would have greater exposure to Dutch and English. Anita and Paulus spoke Dutch at home. They noticed, however, that Joran was beginning to mix Papiamento and Dutch even in basic conversation.

His parents were living a typical ex-pat lifestyle, socializing mostly with other members of the transplanted Dutch community, and generally communicated in Dutch.

Joran, on the other hand, quickly learned Papiamento in order to fit in with his peers. When he spoke it, he was able to find acceptance and escape the teasing that local boys doled out on ex-pats. While he would always remain an outsider, speaking Papiamento demonstrated his desire to be a part of the island community.

When he was old enough for elementary school, his parents decided that Joran would attend the International School of Aruba, a private prepatory academy where English was spoken in the classroom. They knew that Joran needed to learn one language well and, with the potential for higher education at a U.S. university, English was the best choice.

The school was small with an enrollment of about ten children in each grade. Students were expected to follow a dress code. They had to wear white or blue short-sleeved polo shirts emblazoned with the ISA logo and pants or short pants in khaki, black, or navy. The school's lesson plans were the same as those used in the United States and the school had a good reputation. Nearly all of its graduating seniors went on to attend colleges in the United States and the Netherlands.

Anita taught art at the school three days a week, and was always home in the afternoons to help Joran with school assignments and projects. Her husband kept long hours at the office and when he was at home, he didn't appear eager to be involved.

To Joran, his father was remote. However, he rationalized that it was better this way. His father didn't speak English as fluently as his mother, and would not have been as helpful with his homework assignments. Still, sometimes he wished that he would be more involved with the family.

Paulus's government post was not always rewarding and he sometimes grew frustrated. His legal positions didn't always win him favor with the island's ministers, and he was often delegated menial tasks, such as drafting contracts and sorting paperwork. This was dry and boring work, not at all what he had imagined, and he briefly considered relocating the family back to the Netherlands. But, ultimately he decided to stay in Aruba and pursue other career possibilities.

When Joran was fourteen, his father announced that he had been offered an opportunity to become a judge. Although Paulus was excited, accepting the assignment would require three years of training. He would also be off-island for long periods, working on court-related matters on the nearby island of Curaçao, also a constituent country of the Netherlands. Additionally, he would be required to do a one-year stint in the Netherlands as part of the training. Joran loved his father and understood that the judgeship was important to him. However, he still resented his lengthy absences.

Now a teenager, Joran was looking to be more independent. He wanted to be cool like the older island boys in his clique. His mother wished he would make classier friends with his contemporaries at the International School, but choices were few. There were only four or five other boys in Joran's graduating class. Besides, he preferred the companionship of the Aruban boys.

By now, he was fluent in Papiamento and he would often slip into the Creole tongue when he and his friends wanted to communicate covertly. To them, it was like a secret language. It was especially useful when they were picking up women at the bars, nightclubs, and casinos so popular with American tourists.

Since moving out of the main house and into the apartment, Joran had found it easier to get out at night.

The decision to let Joran use the apartment might have been shortsighted, but his parents had had sincere intentions. Joran's increasingly erratic and disturbing behavior was threatening the serenity of the household and Paulus and Anita wanted to shield the younger boys. Moving Joran to the apartment seemed not only logical, but clever. Enhancing his freedom was an unwitting outcome and Joran was soon sneaking off the property almost every night of the week.

Typically, he'd put in an appearance in the main house,

do some homework, chat with his folks, return to the apartment, and after he was sure everyone was asleep, take his exit. If his parents were aware of his nightly truancies, they certainly didn't know where he was going. More often than not, these sojourns were to the poker tables of the Holiday Inn's Excelsior Casino.

SIX

Natalee Holloway's mother had come to Aruba carrying two photographs of her daughter to give to police. Now, standing in the lobby of the Holiday Inn, a salty breeze blowing in from the surf, Beth Twitty realized that she would need a photo of Joran, as well. If he really was the last person to be seen with Natalee, then she needed to track him down. While the desk clerk knew instantly who he was, she had no idea where he lived or how to find him.

Beth remembered that Jug's nephew Thomas had said he'd hung out with Joran at the hotel's casino the night before. There must be cameras inside the Excelsior. Surely the management should be able to find a frame of Joran in a surveillance tape.

"I'd like to look at video from the casino," Beth told the hotel manager, explaining that she believed Joran had been at a gaming table with Natalee the previous evening and she needed a still shot of the young man to distribute. With members of the Holiday Inn staff aware that her daughter was missing, she expected there to be no problem reviewing the footage. Instead, she was informed that the casino operated independently from the hotel. It was now too late in the evening to reach anyone, the manager stated, but perhaps tomorrow something could be done.

The fact that her daughter had missed her flight home didn't seem to alarm anyone on the island. This was Aruba, a carefree island, where people disappeared on benders and romantic liaisons all the time. Eventually, they always seemed to turn up somewhere. But this sort of irresponsible behavior was totally out of character for Natalee.

Beth's daughter was punctual and reliable. For her to miss a flight and completely disconnect from friends and family made no sense at all. Natalee was a straight-A student who had just graduated in the top tenth percentile of her class. It was no small feat when the average GPA of her class was 3.875.

Natalee had been selected for early acceptance to the University of Alabama's School of Medicine and awarded an eight-year academic scholarship that would cover not only her undergraduate work, but all four years of medical school, as well. She knew how to manage her time, and was conscientiously punctual.

She worked part-time after school at an organic market, Harvest Glen, in Birmingham. The mother of one of Natalee's friends owned the store and also employed autistic adults. Over the months, Natalee had developed a special friendship with some of the employees and took them for outings on her days off. She also volunteered at a local cancer center, and was diligent about her Bible study classes. Once, when she knew she was going to miss an afternoon session at the church, she showed up early in the morning to let the pastor know that she would not be attending that day. Although most teens would have simply called, at best, Natalee took great pride in being responsible and accountable. She was not the type of person who would selfishly disappear and leave others to worry.

Natalee's mother was becoming more and more frustrated. Nobody was taking her daughter's disappearance seriously. She couldn't even file a missing person's report for at least another hour.

Not wanting to waste additional time, Eric Williams, the DEA agent, suggested the group drive into town to Carlos'n Charlie's, the bar where the teen was last seen. They located the nightclub on a downtown side street, not far from the harbor. Stepping out of the van into the sticky night air, Beth gazed at the lights reflecting on the water and her worries intensified. How easy it would have been for someone to pull Natalee onto a boat and vanish.

The rowdy, crowded bar yielded no new information. Beth shared Natalee's picture with patrons but no one remembered seeing her. Hundreds of female tourists passed through the establishment every week, a bouncer told her, and without a photograph of Joran the group had little more than a first name and some very vague descriptions.

At this point, Charles Croes's name came into the conversation. Croes owned a cell phone rental company, and perhaps with his help, the team would be able to acquire functioning cell phones in case they needed to split up to search the island. Despite the late hour, they managed to reach him, and he accommodated their request. He agreed to meet them in the parking lot of a Valero gas station.

Waiting in the backseat of the van, Beth was still shaken by what she had just seen at Carlos'n Charlie's. The place had been a madhouse. She saw scantily clad drunken teens grinding against each other on the dance floor. The music was deafening and the smell of marijuana wafted through the air. Imagining Natalee in this place made her feel sick.

The arrival of Charles Croes in his beat-up car puttering into the harshly lit halo of the Valero gas station was a welcome moment. Beth and her friend Jodi climbed into his car. Beth was anxious that no more time be squandered. The two vehicles started back to the Holiday Inn to activate the cell phones. There wasn't a minute to spare. Even though she had been told she would have to wait until morning to look at casino footage, Beth was unwilling to tolerate any further delays. She was sure Joran had her daughter and she was going to find him and get her back.

Striding up to the reception desk, Beth demanded to speak with the person in charge. She made it clear that she wasn't going anywhere until someone showed her the tapes. Her persistence paid off and soon she and Jug were escorted upstairs to review the video.

With the footage on the screen, Beth phoned Thomas in Alabama. "Okay, we are looking at the blackjack tables," she told the teen. "Can you describe this Joran? Where was he sitting?"

Thomas told her to look for the guy with the blue-and-white-striped polo shirt. "There he is!" Beth yelled out, finding a person who met this description.

Hurrying to the lobby, Beth and Jug encountered the Aruban escorts who'd met them at the airport. Earlier Jug had given them several hundred dollars with the hope that the men could use the money to buy information.

The escorts began walking the length of Palm Beach describing Joran to locals. Finally, they found a teenager who knew Joran, and for $100, he gave up his full name and address. He lived with his family on Montanja Street, a back street away from the commercial strip.

To be sure, the Arubans had driven by the house to scout the location. Peering over the gate, they saw a silver Honda parked under a tree. They jotted down the license plate, and presented the information to Beth. The group decided they now had enough information to go to the police. They had a photo, a name, a license plate number, and an address.

Of Aruba's four police stations, the Noord police station, a friendly-looking yellow building with a red tile roof, was closest to the Van der Sloots' orange stucco home. Thirty minutes of coaxing finally convinced the officers there to accompany them to the Van der Sloots' address. Beth wasn't aware that Joran's father had strong ties to the legal community as a judge in training. Police officers were initially hesitant about rousing him in the middle of the night.

It was around 2:00 A.M. when Paulus van der Sloot awoke to an incredible commotion. The family dogs were barking. His middle son, Valentijn, was at his bedside and wanted to know what was happening. The blue strobe lights of police cars crisscrossed the walls, and someone was honking a horn. After dressing quickly, Paulus walked down the dirt driveway to the front gate.

Three people were standing at the gate, two uniformed officers and Natalee's stepfather, Jug Twitty. Behind them were several vehicles, including two police SUVs and a white van carrying a crowd of about ten people.

Paulus didn't know that two men were also hiding behind his house. Matt Whatley and Ruffner Page Jr., members of what locals would soon call the "Alabama Posse," were staking out the rear of the property to thwart an escape attempt if indeed Joran was home and tried to flee.

"A girl is missing and your son was the last one seen with her," one of the officers told Van der Sloot.

"That couldn't be right," Paulus insisted, "because he was at the free tournament at the Holiday Inn and I picked him up in front of McDonald's at eleven o'clock. I'll go inside and get him."

Paulus walked around the patio to Joran's apartment to fetch his sleeping son from his bed. To his surprise, he wasn't there. Then, he tried calling him using his wife's mobile phone. Joran answered on the first ring.

"Where are you?" he asked.

"I'm at the Wyndham." Paulus wasn't completely surprised. The Wyndham Hotel and Casino was hosting a free Texas hold 'em tournament and his son had wanted to participate.

"You are being sought in connection with a girl who has gone missing," Paulus told Joran. "There are people and police at the door and they want to talk to you. Stay put. I will meet you at the Wyndham," he instructed.

Confused, but aware of the severity of the situation, Joran's dark-haired father, wearing his metal-framed glasses, climbed into one of the police vehicles and the convoy headed back to the Palm Beach strip.

The Wyndham Aruba Resort Spa & Casino was on the southern end of Palm Beach. It catered to an elite clientele, more upscale than the Holiday Inn, the host hotel of the graduating class of 2005 from Mountain Brook, Alabama, those past five days and four nights. After pulling up in front of the massive eighteen-story structure with over four hundred guest rooms, a foot race between Beth Twitty and Joran's father, Paulus, ensued, with both sprinting from their respective vehicles past the front desk and into the hotel's glittering Casablanca Casino.

Van der Sloot had the advantage. He knew his way around and headed straight to the rear gaming tables. He wanted to talk to Joran privately before the bristling foreigners were able to locate him. Beth also wanted to be the first to confront the young man and hurried to beat Paulus to her quarry.

Having viewed the casino video footage, she had an idea of what Joran looked like. She thought it bizarre that he would be gambling in a casino after midnight on a school night. The casino was massive. The sounds of laughter and the slot machines ringing reverberated off the walls. The ceiling, sky blue in color, was lit to create a visual effect of perpetual daylight. Beth looked past the dice games and roulette wheels and finally located the poker tables in the rear. When she didn't see Joran, she began asking the pit bosses if perhaps they could point him out to her. Out of the corner of her eye, she noticed Paulus van der Sloot, talking on his cell phone.

His face was growing redder and he was clearly exchanging a few terse words with his son. Hanging up, he told the group that Joran was now at home.

Tempers were running high as they all climbed into their vehicles and returned to the Van der Sloot residence. At 3:00 A.M., the police car carrying Paulus van der Sloot pulled up in front of the family's ranch house. Joran and his friend, Deepak, were standing in the street, leaning on Deepak's silver Honda.

"Why didn't you stay at the Wyndham?" Paulus asked his son.

"I misunderstood," Joran said, matter-of-factly.

Joran then digressed, mentioning that some of the neighbors had come outside and complained about how loud he and Deepak were playing the car's radio while they were waiting for him. Paulus couldn't understand why Joran wasn't taking the unfolding events more seriously. Hadn't he just told him that police wanted to talk to him about a missing girl who had last been seen in his company?

If Joran was at all concerned, he certainly didn't show it. If anything he looked smug and amused when the white van filled with burly Southerners all but emptied, with Jug, his friends, and Lilly, the chaperone, among those prepared to confront him. The police officers got out of their vehicles but did not approach, remaining propped against their squad cars. Beth and her friend Jodi arrived in the car with Charles Croes. He jumped out and joined the assembly in the driveway.

Beth and Jodi heeded the advice of DEA agent Eric Williams to remain in the car, despite Beth's overwhelming desire to be closer to the action.

Paulus van der Sloot noticed the ID tag hanging around Williams's neck. Williams identified himself as a federal agent working with United States law enforcement, although according to Paulus's account, Charles Croes took the lead.

Beth stared out the car window, unable to hear what was being said. She trusted that Jug and the other men would be able to get this rat bastard kid to talk.

At first, there was some confusion as to the identity of the missing girl. For a brief moment, the name Kathleen was being tossed around. However, after Joran was shown a photo of Natalee, he recognized the blonde, particularly her mouth and eyes. "Yes, that's the girl I made out with last night," he said.

In a flowing narrative, one that would later be transcribed in an official police report, Joran described what he claimed were the events of the previous night in graphic detail. He said he met Natalee at the Excelsior Casino, and then hooked up with her again later at Carlos'n Charlie's where he did body shots out of her navel.

"She laid down on the bar, placed a Jell-O shot in her navel, and told me to drink it. Which I did."

Joran explained that he was with his two friends, Deepak, who was now standing beside him in the driveway, and Deepak's younger brother, Satish. He said he bought Natalee a shot of 151 rum and that she chased it down with a swallow of his whiskey and cola.

When the bar closed at 1:00 A.M., Natalee wasn't ready to call it a night. "She was drunk," Joran said.

Before continuing with his story, Joran stopped, looked around at the men gathered in front of him, and asked if Natalee's parents were among the group.

"I'm Natalee's stepfather," Jug declared.

Joran asked that Jug Twitty be moved out of earshot before he continued his story.

Reluctantly, Jug returned to the car where his wife was waiting. He found her talking on her cell phone with Natalee's classmates back in Alabama. A number of the students had gathered at the home of one of their friends in Mountain Brook and were communicating with Beth via speakerphone. To add to the rudimentary conference call, every few minutes one of the airport handlers would break from the group on the driveway to report to Beth what Joran was saying. Beth was relating that information to Natalee's friends.

So far, the Alabama teens on the phone agreed with Beth's spot-on description of Joran. This was definitely the person with Natalee when she drove away from Carlos'n Charlie's. Now, the question was, what had he done with their friend?

Beth and Jug watched anxiously as Joran detailed his night with Natalee to the collection of interested parties: the two friends from Alabama whose daughters were safely home; the chaperone who had agreed to stay behind; the helpful stranger with the complimentary cell phones; the two airport support personnel; the travel agent and dear friend of Beth's; and the vacationing DEA agent. Beth couldn't hear what Joran was saying. But the smirk on his face was infuriating. Her daughter was missing and he seemed amused. His arrogance disturbed her greatly.

By the way he and his friend were dressed, she was having a hard time believing that they had visited casinos that night. They were both in shorts and T-shirts, no more stylish than gym clothes. Beth had heard that Joran was tall, but he was much taller than she had imagined.

Luckily out of earshot from Beth, Joran described how he and Natalee had walked out of Carlos'n Charlie's arm in arm. Once outside, he asked if he could go with her to the Holiday Inn.

"She said that she wanted to see my house," he claimed. "I had told her that that was okay." It was an odd admission, considering that while at the blackjack tables at the Excelsior Casino he'd told the young women that he was a tourist and staying at the Holiday Inn.

Joran said that going for a ride had been Natalee's idea. "So me and Deepak and Satish took Natalee for a ride. I sat together with her in the back of Deepak's car. Deepak was driving and Satish was in the passenger seat.

"She told us to drive past her friends so that they could see the car. Natalee's friends were standing on the corner of Royal Plaza at the southeast side when we drove by. In the car, we started to kiss each other. My friend Deepak drove by Choose-A-Name, Karma Lounge, and after that we drove over the Saskia Road in the direction of the hotels.

"In the car, I touched her breasts and vagina."

In sickening detail, Joran described how he fingered Natalee. He even described the panties she had been wearing that night.

"We drove past all the hotels," Joran continued. "In the car, I told Natalee that I could not go with her to my house. She then told me that she wanted to go to the north coast to see sharks.

"I told her there were no sharks to be seen at the north coast. She answered that there were sharks there and she had seen them already. We decided to drive in that direction.

"On the way, she asked us where we were taking her. She further told us to bring her to the Holiday Inn because the next day she would have to travel back to the United States.

We drove past the lighthouse and after that to the Holiday Inn hotel.

"In the car, she said that her mother was the sister of Hitler and that her family owned a plantation." Joran also claimed that Natalee asked him if Deepak and Satish were his slaves, and told him that back in the United States, where she came from, "black people work as slaves on the plantations."

"The girl was very drunk," he said a second time.

Joran claimed that after driving around, he, Deepak, and Satish dropped Natalee off in front of the Holiday Inn at around 2:00 A.M., and watched the petite blonde stagger toward the lobby as they drove away.

It was a remarkable story. But was it true?

Now, Jug Twitty returned to join the others. Simultaneously, the men voiced their skepticism. "This was not done with subtlety," Paulus van der Sloot later claimed. "They were very accusing and Joran was made aware of the discrepancies in his story." In Paulus's opinion, his son's inconsistencies were very minor and he felt that Joran was being treated unreasonably harshly.

But the discrepancies were glaring. Joran claimed that Natalee wanted to see his house, but he had told everyone he was staying at the Holiday Inn. Natalee's friends said she had been drinking but seemed in control at closing time, but Joran said she was very drunk. None of Natalee's friends remembered Joran doing Jell-O shots out of her navel at Carlos'n Charlie's that night. In fact, they claimed she hadn't even said hello to Joran when she passed him on her way out of the ladies' room. And his story of sexual activity in the backseat was revolting and unbelievable. Natalee didn't even have a boyfriend. It seemed unlikely that she would have engaged in such behavior with someone she had just met in the backseat of a stranger's car with two other men sitting in the front seat.

"No jurisdiction! You have no jurisdiction," Paulus shouted in his thick Dutch accent. "He does not have to talk to you! You have no manners."

Turning to his son, he instructed, "Direct your statements to the officers and not the Americans."

The moment was significant. Then and there Paulus van der Sloot transformed from father to attorney. His hostile tone unleashed a torrent of angry words from the Americans.

"Just tell us where the girl is!" Ruffner Page demanded.

Joran insisted that he dropped Natalee at the Holiday Inn. But the Mountain Brook students on the phone with Beth did not believe him.

"No, he didn't drop her at the Holiday Inn," they shouted into the phone. "She's in the house," they cried. "Go inside and get her!" The Mountain Brook teens were convinced that Natalee had been kidnapped.

Beth was beside herself. Natalee's roommate, Lee Broughton, was adamant. She told Mrs. Twitty that she was in the Holiday Inn lobby until 3:00 A.M. that Sunday greeting her fellow classmates as they returned to the hotel from their final night out. If Natalee had stumbled in, as Joran was claiming, she would have seen her.

"He's lying!" they shouted.

SEVEN

Stephany Flores's eldest brother, Richie, was curled up on the couch next to his young son watching *SpongeBob SquarePants* when he got the call from his brother Enrique. After reviewing the surveillance video at the Atlantic City Casino, Richie had returned home to his apartment in Miraflores to spend some time with Sebastian. His son's first birthday weekend had started out okay, but with his sister missing it had turned into the worst kind of nightmare. Even though he wasn't being rational, Richie found himself feeling guilty for being disappointed with Stephany for not attending Sebastian's birthday lunch that past Saturday.

He had hoped for some sleep and to make the best of the remaining hours of his weekend with his son. After shared TV time and a big kiss, they had both turned in, hoping for a good night's sleep, but no one in the Flores family would get any rest that night. Richie had just nodded off on the couch in the living room when the vibration of the cell phone in his pocket snapped him back to life.

"The guy on the video with Stephany is a killer," Enrique blurted out, unsure where to begin.

"Slow down, Kee-Kay," Richie said, addressing his brother by his childhood nickname. "What do you mean, he's a killer?"

"Carolina Googled him. He's done this before," Enrique replied, detailing what the family had learned since dispersing at the casino.

Richie listened in horror as his brother told him about Carolina's gruesome discovery. The Dutchman, Joran van der Sloot, who was last seen with Stephany, was suspected in the murder of a young woman in Aruba five years before.

Richie could hear his stepmother weeping in the background as Enrique pointed out the similarities in the two women's disappearances.

"They both disappeared on May thirtieth. He took Stephany on the five-year anniversary of the first girl's abduction," Enrique said, his anger rising.

Richie sat rigid and upright on the gray leather couch listening intently to every detail. Like Stephany, the girl in Aruba had also met Joran in a casino, and despite countless searches her body had never been found.

"I'll be right over," Richie said. Waking the nanny, he apologized for the last-minute request at such a late hour. He had to find his sister.

Upon hearing this latest development, Richie knew that Stephany was in grave danger, and he and Enrique needed to actively join the search. Miraflores was their backyard, after all. The two men knew the hotels that foreigners tended to frequent. If Van der Sloot was still in the area, they would find him.

Just after midnight, Richie pulled his dark-colored four-door BMW up to the curb in front of his family's home. The lights were all on and Enrique was waiting for him by the front door. In his hand, his brother held a photo of Stephany as well as a photo of Van der Sloot that his wife Carolina had printed from the Internet using Stephany's computer.

"Maybe someone will recognize him," Enrique said, shrugging. He was determined to find his sister, but, from what he had read about Van der Sloot's past, realized this was probably not going to end well.

In the photograph, which appeared to be several years old, a smiling pimple-faced Joran was holding open a zippered sweatshirt revealing a light blue T-shirt emblazoned with the words, "It's Not Nice to Stare."

Armed with the color photos, the two brothers began driving from hotel to hotel. Van der Sloot was a tourist after all; he must be a hotel guest somewhere. Their first stop was La Casa Roja, a budget hostel they knew was popular with Dutch tourists.

It was approaching 1:00 A.M. when the Flores brothers rang the doorbell of the three-story restored colonial mansion painted a deep shade of red and encircled by a bright yellow wrought-iron fence. The owners were Hare Krishnas who ran a small vegetarian restaurant out of the guesthouse. In spite of the late hour, they welcomed the brothers inside. However, neither they nor the other guests recognized Joran from the photograph.

From there, the two began a grid search of the bars, casinos, and hotels around the Atlantic City Casino, but no one recognized Van der Sloot's photo. In the middle of the night, the streets were almost empty.

On a normal evening driving around together, Richie and Enrique would have been laughing and listening to the radio. But tonight an awkward silence chilled the car as they hurried through bars, hotels, and restaurants. They both knew that Stephany was more than likely dead and neither of them wanted to put it into words.

Three days had passed since she'd last been seen in the company of a suspected killer. Their sister was not one to be exploited, but physical strength had its limits. They'd both viewed the casino video and saw how Van der Sloot had towered over her. If his intention was to kill her, she would not have had much of a chance.

The temperature continued to drop as the night wore on and the air felt cool and damp. Shortly before 3:00 A.M. Richie's cell phone rang. "That's probably Dad," he said, reaching to answer it.

However, he did not recognize the man's voice on the other end of the line and never learned his identity. He had news about Stephany.

"Go to the Hotel Tac on República de Panamá," the caller said before hanging up abruptly. Richie wasn't sure what to think, but immediately headed toward the location.

He had driven past the Hotel Tac many times on his way to and from business meetings and nights out at restaurants and nightclubs. It was next to the Primax gas station and across the street from the giant Wong grocery store where he sometimes did his food shopping. He was now so filled with anxiety that he drove to the wrong location a few blocks away on Paseo de la Republica. With a bang on the steering wheel, he corrected his mistake and turned around.

The two brothers were unprepared for what they encountered as they approached the correct hotel. The entire block was awash in police lights. Investigators were gathered on the sidewalk outside the gaudy gold rectangular structure with black-tinted windows. Above them, the name of the hotel was written in bold green capital letters. The ground floor of the hotel housed a small "casino," nothing more than a gaming room filled with digital slot machines that rarely had more than a handful of customers who played with quarter-size tokens bearing the hotel's name.

What an awful place to wind up, Richie thought. It looked like a hot-sheet motel, one of those by-the-hour places where couples met for quick sexual encounters.

Although the brothers weren't certain, they feared the worst. Richie and Enrique got out of their car, walked up to the yellow police tape, and identified themselves to a uniformed policeman.

"Stay where you are," the officer instructed. "I'll get a detective."

Soon a grim-faced detective approached the two men and gently informed them that their sister was dead. A hotel employee had found her body earlier in the evening. It appeared that she had been there for several days.

"I'm very sorry," the officer told Richie and Enrique. "There's no sign of Van der Sloot in the hotel."

Not wanting his father to learn about Stephany's murder on the news, Richie ran to his car, leaving Enrique at the scene, and raced back to the family's house in Surco. One of the most difficult conversations of the young man's life followed. His father did not take the news well, and demanded that Richie take him to the crime scene.

Ricardo Flores Sr. usually did all the driving. He was, after all, a race-car driver. But having already taken an anti-anxiety medication, he wanted Richie behind the wheel.

When the time came, Richie volunteered to make the identification of his little sister himself. He did not want the task, but he wanted to spare his father additional anguish. This was not the first time he had stepped in to ease his father's suffering. When he was fourteen years old, he was asked to identify the body of a dead aunt because his father said the stress would make him faint.

Not only had the young Richie identified his relative, but he had then been instructed to help dress the corpse and lift it into the coffin. The horror of having some skin come off his aunt's ankle in his hand was a haunting moment he would never forget.

At the time, Richie had been angry with his father for asking him to do such a grown-up job. But now, he felt better prepared.

Head down, heart racing, he nervously followed the officers up the stairs, stopping outside of Room 309. Several plainclothes detectives braced him for what he was about to see, standing just beside him as he entered the tiny room. His sister's body was on the floor, covered in dried blood, so badly beaten that she was hardly recognizable. But it was Stephany. There was no doubt.

Stepping out onto the sidewalk, Richie locked eyes with his father who appeared so much smaller than the proud, fearless man who raced cars on steep mountain roads for sport. He looked broken.

With gentle sympathy, he admonished his father not to climb the stairs to the third floor. Investigators agreed, telling the elder Flores that he should remember his daughter the way she was.

The three Flores men remained outside on the sidewalk as police secured the hotel. Ricardo was doing his best to contain his emotions when he heard his wife's frantic cries.

"Where is Stephany?" she was yelling. "Where is my daughter?"

Looking back toward the commotion, he saw Mariaelena pushing her way through the crush of reporters and bystanders that continued to grow on the sidewalk just beyond the yellow crime scene tape. Bundled against the cold, she looked worn out. Her brown eyes were puffy and red, and tears channeled down her face. Carolina, Ricardo's daughter-in-law, was with her.

"Let them through," someone yelled. "She's the mother."

With all the pandemonium, Ricardo was unable to prevent his wife from seeing the coroner's van backed into the hotel's driveway, its doors open as if waiting for a passenger.

"No! No!" she shrieked. "I want to see my daughter!"

Without thinking, someone in the crowd announced she was dead.

The news was too much. Stephany's mother collapsed on the sidewalk. She was carried back to the family's Mercedes while relatives called for an ambulance. Paramedics arrived within a few minutes and administered medication to help calm her. Even so, she was in no condition to remain on the scene and Richie volunteered to drive her home, where caring relatives were waiting. Although Richie wanted his father to accompany her, Ricardo refused to leave. He insisted on remaining outside on the sidewalk until his daughter's body was removed from the hotel.

Upstairs, officers were waiting in the hallway outside of Room 309. All hotel employees were forbidden from entering the chamber where Stephany's body lay sprawled on the floor. They weren't allowed to leave the hotel, either. Everyone was waiting for homicide investigators to arrive.

Captain Juan Callan was on duty that night. At forty-six, the compactly built policeman had been a member of the Peruvian National Police Force for two decades, the last eight years working homicide. His detective work was legendary in law enforcement circles, as was his affinity for motorcycles, particularly Harley-Davidsons.

Callan's four-man team had been clearing backlogged paperwork at police headquarters in Central Lima when their commander, General Cesar Guardia, alerted them to the dead body found at a hotel in Miraflores. General Guardia was the director of Peru's criminal investigations division and made it clear to his lead detective that this was a high-profile case with international implications. The dead woman was the daughter of a famous race-car driver, and the prime suspect, Joran van der Sloot, was a Dutch national and suspected murderer who was last seen fleeing in a car similar to Stephany's.

Callan, grabbing his signature leather jacket from the coat rack, quickly briefed his team members on the investigation unfolding in Miraflores. The body had been there for several days, meaning Van der Sloot had a significant jump on them. Callan had heard about the Flores case on the news but hadn't followed it closely. He knew his colleagues in the kidnapping division had been working around the clock since the woman had been reported missing.

During his career, Callan had been involved in nearly fifty homicide cases, including the high-profile 2009 murder of Peru's beloved folk singer, Alicia Delgado, known throughout South America as the "Peruvian Princess of Folk Music." The vivacious fifty-year-old redhead had been discovered hanging by a leather belt in the closet of her home in Santiago de Surco, not far from the Floreses' residence. She had been stabbed nine times, and Callan and his team were charged with tracking down her killer.

While policework didn't pay well—rookie cops made about $500 a month—Callan was passionate about his job and often attended seminars and took classes at the police academy to stay on top of the latest forensic techniques. He was the lead detective of Homicide Team 2 and his four-man squad was made up of some the city's brightest investigators.

His most experienced officers, Macedonio Ugarte and Jose Castro, were ten-year veterans of the division. With a full head of wavy gray hair and tinted eyeglasses, Ugarte was known for his stern, no-nonsense approach. Castro, by contrast, had jet-black hair and put witnesses at ease with his disarming smile.

Miguel Tong and Frank Gonzalez, the younger members of Callan's team, couldn't have asked for better mentors. The baby-faced Tong had joined the squad in 2007, and he and Callan were *compadres,* friends, whose families socialized outside the office. Callan was the godfather of Tong's young son.

Gonzalez, nineteen and reed thin with a buzz cut and goatee, was a rookie, and had been recruited right out of the academy. His fellow officers liked to rib him about his serial dating and his reputation as a ladies' man.

The detectives arrived at the Hotel Tac in unmarked vehicles. Their black police vests with official patches and the word "Homicide" in bold yellow letters identified them as law enforcement personnel.

It was a frenzied scene. Members of the local media were trying to get inside the hotel and swarmed investigators as they climbed out of their cars. The victim's father immediately confronted Captain Callan. Ricardo Flores was on the sidewalk and begging to be let upstairs to see his daughter. Callan ordered uniformed officers to keep the reporters at bay. Taking Ricardo aside, he explained that his son Richie had already identified the body and for the moment no one else was allowed to enter the hotel.

Eager to begin the investigation, Callan instructed Ugarte, the team's gray-haired veteran, and Gonzalez, the rookie, to go with him to the third floor. Checking the door to Room

309, he noted no signs of forced entry. The window was open. The smell of decomposition was faint but unmistakable. Callan and his men surveyed the bloody scene before slowly backing out of the room. The CSI team and a representative from the prosecutor's office were on their way and he did not want to do anything to compromise the evidence. He had a daughter of his own, and exiting the room he thought about Ricardo Flores. Callan promised himself he would bring Stephany Flores's killer to justice.

Wasting no time, Callan began interviewing hotel staff and quickly discovered that a guest on the fourth floor had returned to the hotel earlier in the evening, worried about Joran van der Sloot.

Adeli Marchena, the receptionist who had discovered the body, told Callan that Elton García, a guest for more than a month, had come into the lobby shortly after she had found the body. He seemed worried that Joran and the missing Peruvian woman whose disappearance was being followed on the news had both been kidnapped. Adeli thought the timing of García's inquiry was strange. The police had been summoned by her boss but they had not yet arrived, and here was García at the reception desk, inundating her with questions about Room 309's resident. Her exchange with the man in Room 406 was disturbing enough to compel her to mention it to the homicide investigators.

Callan agreed. A man of priorities, he had a killer to catch and if García could lead him to Van der Sloot he needed to be interviewed as quickly as possible.

Callan took the stairs up to the fourth floor to interview the possible witness in Room 406. The guest registry had listed García as Albanian, and Callan was a bit surprised when the square-jawed man in the jean jacket who opened the door addressed him in Spanish.

Callan made a rapid assessment of García. The thirty-five-year-old had a thick tousle of jet-black hair feathered with a bit of gray, long thin sideburns, and a "soul patch," a thin clump of beard just beneath his lower lip. He looked like he hadn't slept in days.

After introducing himself and referencing Van der Sloot, the experienced detective took a conversational tone. He knew the interview process could be intimidating. Taking a seat in one of the simple wood chairs, he invited García to do the same. García's room looked identical to the one on the third floor: cheap gray carpet, white walls, a queen-size bed with a floral comforter, two chairs, and a small night table.

In response to Callan's questions, García explained that he had been born in Albania, but was married and lived in Uruguay, where he ran a small business. He had come to Lima the last week of April to participate in the Latin American Poker Tour.

Callan thought it strange that García would have arrived in Peru more than one month before the tournament was set to begin, and that a married man would leave his wife at home for so long, but he kept his skepticism to himself.

García explained that earlier in the evening he had attended a dinner party at La Rosa Náutica, a sprawling bar and restaurant on Pier 4 of the Lima Beach Circuit, at the base of the cliffs below Miraflores. The event was being hosted by the Atlantic City Casino to celebrate the kickoff of the Latin American Poker Tour. This was the first time the tournament would be held in Peru, and local celebrities and government dignitaries were expected to attend.

The Atlantic City Casino was providing shuttle buses to and from the venue, which boasted 360-degree views of the Pacific Ocean from floor-to-ceiling windows. There would be cocktails, dinner, and live entertainment.

García explained that even though Joran was not registered to play in the tournament, he told him he had come to Lima for that purpose only. Joran knew that some of the best players in the world would be at La Rosa Náutica that night. By 11:00 P.M., when Joran had still not arrived, García said he started to worry. He did not know Joran well, but his failure to show up had him concerned.

He had seen the missing persons reports about Stephany Flores on the news. "The players at the Atlantic City were also talking about it," he said. The news and the Internet had suggested kidnapping as a possible motive, and García thought Van der Sloot might be a victim, as well.

As the conversation continued, Callan discovered that García was acquainted with Stephany as well as Van der Sloot. Not only did García know Flores, he told the detective that he had been the one to introduce Joran to her at the poker tables one night. Although he hadn't seen Joran at the casino for several days, he hadn't made the connection that his friend was missing until he failed to turn up at La Rosa Náutica. Joran was a Dutch foreigner, and unless he was checking in with someone at home on a regular basis, no one would even know he was missing, García reasoned.

García said he expressed his fear to one of the table supervisors, a young woman named Katy Herrera. He had asked Katy to call the Hotel Tac to see if Joran was there.

Making calls for clients was not something that Katy normally did, but hearing García's concerns she agreed to place a call on his behalf. Katy was also aware of the news reports about Stephany Flores. Members of the young woman's family had been at the casino hours earlier that very night reviewing video footage, and word around the casino was that they had seen a tape of Stephany and Joran leaving the casino together.

During her three years at the Atlantic City, Katy had come to know Señorita Flores as a regular at the gaming tables. She had seen her sitting with the Dutch foreigner on two separate occasions that past week, and remembered the two of them playing together in an upstairs poker room when she left in the early hours of Sunday morning. She hadn't thought much of it at the time. Joran was a quiet person and seemed devoted to the task of playing poker. He'd been coming to the casino for about three weeks, and told her he was in town for the Latin American Poker Tour.

On Saturday, May 22, Katy saw him at the casino. She invited him to attend Sunday services at the Emmanuel Evangelical Church in downtown Lima and handed him a brochure, "Steps to Receive the Lord in Your Life." The following morning, Katy arrived at the church accompanied by a friend and was pleasantly surprised to see Joran there. After the service, she walked with him out to the street and helped him hail a cab. This was the only time she had ever seen him outside of the casino.

García gave Katy the telephone number for the Hotel Tac and she placed the call from a pay phone in the employee cafeteria. But Joran wasn't there.

That would explain the call to the receptionist earlier in the night, Callan thought, tapping on his notebook with his ballpoint pen. But why hadn't García made the call himself? He was fluent in Spanish and had been a guest of the hotel for more than a month.

"Can you tell me where you were at 5:20 A.M. on the morning of Sunday, May 30?" Callan asked. If this hotel guest had anything to do with the murder in 309, he didn't want him to have the opportunity to concoct an alibi.

García claimed he was nowhere near the Hotel Tac the morning Stephany was last seen alive. He had stayed up most of the evening playing poker at the Atlantic City before heading to the Tequila Discotheque in San Isidro with several casino employees. The group partied until well past dawn, and he didn't return to the hotel until ten o'clock that morning.

Callan made a note to check out his story. "Can you describe your relationship with Joran?" he asked García, who was now growing impatient.

"We weren't friends at all," he said. "I only knew him from sight and from having played poker with him at the free table at the Atlantic City Casino."

"And Stephany Flores? Where and when did you meet her, and to what degree were you friends?"

"I met her on May 23, at around 9:00 P.M. at the Fiesta Casino, across the street from the Atlantic City Casino." García related how she had made $700 from a ten-dollar investment during a poker game that night.

Callan studied the man's face, his square jaw, and the long, thin scar hidden beneath a thick, bushy eyebrow. He had small hands, and his skin was soft. His nails were well trimmed. He was definitely not a person who engaged in any kind of manual labor.

"Do you have any knowledge of what type of car Stephany drives and can you tell me if you drove it at any time?"

"I didn't know that Stephany had a car, and furthermore, I have never driven a vehicle in Lima. When I arrived at the hotel tonight I asked the receptionist if Joran was in his room. She said he wasn't there and that police were on their way because they found a dead woman in his room.

"What's going on?" García demanded. "Was it Stephany Flores?"

"You tell me," Callan fired back.

García grew uncomfortable, realizing he was indeed being interrogated. He reiterated that his relationships with Stephany and Joran were extremely casual, not much more than recognizing each other for a hello.

"What do you know about Stephany's murder?"

"I don't know anything about a murder. I heard about her disappearance from the press and the Internet. The players were talking about it and I worried about her because I knew who she was.

"When Joran didn't arrive at the party at La Rosa Náutica, I worried about him, too, thinking that maybe he had also been kidnapped."

"Do you know if either Stephany or Joran registered to participate in the Latin American Poker Championship?"

"They are not registered," García said. "Only three hundred of the best players in the world are participating in the tournament. And I am participating."

The man's arrogance was not lost on the detective. "When was the last time you saw Joran van der Sloot?"

"On Sunday night, May 30, playing poker at the Atlantic City Casino. I think it was around ten."

Unzipping his coat, Callan leaned forward in the chair. "Can you explain how it is that you and Joran came to be staying in the same hotel?"

"Purely by coincidence." He elaborated that many of the

players, even the local ones, stay at the Hotel Tac because it's cheap and close to the casino.

"Besides you and Joran, how many other players are staying at the Hotel Tac?"

García responded tentatively that he knew of no others, only Joran.

"Can you please describe your relationship to Joran?"

He repeated that they weren't friends, merely friendly travelers in a foreign city. He had played poker with him once or twice at the casino and that was all.

"Have you ever been in his room? Room 309?"

"No, I never went into his room."

"Can you tell me in which country you met Van der Sloot?"

"I had never seen him before this visit to Peru."

"Do you know where Joran is from?"

"He told me he lives in Aruba, but he is Dutch."

The police captain nodded. He was suspicious. His years as a detective ingrained him with instincts and talents to glean information from things not spoken. Even though García claimed to have met Van der Sloot for the first time in Peru, he suspected the two had a history; perhaps they knew each other from Aruba. Discovering Joran's phone number plugged in with García's cell contacts kept Callan's suspicions percolating.

Closing his notebook, the detective got up from his chair. "We need you to look at the body. You need to tell us if she is the one from the casino."

The Uruguayan poker player became visibly shaken and was unable to comply, not unusual in corpse identification requests.

Instead, Callan produced the victim's identification card, discovered in Van der Sloot's room, to show García.

"Is this the woman from the casino?"

"That's her," said García. "That's Stephany."

While Callan questioned the hotel guest in Room 406, members of his squad fanned out through the hotel, questioning employees and waking guests. Police were puzzled about the length of time that had elapsed from when the murder occurred to when Adeli discovered the decaying corpse in Room 309. From the state of decomposition, the body appeared to have been there for at least three days. Yet, no one had smelled anything unusual. Another troubling event, the employees of the hotel called the hotel's owner about the body *before* they alerted police.

Investigators were suspicious, with payoffs a problem for law enforcement. Did Van der Sloot have any accomplices? Had he paid an employee to stay silent, or perhaps abet his escape by keeping the room locked and untended?

The fact that no one from the hotel had entered the room for such a long period seemed both strange and suspicious to investigators. This was a hotel and one would expect that the housekeeping staff would have made occasional visits to the room over three days, if for no other reason than to clean the room or turn down the bed. The fact that Joran was delinquent on his rent caused even more distrust. How had Stephany's badly decomposed body gone unnoticed for so long? The open window had dissipated some of the smell, but the mystery of the undetected stench, foul and unmistakable, certainly could not be ignored.

Police quickly located the owner of the Hotel Tac, Kuan Bo, a twenty-six-year-old Chinese immigrant who spoke fluent Spanish. Bo told investigators that he first learned of the body in Room 309 when he received a call from a hotel employee on June 2 about forty minutes past midnight. He had been resting at home in Miraflores about fifteen blocks away when his cell phone rang. But instead of dialing 105, the Peruvian equivalent of 911, he raced to his hotel to assess the situation for himself.

A short time after arriving, he called the emergency number from the reception desk. According to Bo, the first police officers didn't arrive for another hour.

Kuan Bo told the officers that he had no idea who Joran van der Sloot was. He explained that he had no regular presence at the hotel. He usually stopped by once a week to make sure everything was running smoothly. He employed managers to supervise the day-to-day business. In fact, he hadn't even seen the name Van der Sloot until he looked up Room 309 in the guest registry when he was dialing 105 and discovered that the Dutchman had been a guest of his hotel since May 14.

Kuan Bo described the closed-circuit video system the hotel used for surveillance. While he was waiting for the police to arrive, the owner had done a bit of video sleuthing on his own. He had isolated footage of Joran entering the lobby several days earlier in the company of a female guest. He only had enough time to review a very small portion of the tapes. The entire hotel was fitted with cameras.

With days worth of tape and many camera angles to scrutinize, the work was tedious, but the team assembled a chilling video time line. The actual murder was committed out of detection, with no cameras monitoring the interiors of the guest rooms. What *was* recorded was invaluable. Joran van der Sloot's movements, from the time he entered the hotel lobby with Stephany Flores in the early morning hours of Sunday, May 31, until he escorted her into his third-floor guest room minutes later, were there.

Assembling the video time line was not completely straightforward. Not all cameras were in sync with the actual time, detectives discovered. Discrepancies of up to ten minutes were found. The images, however, were powerful and unmistakable.

After arranging the footage into a chronological sequence, the detectives reviewed it from beginning to end in disbelief. Evidence like this was rare in their line of work.

Sitting in front of a video monitor, investigators first screened footage from cameras 11, 15, and 16, which were trained on the lobby and reception desk. The video, marked with a time code of 5:20 A.M., shows Joran van der Sloot approach the reception desk to request his room key. On the tape, Van der Sloot is seen wearing a wrinkled beige long-sleeved shirt and blue jeans. He flashes the receptionist a broad smile as she hands him the key. Twirling the key from the end of the plastic keychain in his left hand, he looks confident and amused. His companion, Stephany Flores, trails behind, head hung low. Her movements seem sluggish, almost as if she had been drugged. Stephany is wearing a black T-shirt and a dark pair of jeans.

Key in hand, Van der Sloot and Flores take the stairs up to his room on the third floor. Moments later, another camera positioned near the door to Room 309 shows Stephany following Joran into the hotel room. They enter his room like two strangers getting on an elevator, no signs of playfulness or flirtation. Joran does not even extend the fundamental courtesy of allowing ladies to go first. He can be seen turning on a light from a switch just inside the entryway before the door to the room closes.

Several hours pass before Joran exits Room 309, without Stephany. He steps into the brightly lit, linoleum-floored hallway. Emerging at the lobby level, he walks past the reception desk. He has changed his clothes. He is now wearing a red, white, and black striped short-sleeved shirt. The reception area camera records him in the lobby. He does not deposit the room key with the receptionist, as is customary. He leaves by the hotel's front door at exactly a minute after 8:00 A.M.

Eleven minutes later, 8:12 A.M., Joran returns to the lobby's stairwell carrying two disposable paper coffee cups, one in each hand, and heads up to the third floor. He enters his hotel room.

At 8:35 A.M., carrying the same cups, he comes out and looks up and down the hallway. He closes the door and locks it using his room key. Soon, he gestures, as if he is knocking on his door. He lingers for a few minutes pacing around in circles, shifting his weight back and forth, before finally staring directly into the camera.

He walks downstairs to the lobby. He approaches the reception desk smoking a cigarette and exchanges conversation with the receptionist. He makes a hand signal, as if he is holding a key and turning an imaginary lock.

At 8:39 A.M. a hotel employee, Reynaldo Cruz, unlocks

the door for the Dutchman with a spare key. Joran stands behind him, the cigarette pinched between his thumb and forefinger, the two cups of coffee in his left hand. He looks nervous.

Reynaldo Cruz, in a blue-and-white hotel uniform, pushes the door open a crack and walks away.

Van der Sloot again enters the room. Fifteen minutes later, he emerges from Room 309 for the last time, wearing a small green backpack on his back and carrying a beige case in his left hand.

Moments later, the lobby camera records him in his final departure from the Hotel Tac. He says nothing to the receptionist as he walks out into the morning sun, climbs into what appears to be Stephany's Jeep, and disappears. The haughty, high-flying Dutchman; the wannabe poker king; the Papiamento pimp is gone.

After replaying the tapes several times, the detectives concluded that Van der Sloot had been aware of the cameras, but not necessarily before he and Stephany had entered the room. He appeared to be acting when he pretended to puzzle about being locked out and knocking. After all, he had just locked his own door.

The police theorized that the hapless victim was dead before 8:01 A.M., the beginning of the coffee-run drama. They figured that Joran had purposely staged the coffee run to craft an alibi, trying to falsely establish an opportunity for an alternative perpetrator. But when Cruz, the employee he had summoned to gain access to his room, only opened the door a crack, and therefore did not discover the murder scene, the plan failed.

The last time Joran was seen on tape was when he pulled away from the Hotel Tac in what was most certainly Stephany's Jeep. However, detectives continued reviewing several days worth of footage from outside Room 309, astounded that no one was seen entering the room until night clerk Adeli Marchena discovered the body three days later. This lapse on the part of the hotel demanded answers.

"Do you know why your employees did not clean the room from May 30 until June 2?" homicide investigator José Silva asked.

Kuan Bo explained that unless a guest specifically requested a cleaning, staff had no reason to enter a room. But during an interview with Reynaldo Cruz, the man who had let Joran into his room using a spare key, and one of four employees on the hotel's housekeeping staff, Cruz told Detective Silva that part of his duties were to clean the rooms every day. As far as he knew, there had been no order to avoid Room 309.

A police report later questioned the system that Bo described. Establishments in the category of the Hotel Tac, while inexpensive, almost always prided themselves on daily chambermaid service. And according to housekeeper Reynaldo Cruz, the Hotel Tac was no exception.

Given this lapse, investigators did not rule out complicity from hotel staff. The report concluded that the Hotel Tac could face "penal and administrative responsibility" sometime in the future. The sloppiness had given a fugitive a three-day lead in his flight from justice and had hampered the investigation.

Room 309 was an evidentiary gold mine. Police investigators produced fifty-three color photographs and a detailed, hand-drawn sketch of the room before they were done.

Investigators were quick to realize that the long-sleeved shirt that the victim was wearing, now soaked in blood, was the same shirt Van der Sloot had been wearing when the two entered the hotel. It appeared the suspect had dressed the young woman in the shirt after killing her. Why someone would put his clothes on a victim was chilling to contemplate.

According to an initial report, "The front of the shirt and the left sleeve are not buttoned up, nor are the left and right front pockets. The shirt on the victim's body is loose and looks as if it is many sizes too big."

Scrapings were taken from under the victim's fingernails for DNA analysis. Police noted that no hair from the assailant or other clues were visible or obvious. The fingernails of both hands appeared broken and jagged as if she had put up a violent struggle.

Police left the room with evidence carefully boxed, bagged, and tagged, including five credit tickets from the tables at the Atlantic City Casino; a pair of bloody, light-blue All Star sneakers, size six and a half; a pair of bloody blue jeans, size thirty-six; and many other items including cigarette lighters, clothing, and an empty black canvas case. They also found a piece of paper torn from page thirty-eight of an appointment book with the handwritten words "Tony Igmaci $600" and two illegible signatures.

Nearly empty plastic Coca-Cola bottles and disposable paper cups from Holly's Coffee were recovered and sent for toxicological testing. Cigarette butts collected from the ashtray were also collected and labeled.

A Prince tennis racquet discovered on the floor near the TV stand was initially treated as a potential murder weapon. But the racquet had no more than usual-use wear and tear, paint scratches, and minimally frayed strings. No signs that it had been used in a violent action were evident. Later, lab tests would confirm no trace blood or anything else of criminal interest on the racquet. Most likely Joran always had his tennis racquet with him. He played competitive tennis in his youth and had probably been looking to find a pickup game in Peru.

Of considerably more interest, Stephany's "flower power" wallet lay on the floor, emptied of its cash and credit cards. Her black Nextel phone, which family and friends had been calling for days, lay silent on a countertop, its battery drained.

Homicide investigators conducted a cursory examination of the body, knowing a full autopsy would be performed later that day. The victim was covered in bruises and in an advanced state of putrification, bloated almost beyond recognition.

Blood that had oozed from the nose was clotted. Dark bruising circled both eye sockets. Both knees had red bruising and the multiple bruises on the feet were grotesquely greenish. Contusive wounds to the back of the second finger of the right hand and abrasions on the chin and right cheek added to the inventory of obvious injuries.

The bruising around the neck was curious. The police could not determine if the marks were produced by manual strangulation or hanging. The crime scene did not support any obvious sexual assault but swabs were collected for further testing.

While no shoe prints were found in the room, there were recoverable fingerprints everywhere, on the outside of the transparent ashtray on the nightstand, on the plastic soda bottles, three disposable cups, and on the gaming tickets from the Atlantic City Casino.

Under the supervision of Captain Marco Vargas, crime scene technicians now sprayed the room with luminol to test for blood. Luminol reveals invisible blood by chemiluminescence; it glows when it mixes with a specific reactive agent. At crime scenes, the reactive agent is the iron in the hemoglobin of human blood. After luminol is applied, even trace amounts of blood emit an eerie blue light.

The test was both shocking and revealing.

Vargas and his team sprayed the luminol brand Bluestar in the room, on the carpet and walls, and in the bathroom. When they turned off the lights, glowing traces of luminescent blood were everywhere: under the bed, on the floor by the dresser, and on the bone-colored tile of the bathroom floor.

Vargas now turned his focus to the bathroom. Not only did the sink test positive for blood, but the shower floor also glowed with the evidence.

The suspect appeared to have showered before fleeing the scene.

Based on the first collection of evidence in the investigation—the surveillance tapes, the physical evidence in Room 309, the Internet profiles of Van der Sloot—the police developed a straightforward working theory. They believed Stephany had been lured to the room, was beaten, robbed, possibly even tortured in an attempt to get the passwords to the credit cards that were missing from her wallet, before finally being strangled. Van der Sloot's modus operandi, they concluded, was selecting his victims in casinos and/or gaming rooms where women who play these games go. Through deceit, he obtains his victims' money. Plain and simple, this was a robbery turned homicide.

The deadline for registering for the the Latin American Poker Tour at the Atlantic City Casino was Sunday, May 30. The U.S.$2,700 entry fee could be paid in person at the gaming tables or online. It was possible that Joran needed Stephany's credit card numbers to pay the entry fee for the tournament. Perhaps he had lured Stephany to his room with hopes he could convince her to loan him the money to register and she had refused?

Like in the U.S., under Peruvian law all individuals are presumed innocent until proven otherwise. However, the five detectives working the case knew they had their man. Now they needed to find him.

EIGHT

From the moment the trip was presented, Natalee Holloway's father, Dave, had been opposed to his daughter traveling to Aruba with her classmates. He had heard the pitch— everyone's parents were allowing it; last year's identical trip had been uneventful; Natalee, more than anyone, deserved a graduation trip. He didn't care what the other parents thought. He did not like the idea.

He had fears about safety. He was concerned that seven chaperones for 124 teenagers were insufficient. Common knowledge held that the island's tourism slogan, "One Happy Island," hinted at Aruba's drinking age, young and barely enforced. In Dave's opinion, an 18:1 student-to-chaperone ratio, even with the utmost diligence, was inadequate.

Besides, Dave and his second wife, Robin, were old-fashioned and thought the $985 cost for a five-day jaunt was too extravagant for high schoolers. Holloway was a conservative man in his midforties with bushy brown hair combed to one side and a charming gap between his front teeth. He was a responsible and loving father.

He knew, however, that in spite of his misgivings, the trip would likely take place even without his blessing. His ex-wife, Beth, had sole custody of their two children and she'd been the one to sign the consent form for the five-day Caribbean getaway.

Still, despite his trepidation, Dave gave his daughter a check for $500—half the cost of the vacation—as a gift, telling Natalee to do with it as she pleased, knowing she would probably use it to finance the trip to Aruba.

Even if she had left that May morning without his full approval, he never expected the telephone call he received on Monday, May 31. There had been a barrage of confusing and contradictory phone calls. The first call was from his son, Matt, saying that Natalee hadn't shown up for her flight. Next came word that she had last been seen leaving a bar in the company of a Dutch tourist, described by Natalee's friends as a nice kid. When Matt called again late in the evening saying that Natalee was okay and had only missed her flight, Dave was naturally relieved. Matt explained that she was flying in the next day. But Matt himself was misinformed; a flight for Natalee *had* been booked on Delta Airlines for the following day by an optimistic chaperone. The booking, however, was based on hope, not knowledge.

Natalee Holloway was born in Memphis, Tennessee, on October 21, 1986. She was the first child of David Edward Holloway and Elizabeth Ann Reynolds, college sweethearts. They met at the University of Arkansas in Little Rock where Dave earned a bachelor of science in business management and Beth completed a BS in speech pathology with a minor in special education.

After graduation, they moved together to Memphis, a thriving musical town on the banks of the Mississippi, where they married in a church in front of glowing parents and approving friends. Memphis was a lively city rich in culture and history. It was the birthplace of rock 'n' roll and the town where Johnny Cash, Elvis, and B. B. King began their musical careers. The city was also the backdrop for several of John Grisham's bestselling legal thrillers, including *The Firm*.

Here in Memphis, Natalee Ann was born. Dave and his young wife were elated with the arrival of their daughter, who shared her mother's fair hair and light complexion and her father's almond-shaped eyes and broad, inviting smile. Two years later, their son Matthew was born. Matt was a stocky, sweet-natured boy who shared his father's facial characteristics and gentle, down-to-earth personality.

When Natalee was three and Matt was just learning to walk, the family moved to Clinton, Mississippi, a three-and-a-half-hour drive due south and a world away from the blues and barbecue of Memphis's Beale Street. Clinton was a rural town with single-family, red brick homes that was popular with both young families and retirees. There wasn't much excitement. The change of pace from bustling Memphis to pastoral Clinton was drastic and difficult.

Soon, Beth and Dave became acutely aware that they were no longer compatible. When Natalee was seven and Matt was five, they divorced. The custody battle was messy and protracted. Beth eventually won sole custody of the couple's two children. Bitter feelings lingered, and the couple limited their interactions to matters concerning the children.

In 1995, Dave remarried. His new wife, Robin, was a quick-witted blonde who, like her groom, was intensely religious. Funny, gracious, and several years younger than her husband, Robin was a nurturing stepmother to Natalee and Matt. They both developed a strong affinity for this new member of the family.

After the wedding, Dave and Robin moved to Jackson, Mississippi, about thirteen miles from Clinton and a straight shot on Highway 20. But Dave didn't like being separated from his children by even this short distance, and he and Robin moved back to Clinton the following year. Although Dave and his ex-wife rarely spoke, he played an active role in raising Natalee and Matt. He made the most of his alternate weekends and filled them with children-oriented activities. He and Natalee enjoyed a nighttime ritual of creating fantastical stories together.

In 2000, Beth remarried, as well. Her bridegroom was George Twitty, nicknamed "Jug." Natalee was fourteen and Matt was twelve when she and the children moved to Mountain Brook, Alabama, to settle comfortably into the home of her new husband. That same year, Dave and Robin relocated to Meridian, Mississippi, a racially diverse city about twenty miles from the Alabama state line, and 150 miles from Mountain Brook. Dave worked as an insurance salesman, and Robin was preparing to make a family of her own. Two daughters, Brooke and Kaitlyn, soon made their entrance into the Holloways' Meridian household.

Natalee and Matt visited every other weekend and stayed with Dave and Robin for longer stretches during summers and on holidays. Family time was spent watching movies at home, but occasionally, for a special treat, they trekked to the local shopping mall to catch a new release on the big screen. Sunday mornings in Meridian were spent at the Poplar Drive Springs Baptist Church, and Natalee always made sure to pack her Sunday best.

When Natalee was sixteen, she got her driver's license, and her visits to Meridian became less frequent. Like a typical teenager, being with her buddies in Alabama trumped weekends with her dad in Mississippi. Still, Dave and Robin often traveled the 150 miles to Mountain Brook to watch Natalee perform with her high school dance squad, the Dorians, during halftime at the Mountain Brook's Spartans football games.

Natalee's senior year was a scramble of obligations: school; volunteer work; the part-time job at the health food store; church activities; rehearsals with the dance team. Dave certainly understood, and he and his new family treasured whatever dates they were able to schedule together. Earnest wishes for more time were impossible to fulfill.

Natalee's graduation day, one day before her trip to Aruba, was the last time the father and daughter were together. That day, Dave and Robin and their two daughters arrived at Beth's house to pick up the tickets for the commencement ceremony. Natalee insisted that they all come inside. She wanted Brooke and Kaitlyn, ages two and seven, to meet Macy, her Shetland sheepdog, whose nails she had playfully painted with polish. She also wanted to show them her light-purple bedroom decorated with her *Wizard of Oz* memorabilia, a collection she'd been passionately amassing since eighth grade.

The invitation inside was awkward. They had not all been under the same roof in years. In hindsight, Dave, with his unshakable faith, believed that the Lord had played a role in creating this precious and indelible memory. All the family strife was unimportant. This day, May 24, 2005, was Natalee's day, and the family was together.

Now, less than one week later, phone calls were bringing him horrible news. His daughter had simply vanished.

Dave wasted no time contacting family. Everyone wanted to leave for Aruba immediately but there were no commercial flights until morning. His ex-wife had a friend with a private plane, but he didn't have such connections.

When Dave, his brother Phil, and his brother-in-law Michael stepped off the commercial jet at Queen Beatrix International Airport on June 1, no team of prearranged personal escorts met them. However, they managed to solicit a map of the island and directions to the nearest police station from employees at the rental car counter.

Dave had assumed that on such a small island, the disappearance of an American tourist would have been high priority for law enforcement. But the officers at the first two precincts he visited knew nothing about his missing daughter. Finally, he was directed to the Noord Police Station where he found a detective who was familiar with Natalee's missing persons investigation.

From the moment they shook hands, Detective Dennis Jacobs, a 350-pound narcotics officer who announced he was in charge of the investigation, disturbed Dave. He did not extend condolences about Dave's daughter or reassurances that they were on top of the case. Instead, he posed the question, "How much money do you have?"

Dave was in such disbelief he assumed he must have heard the question incorrectly. He returned to the issue and asked what was being done to find Natalee. If this man was in charge, why wasn't he out looking with the police search team? In fact, *was* there a police search team?

The detective did not seem to be taking Natalee's disappearance seriously. He had been the one to process the missing persons report filed by Dave's ex-wife, but, like he had been quick to explain to her, his own theory incorporated no foul play or alarm.

"This happens all the time," he stated matter-of-factly. "She'll probably turn up in a few days."

Dave couldn't believe the callous treatment he was receiving. The detective even had the gall to suggest that Dave indulge in a cocktail from the very bar where his daughter was last seen. Everything about this police officer seemed offensively inappropriate. Dave quickly realized that he was on his own.

What Detective Jacobs hadn't told Dave Holloway was that he and a fellow officer, Sergeant Shaniro Kelly, had spent the prior morning interviewing Joran van der Sloot, one of the three men last seen with Natalee. The interview, taken in Papiamento at 11:20 A.M. on Tuesday, May 31, was the first of more than a dozen statements the teen made to police about his night with Natalee.

His story was similar to the tale he'd told the group of Americans from Alabama in the driveway of his home that past Monday night. But there were some new details. Joran painted Natalee as both drunk and belligerent, saying that when he and his friends, Deepak and Satish, pulled up in front of the Holiday Inn after the journey to the lighthouse, Natalee opened the car door and fell to the ground.

"I went out by the same door and helped her get up," Joran told the detectives. "The girl told me not to touch her and pushed my hands away. I watched as she then walked in the direction of the lobby of the Holiday Inn. I had not seen anyone in the lobby. My friends Deepak and Satish had told me they had seen a dark-skinned man in the lobby. They further told me that this man was a guard."

Joran claimed that Natalee was leaning against one of the orange columns near the entrance to the resort when the three drove away.

Detectives had also interviewed Deepak and Satish Kalpoe at the Bubali Police Station, a small, run-down-looking cement facility on the beach next to the Wyndham Hotel. Deepak's statement was also taken in Papiamento, while Satish spoke with the officers in Dutch.

Like Joran, the brothers agreed that Natalee was drunk. They claimed she approached their Dutch friend at Carlos'n Charlie's, and begged him to join her on the dance floor. Deepak said Joran had declined her invitation; Satish remembered that Joran had indeed danced with the "white girl" that night.

The brothers each recounted standing at the bar, drinking whiskey and Cokes and shots of Bacardi, but neither man mentioned the body shot that Joran claimed to have sucked off Natalee's stomach.

Deepak told the officers that when Natalee's friends saw her hanging out the rear window of his car, they were upset. "A young person came over to my car and told her to get out of my car," Deepak recalled. "I parked my car and I told the girl that she should go with her friends. She refused to do this. She said that my car was beautiful and she wanted to drive around for a while.

"Joran asked if she was certain that she wanted to drive around with us. And the girl answered, 'Yes.' I told Joran that I didn't think it was a good idea that she remain with us because she was drunk and I didn't want any problems," the elder Kalpoe volunteered.

During the drive, Deepak said that Natalee and Joran were kissing and Joran was touching her breasts. He also claimed that at one point, when they had reached the lighthouse on Arashi Beach, the northernmost tip of the island, Natalee fell asleep. "I told Joran to wake her up and ask her what hotel she was staying at. I heard the girl tell Joran the Holiday Inn."

Satish's initial statement to police was remarkably similar to his brother's, particularly the part about dropping Natalee at the Holiday Inn. Like Deepak, the younger Kalpoe recalled that Joran was kissing and touching Natalee in the backseat of his brother's car, and that she appeared drunk. The two brothers also recounted how Natalee spilled out of the backseat and onto the pavement in front of the Holiday Inn, and had refused Joran's help getting inside.

Like Joran, they also described a "dark-skinned" man standing in the lobby who they claimed must have been the last person seen with Natalee Holloway.

"He's approximately one-point-eight meters tall, he has a heavy-set body, he has close-cropped hair, he wore a black T-shirt, he wore black cotton long trousers, which most of the guards wear, he had a walkie-talkie in his hand and spoke by means of the walkie-talkie," Deepak described. "If I see the guard again, I will recognize him."

Satish's description of the security guard mirrored his brother's. However, unlike his brother, he told the police that he did not think he would be able to recognize him again.

Neither Beth's nor Dave's groups were apprised of these interrogations, or any other actions that were taking place on behalf of their daughter. Beth was sure she had seen Deepak's car in the parking lot of police headquarters on the morning she came to give an official statement to the police, but detectives failed to mention that they had spoken with the three young men.

Before Dave and Detective Jacobs parted ways at the Noord Police Station that day, Jacobs cautioned him that he had received reports that his ex-wife and her party had been knocking on the doors of crack houses in some of Aruba's seedier neighborhoods following up on "tips" provided by local drug addicts in exchange for cash. The detective warned him that this was a dangerous and unfruitful way of doing business and he should persuade her to refrain.

Aware that Beth and Jug had the "drug deal gone wrong" angle covered, Dave and his group began searching the remoter beaches and backcountry. He hoped he'd find his daughter alive, but he was aware that if she had been killed a freshly dug grave was more likely to be found.

Beth did not coordinate her search strategies with Dave. Her parallel efforts had her plastering "Missing" posters of Natalee across the length and breadth of the island. The posters featured two color photographs of Natalee and a physical description: blue eyes, long blond hair, five feet four, 110 pounds. Soon everyone in Aruba was aware of the young woman's disappearance. But the story was about to be international news.

Frustrated by what she perceived as police ineptitude, Beth turned to the cameras, first granting an interview to a local TV station. By June 2, the family's heart-wrenching plight ran in *USA Today* and had been picked up by the cable news network CNN. Soon all the other networks followed.

Speaking to the camera, hoping her daughter was somewhere where she could hear her, Beth Twitty held up two cell phones and said, "Natalee, you can reach me on your cell phone. I have it, and it's set up for international use now. And I also have my cell phone. It's set up for international use. So please call me. And I will stay here until I find you."

Natalee's story had all the ingredients the media savored when looking for a sensational news event. A beautiful blonde; a smart, college-bound high school senior; an upscale, up-standing citizen vanishes in an exotic Caribbean paradise. Every parent's worst nightmare of child abduction was captured in Beth Twitty's anguish. Natalee was a sister, a friend, a classmate, a fellow American, a collective daughter vanishing in the prime of her life.

Her missing persons case was becoming mainstay cable news fodder, which had recently been dominated by pop star Michael Jackson's arrest on child molestation charges.

When Beth and Dave first landed in Aruba, local interest in their daughter was moderate. Now it seemed the whole island was looking for Natalee. For six days, police officers, members of the Royal Dutch Marines, and hundreds of volunteers, including Aruban citizens and American tourists vacationing on the island, combed the beaches and hiked the desert looking for any fresh disturbances in the earth. By Saturday, June 4, ten investigators from the FBI joined the three agents who had already been dispatched to the island.

Dutch coast guard officers searched the waters, as helicopters flew overhead. Volunteers from Aruba's Search and Rescue Federation, the Aruban Red Cross, and other local organizations joined Dave in the daily land searches. The men would come back dehydrated, sunburned, and covered with scratches after hours of scouring the cactus-strewn terrain in the searing heat. In churches across Aruba, congregations prayed for Natalee's safe return, a gesture that touched her deeply religious parents.

The reward money being offered for information leading to Natalee's safe return was growing and now stood at $50,000. The Aruban Tourism Board and local business owners donated $20,000, and $30,000 was raised by the Holloway and Twitty families and their supporters back in Alabama. Still, no worthwhile leads fomented.

Beth had been staying in her daughter's room at the Holiday Inn since her arrival on Aruba. Four days had passed investigating hunches, probing the police, and pasting posters when a knock on the door brought her news. A hotel employee in freshly pressed whites came to Room 7114 and told her they had located the video footage from cameras outside of the lobby. They thought they had spotted Natalee.

The employee escorted Beth and Jug to a nearby room where they found a group of uniformed police officers around a video screen. "Is that her? Is that Natalee?" one of the officers asked, pointing to a young woman with long blond hair entering the lobby.

In her heart Beth wanted to believe it was Natalee. She wanted to say, "Yes, that's her." But, she recognized the fair-haired teen in the grainy video as Natalee's friend, Madison, by the way the young woman walked, by the way she carried herself.

Shuttling through the video of the rest of that evening, there was no sign of Natalee. There were no signs of Joran, Deepak, or Satish, either. Beth remembered the scene that Joran and Deepak had been willing to re-create the night of the confrontation in the Van der Sloots' driveway. Everyone, Joran and Deepak included, had returned to the Holiday Inn. There, Joran and Deepak had performed a convincing reenactment of the events, demonstrating exactly where they had dropped off Natalee.

"We pulled up right here," Joran had said, pointing to a spot on the roundabout in front of the hotel lobby. "As soon as she got out of the car, she fell down and hit her head. She was so drunk."

If the story had been true, the cameras would have recorded the incident. The boys had concocted the entire story. The story and the video footage did not match. Furthermore, there was no "dark-skinned" security guard on staff, not that night or any night.

The three young men had flagrantly misled the police. The evidence of what was *not* on the tape proved it. Everything Joran had said had been a lie. Beth was now confident investigators had all the information they needed to arrest him.

NINE

JUNE 2, 2010
LIMA, PERU

Ricardo Flores made a vow to himself not to leave the Hotel Tac until his daughter's body was removed from the hotel. Just after 4:30 A.M., when Lima was still dark, Detective Tong and two other officers wheeled the gurney, supporting a casket draped in black, up the ramp from the hotel's underground parking garage. The coroner's gunmetal-gray van stenciled with the words "DIRINCRI HOMICIDIOS" was parked at the top of the ramp waiting to receive the body and take it to the morgue, a twenty-minute drive. The sidewalk was illuminated with a steady stream of flashbulbs as reporters and news crews jockeyed for the right angle from which to capture the "money shot."

Stephany's father understood the feeding frenzy that occurs when reporters and photographers try to capture the scene of a murder and a body's removal, especially when famous people are involved. He was so grateful that a friend had provided a proper casket so that his daughter would not have to suffer the indignity of being carried out in a body bag for the entire world to see.

Captain Juan Callan told Flores that his daughter's body would undergo an autopsy later that morning. He'd have someone in the department phone him as soon as he knew more. A lump grew in Ricardo's throat as he watched the coroner's van carrying his beloved Stephany pull onto the street. "Let's go home," he murmured to his sons, climbing into the passenger seat of Richie's car.

Turning onto Avenida Benavides, Ricardo looked back over his shoulder and noticed a caravan of news vehicles tailing them. They wanted a statement, a reaction from the grief-stricken father. He would have to speak to them in the future, but at the moment he simply wanted to be home holding his wife, whom he had last seen collapsed in grief on the sidewalk. Without the support of his sons, Richie and Enrique, in the car with him, he would not even have been able to endure the short drive.

Richie used the quiet in the car to gently recount the grisly scene he had witnessed in the hotel room. Because there was blood everywhere, he wrongly assumed that his sister had been stabbed to death. He spared them the physical injuries to his beautiful sister's face.

The three men strode into the house, arriving just ahead of the media. Ricardo found Mariaelena curled up on the couch in the living room. The sedative she had been given by the paramedics had helped, but her face was contorted with grief, tears running down her cheeks. Kneeling down, he kissed her on the forehead, stifling his own tears with great difficulty. As the patriarch of the family, he needed to remain strong.

Sitting beside his wife, he watched as the morning sun rose from the east. The dawn of another day without Stephany, he thought. He missed her so much. There was nothing to do now but wait.

Just after 8:00 A.M., the phone rang. As promised, Callan was keeping Flores updated.

"Van der Sloot has already fled Peru," the officer on the phone related. Police had just spoken with Interpol and had been informed that Joran had crossed into Chile near the

Peruvian border town of Tacna on May 31 at three in the afternoon, two days earlier. Van der Sloot was moving south and investigators worried he was headed for Argentina.

Hanging up the phone, Ricardo looked out the window to where dozens of reporters were camped out in front of his house. He was a savvy entertainment promoter and he realized he could use the media to his advantage.

Flores's relations with the press were sometimes good, sometimes not. Several years earlier, he had promoted a Michael Jackson concert in Lima and had sold thousands of tickets. But the King of Pop had failed to honor his commitment and the show had to be canceled. The press had heckled Ricardo for months.

The cancellation had not been his fault, but reporters suggested that Jackson had never been booked and accused Ricardo of fraud. Although he was vindicated in a formal investigation, he struggled to forgive the press.

Now, however, they were needed and he needed to manage them to his benefit. Ricardo wanted the press, with its ability to disseminate information, to help in Joran's capture. He wanted everyone to be familiar with Joran's image and knew talking to the media would keep the case in the headlines.

Striding to the bathroom, Stephany's father splashed handful after handful of cold water on his face before combing his hair and putting on a clean white shirt. He was exhausted but rose to the task as he stepped outside to address the cameras and microphones. The time for him to speak had arrived.

At 8:35 A.M., Ricardo Flores emerged from his house, flanked by his two sons. Only three hours earlier he had watched helplessly as his only daughter's body was wheeled from a tourist hotel. Now, he was determined to see that her killer be brought to justice.

Standing in front of the mahogany door of the family's garage, Ricardo delivered his message.

"I am doing this out of consideration for other families," Ricardo began, "so that this does not happen to them."

Because of the notoriety of his daughter's alleged assailant,

Stephany's murder was fast becoming an international story. Television crews from the United States and Holland joined the local journalists standing on the other side of the security gate surrounding the Floreses' home.

His tone was calm and monotonic as he explained to reporters what he knew about Stephany's last evening: She had been with friends. She met Van der Sloot in a casino. He had somehow lured her back to the hotel where he murdered her. "Van der Sloot is now on the run, possibly headed to Argentina, and I need your help in bringing him back to Peru," Ricardo lamented. "This was not the first murder he committed. He did the same thing in 2005. But because he was underage and there was no evidence, he had walked away to kill again.

"Van der Sloot was previously implicated in the murder of a teenager in Aruba," Ricardo continued, staring directly into the cameras. "Her body was never found. This time Van der Sloot must be stopped before he kills again.

"I don't want this to happen to other families," Ricardo implored. "I don't want other families to go through what we are going through now.

"I know my daughter was stabbed," Ricardo told the cameras, his calm demeanor replaced by a tragic faraway stare. "There was definitely a struggle, but I imagine an autopsy will provide more answers."

"This is my daughter's killer," he finished, holding up two photos of a teenage Joran, dressed in a lime-green striped polo shirt.

Ricardo Flores was utterly exhausted, unable to speak another word. He broke down completely in free-flowing tears and breath-choking sobs. Richie and Enrique took over the microphones.

Meanwhile, at Lima's central morgue nine blocks east of the Palace of Justice, Stephany's body had been wheeled into a chilled autopsy suite. Unlike Miraflores, the neighborhood of Santos surrounding the morgue was a desperate and violent place, a barrio of "one-sink alleys," districts so poor that residents of the many dead-end streets shared a communal faucet for laundry, cooking, and bathing. Dressed in white lab coats, Dr. Juan Martin Villalobos and his assistant, Sergio, carefully lifted the badly decomposed corpse onto the stainless steel table in preparation for the *necropsia*.

Dr. Villalobos glanced over the paperwork that accompanied the body, a three-page, handwritten, all-purpose form completed shortly before 6:00 A.M. when the cadaver was removed from the crime scene at the Hotel Tac. Skimming through Captain Juan Callan's crime scene notes, he read aloud for the benefit of the other three individuals in the room: Sergio, his assistant; Dr. Judith Maguiña, another forensic pathologist; and a representative from the Public Ministry.

From Callan's notes, Dr. Villalobos read to the team that the body had been discovered on top of a blood-soaked sheet. A tennis racquet had been found amid the clothing and other items near the body, but had tested negative for blood. If the racquet had been the murder weapon, the body would have presented bruises matching the patterns and dimensions of the racquet. The coroner noted that none were present.

Callan's notes also indicated that the body was cold to the touch. A window of the hotel room had been left open and the body temperature of the victim had dropped to room temperature. The pathologist didn't need a form to know the victim had suffered a violent and unnatural death. Looking at the body, this was unmistakably a homicide.

Stephany's head alone told the story of a violent struggle. Both eyes were circled in dark blue-red bruises, her nose crushed and nearly flattened. More bruises covered her cheeks and chin and a bloody, viscous fluid oozed from her left ear. There were signs of petechial hemorrhaging, small blotches created as capillaries explode, on her face. These tiny red pinpoint marks occur when pressure is applied to the neck, a classic sign of strangulation.

Hitting the record button on a small digital recorder, Villalobos announced that he was ready to begin. He started with the basic information. The twenty-one-year-old student on the table before him was dressed in a black sleeveless T-shirt, a long-sleeved beige button-down shirt "soaked in blood on the back from the neck to the bottom," a brown bra, and red underwear. Pausing, he noted that beneath the underwear was a sanitary napkin completely soaked in blood. The victim had been menstruating.

With the assistance of his lab tech, Villalobos cut away the clothing before removing Stephany's jewelry—a white metal watch by Rip Curl, a silver ring, and two black-and-gray pendant earrings.

Stephany's once dark brown eyes were now protruding from their sockets. A contact lens was missing from the right eye. "Pupils are opaque, fixed, and dilated with time of death occurring between two and three days," he dictated into the recorder. It was just a ballpark guess. With a more recent death, he would have inserted a thermometer into the liver. A temperature reading from this organ would have narrowed the window considerably, but with a stone-cold corpse, the measurement would have been useless.

Turning back to Callan's notes, Villalobos saw that the body had remained in the same position since the time of death. This was a fairly easy conclusion to reach given the victim's fixed lividity. When a person dies, the heart stops pumping blood. Lacking pressure, the blood begins to settle and pools in the parts of the body closest to the ground and they take on a darker hue. The victim's coloring was consistent with a body lying on the floor in the same position for several days.

Rigor mortis, a natural stiffening of the body, which occurs in the hours immediately after death, had come and gone. Stephany's battered corpse was limp and flaccid. Putrefaction had begun to set in and her once beautiful oval face was now a horrifying kaleidoscope of green, blue, and purple. Taking some measurements, Villalobos noted that Stephany measured five feet six inches tall and weighed 154 pounds. She appeared well nourished and hydrated and had no tattoos.

Working his way from top to bottom he found two old scars, unrelated to recent events, one on her torso and another on her right leg. Her upper body presented more recent injuries including multiple bruises predominantly to the left-hand side of her face, neck, chest, arms, and abdomen. Her straight, once luxurious, chestnut-brown hair was caked with blood. A sickening red fluid oozed from both nostrils as dried blood mixed with other secretions created when a body decomposes. Her lips appeared blue and moist to the touch. Her teeth were intact.

Bruising around the neck was consistent with strangulation. More bruises and lesions were present on her chest. Her stomach appeared distended and was covered with bruises and lesions, as well. More bruises, lesions, scrapes, and cuts covered her upper and lower extremities. The second finger on her right hand had battle injuries. She had fought hard, but in vain.

Villalobos found no sign of recent sexual activity. In fact, based on examination, Stephany Flores was a virgin.

Readying his scalpel, saw, and other forensic tools, Villalobos began the internal exam. There were no signs of trauma to the top of the cranium, but there were internal lesions on the scalp and the rear base of the skull. The soft tissue of the brain, in an advanced state of putrefaction, had turned brittle. Its degraded condition made it difficult to handle, but it showed that the young woman had suffered devastating internal injuries. Villalobos discovered a hemorrhage to the dura mater, the tough fibrous membrane that envelops the brain and spinal cord. Another hemorrhage was found in the fossa media, home to the brain's temporal lobes, which control speech, vision, and memory. Subarachnoid hemorrhages of the cerebellum were noted.

Essentially, blood vessels just outside of Stephany's brain had ruptured, allowing blood to flow into the empty space between the brain and the wall of the skull. The buildup of blood would have created pressure on the brain resulting in an intense headache, nausea, vomiting, and perhaps even unconsciousness.

But Villalobos doubted the brain injuries themselves were enough to kill this young woman. Had the assailant inflicted these injuries alone, in all likelihood Stephany Flores could have been saved.

Working his way down, Villalobos probed his fingers into the muscle tissue of Stephany's neck. There, he discovered bright red hemorrhaging lining the third, fourth, and fifth cervical vertebrae, indicating she had been choked. Although it was an ugly injury, it was not necessarily fatal. Her neck had not been broken, contrary to prematurely leaked news reports.

The actual cause of Stephany's death was not as straightforward as Dr. Villalobos had hoped. An X-ray of her hyoid bone, a fragile bone in the neck positioned under the jaw, raised the possibility that Stephany may have been alive but unconscious for quite some time before succumbing to her internal injuries. When the horseshoe-shaped hyoid bone is broken, it almost certainly means strangulation, but Stephany's hyoid was intact.

Removing the liver, spleen, lungs, and pancreas to send off to the lab for pathologic study, Dr. Villalobos discovered a white, plastic gastric band in the young woman's stomach. Stephany, it appeared, had struggled so much with her weight that she had a surgically placed bariatric band.

Toxicology results from the samples revealed the presence of amphetamines. The discovery of amphetamines in Stephany's system prompted a range of speculation and theories. The first speculation, leaked soon after the discovery, suggested a date-rape drug scenario, supported by video footage of Stephany entering Joran's hotel room. In the film, her motion is slow and shuffling. Her submissive position behind Joran reinforced the possibility of being drugged.

Amphetamines, however, are not a classic drug associated with date rape. In fact, amphetamines are stimulants with effects just the opposite of sluggishness and lethargy. More likely, Stephany's behavior on the video was the consequence of extreme fatigue and alcohol consumption. The tape in the hotel is time-stamped 5:20 A.M. And the casino footage had shown her sipping a glass of wine.

A more nefarious theory explored the possibility that Stephany was a recreational drug user or even a drug abuser. In the world of drugs, assassinations and murders are commonplace and debts are paid with lives. A blister pack for medication found in Stephany's Jeep lent support to this idea. However, additional tests for cocaine, barbiturates, marijuana, and other illegal drugs came back negative.

The blister pack in the Jeep contained nothing more than over-the-counter cold medicine, and made sense—before she went out, Stephany had complained to her father about not feeling well.

The presence of amphetamines most likely had no bearing on the criminal investigation. The gastric band in Stephany's stomach was evidence enough of her strong desire to control her weight. Amphetamines are commonly used as appetite suppressants; therefore, with the most popular uses for over-the-counter amphetamines being energy enhancement and weight loss, the mystery of the drug's presence in Stephany's system could be resolved.

The deteriorated condition of Stephany's body made it impossible to get a blood sample from her remains. Instead, a sample was obtained from the blood-soaked shirt found on her body. Stephany was type A. No other blood but hers was found at the crime scene. If her assailant had been injured during the violent struggle in Room 309, he had left behind no blood evidence.

Perhaps the most disturbing finding in the autopsy was the possibility that Stephany may have been drifting in and out of consciousness for hours after her attack, helplessly lying on the hotel room floor. Her arms, fingers, and legs were blue and cyanotic, indicating that the deficiency of oxygen in her blood occurred *before* she died, rather than *after* she died.

Combined with the discovery of blood traces in the shower stall, the scene became complete: the horrifying scenario had

Joran showering off the evidence as Stephany, alive but barely conscious, lay on the hotel room floor.

As for cause of death, Villalobos's conclusion was surprisingly noncommittal. He explained that Stephany's body had remained undiscovered for two to three days, had been in bad shape and had been, in his words, "in a state of putrefaction that makes an autopsy difficult."

He concluded that Stephany's death had been caused by the combined result of damage to the brain and cervical trauma due to choking. Villalobos also determined that the "causing agent" for Stephany's injuries was a blunt instrument. Because the tennis racquet had been ruled out, the investigating detectives needed to reach their own conclusions regarding the causing agent. All the evidence pointed to a rage killing.

Callan and his team suspected that the blunt instruments used to kill Stephany were Van der Sloot's fists—that the Dutch traveler had savagely beaten the young woman for her cash, which he needed to gamble. After smothering her and rendering her unconscious, he posed her body to make it appear as though she had been the victim of a violent sexual assault. He then began his coffee-run charade to help create opportunities for other assailants and alternative explanations for her horrifyingly unnecessary death.

TEN

JUNE 4, 2005
ORANJESTAD, ARUBA

Beth Twitty's impassioned pleas for the safe return of her missing daughter seized headlines in the United States and the family's ordeal became a media obsession for the cable news shows. The story of the missing Alabama student was a ratings coup; viewers couldn't get enough.

The escapade of Jennifer Wilbanks, the runaway bride who then reappeared a few days later with a fabricated kidnapping tale, had been the splashy headline only a month earlier. Now Natalee's case, with no body and no bloody crime scene, let imaginations run wild about her fate—from a voluntary runaway to a sex-slave captive to a victim of murder. Her beauty and her mother's persistent wrenching pleas made her story stay in the spotlight.

Aruba's deputy police chief, Gerold Dompig, later claimed that Beth's decision to go before the media so early in the investigation pressured him, and under intense media scrutiny he made hasty decisions that he wouldn't have normally made, including the premature arrests of people who shouldn't have been suspects.

Natalee had been missing for six days when Dompig, a well-groomed black man with close-cropped hair and a neatly combed mustache, stood before the cameras and delivered a cryptic message.

"We are working diligently," he said of his department's investigators. "I want everybody to hold his breath for the next twenty-four hours. There will be developments after this weekend."

Without mentioning any names, Dompig, the police department's second-in-command under police chief Jan van der Straten, told reporters that two Surinamese men and a Dutchman were the investigation's three most important leads. They admitted they had dropped Natalee at the hotel the night she went missing. He stopped short of calling the men suspects, instead referring to the three as "persons of interest."

In response to questions, the deputy police chief spelled out his department's three theories. "One is, as you all know, that these persons of interest might have done something wrong to Natalee. That's one area. The other area is that Natalee is just missing, in terms of being somewhere else for whatever reason. And the last theory is, of course, kidnapping."

Beth Twitty had seen the videotape from the lobby of the Holiday Inn. She knew that her daughter had not come back to the hotel as Joran had explained. She also did not believe the boys' story about the black security guard. Imagine her overwhelming dismay when she awoke on the morning of June 6 and learned that two dark-skinned security guards had been arrested—and not Joran and the Kalpoe brothers.

In a predawn raid, Aruban police had stormed the homes of two black men who, until recently, had worked as security guards at the Allegro Aruba Grand about a mile down the beach from the Holiday Inn.

Security guard Antonius "Mickey" John was asleep in his bed when a police tactical team knocked on the door of his cream-colored house with a pink tile roof on Van Speyk Street. The house was next to a drive-in Burger King in a nearly all-black neighborhood in Sint Nicolaas, Aruba's sec-

ond largest city. Sint Nicolaas was on the south side of the island. Many of its residents were former citizens of the British
Caribbean islands but had come to Aruba in search of jobs.
Mickey John and his family lived just off Bernard Street, the
city's main road, in a poor area where many of the rectangular cement houses were run-down and in varying states of
disrepair.

The house was so close to the Sint Nicolaas Police Station that the Johns could see a corner of the blue-and-white
stucco façade from their front porch. The Valero Oil Refin-
ery Company, then owned by American oil giant Valero,
operated a plant several miles south.

Before sunrise, John was dragged from his bed, handcuffed in front of his mother, and led to an awaiting unmarked
police vehicle. The arresting officers, including Dennis
Jacobs, were in plainclothes. They dismissively ignored
John's hysterical mother, Amy, and refused to tell her why her
son was being taken into custody. Someone had tipped off the
media and cameras captured the arrest.

Although fluent in English, John spoke little Dutch. He
was ten when he moved with his mother to Aruba from their
native Grenada. He had attended English schools on Grenada and Trinidad, and completed his secondary studies in
English on Aruba. Standing five feet ten, with broad shoulders, and deep-set brown eyes, John was a self-described
"Rasta man" who liked to quote from the Bible. Around his
neck, the twenty-one-year-old wore a heavy gold chain with
a sizable marijuana leaf–shaped medallion and he wore a
gold hoop earring in each ear.

He had never been in trouble with the law, and had no
idea why police had come for him. John knew he had done
nothing wrong and grew concerned when police started asking questions about the missing American woman. By then,
everyone on Aruba was familiar with the case. John had seen
the posters of the pretty blond teen on buildings and in windows of stores and bars everywhere he went.

There was something about the demeanor of the investigators, however, that seemed sympathetic. He would later

recall that he was treated well by the arresting officers and sensed it was because they knew he was not guilty of any crime. He hoped he was not being framed. He was a black man living on a Dutch colony and knew that racial inequality was a serious problem.

During the first of two interviews police conducted with John, he explained that he had worked at the Allegro Grand Hotel on Palm Beach up until May 31, 2005. Specifically, he was employed by the A.S.I.S. Guarding Company and his assignment had been as a security guard at the Allegro Grand. The luxury hotel, a gorgeous four-hundred-room, nine-story resort, was undergoing a $25 million makeover and had been closed to overnight guests for nearly a month; only the casino had remained open until May 31. At that time, the casino was also closing for renovations. The contract for security services between the Allegro Grand and A.S.I.S. Guarding expired at midnight May 31, and would not be renegotiated until the hotel reopened. Therefore, John found himself temporarily unemployed, awaiting a new post from A.S.I.S. The prime slice of oceanfront real estate was two blocks from the Holiday Inn.

"What hours did you work on the night of May 29 into May 30?" asked Sergeant Clyde Burke.

"I worked from 6:00 A.M. until two o'clock in the afternoon," John said in a smooth Caribbean accent. "I remember this clearly because there was a festival on the beach of the Holiday Inn. The Soul Beach Music Festival." The Memorial Day weekend event had been a boon for tourism and had featured Grammy winners Lauryn Hill, Boyz II Men, and Wyclef Jean. Tickets for the festival had been included in the five-day vacation package purchased by the Mountain Brook students.

"On Monday, May 30, I worked from 6:00 A.M. until 2:00 P.M. That same evening I worked from 11:00 P.M. to 7:00 A.M. the morning of May 31."

When asked about his uniform, John described the dark blue trousers and white vest provided by his employer. "I generally wear a black windbreaker when I'm working the night shift," he explained.

The dark-colored slacks and black jacket matched the outfit that Deepak and Satish Kalpoe had described to police.

John said that during his two-year assignment at the Allegro Hotel he worked as a casino monitor during the day and as a security guard outside the hotel in the evenings, a time when the tourists were more likely to begin to get rowdy. When not stationed directly in front of the Allegro Hotel, John was on foot patrol along J. E. Irausquin Boulevard.

"Do you ever go to other hotels when you are working?" Burke asked.

"I sometimes walk to the Radisson and the Holiday Inn," John replied.

"When was the last time you were at the Holiday Inn?"

"On Sunday, May 29, around noon I went to the hotel for the celebration on the beach. I also went on Sunday, May 29, around 9:00 P.M.," John said, explaining that his girlfriend from Boston had been in town and that was where they had agreed to meet. The two had spent several hours at the sports bar in the Holiday Inn, the same bar where Joran had run into Natalee and her group. He and his date remained there until midnight before heading home.

John recalled seeing a group of young people at the bar that night, but said they left before he did.

"I'm not the only guard who wears a black jacket," John maintained, venting bewilderment over his arrest.

"Did you kill Natalee Holloway?" Burke asked.

"I have not kidnapped or murdered anybody. I would never do that. I know that tourism is important to Aruba and I would never do anything to jeopardize this, it brings in money and also jobs," John declared. "I have lived here ten years and I work hard for my money.

"I know that at the Holiday Inn many of the so-called beach-bums hang around and sleep there at night. You should question them."

John pointed out that he had to be back at the Allegro Hotel at 6:00 A.M. the next morning. "I'm not going to be out partying if I have to be back at work at 6:00 A.M."

As John sat across the table from detectives, anxious, nervous, and mystified, police officers were being dispatched to conduct a room-by-room search of the Allegro Grand. It was an active construction site with hundreds of empty rooms, making it an ideal place to stash a body.

Searches were also commencing on other parts of the island. Some groups were scouring the barren, cactus-strewn areas that surrounded John's house and neighborhood. Hundreds of people had volunteered to comb the sixty-nine miles of Aruba's beaches, especially the beach in the vicinity of the California Lighthouse where Van der Sloot and his friends claimed to have driven with Natalee on the night she disappeared.

While the police continued to interview Mickey John, his friend and fellow security guard, Abraham Alfred Jones, was led into an adjacent room for questioning. Jones, a gregarious man with a slight beard and a penchant for baseball caps, had also been roused from his bed and taken into custody by undercover officers that morning. He told police his story. He was twenty-nine, born and raised in Aruba. His friends called him "Maca." He lived with his common-law wife, Cynthia de Graaf, and their young daughter on Vuyst Street, a few blocks from the Johns family in Sint Nicolaas.

Jones gave his statement in English, not in either official language, Dutch or Papiamento. In his security guard position at the hotels, he often conversed with tourists, who were overwhelmingly Americans, and his English was strong.

Jones told detectives that he began working as a security guard in 2002 and, like John, wore dark-blue trousers and a white shirt when on the job. In the evenings, he donned a black Adidas jacket with three white stripes. He carried a walkie-talkie while patrolling the grounds of the hotel. He claimed that on May 30, he worked the day shift alongside "Bolo," his nickname for Mickey John, and another Aruban guard.

"I worked the shift from 7:00 A.M. to 3:00 P.M. then 3:00 P.M. to 11:00 P.M. then 11:00 P.M. to 7:00 A.M.," he said, describing what essentially was a twenty-four-hour workday.

"After my shift, I sometimes go to the Holiday Inn to enjoy the live bands."

"Do you ever leave your post at the Allegro Hotel in the evenings?" Detective Jacobs wanted to know.

Jones explained that his employer provided security to other hotels in the area and like Mickey John he often walked up and down the entire strip, always alone. "The three of us can never be gone at the same time while on night duty."

Jones told the investigators that the previous Thursday he and John had shared a couple of drinks at the sports bar at the Holiday Inn. He and John thought this bar was one of the better spots to find some action.

"Did you ever meet or speak with the girl on the posters?" Burke asked, referring to the American teen, Natalee Holloway.

"I read in the newspaper about the girl being missing, but I have never met nor spoken with her."

"Do you sell or use drugs?"

"No."

"How about John, is he a dealer?"

"John smokes marijuana, but I do not believe he is a drug dealer."

"Do you punch a clock at the hotel?" Jacobs asked.

"Yes, the punch clock is in the timekeeper's office."

"Does John have a car?"

"He has a gray Suzuki Vitara, but it is broken. Lately he has been driving a red four-door Toyota Tercel that belongs to his mother."

After the interrogations, Mickey John and Abraham Jones remained in custody in separate facilities. Neither man was told why he was being held, or what charges might be filed against him. Meanwhile, the press was reporting that both men were being detained on suspicion of kidnapping and murder.

Mickey John was transported to the Sint Nicolaas Police Station within sight of his house, but he was not permitted to have any visitors, family or otherwise. For nine days, he was locked in a small cell, where his bed was a slab of poured concrete. His meals consisted of dry chicken and fish, mashed potatoes, and lettuce. Despite his chronic acid reflux, he was denied his medication.

"You're in a cage like chickens," he said of his extremely difficult incarceration.

To relieve his isolation, he sang reggae songs endlessly and tried to stay calm using meditation.

Abraham Jones was taken to a different police facility in Noord. Jones's mother publicly denounced her son's detention, insisting there was no evidence linking him to Natalee Holloway's disappearance. His wife agreed. Cynthia was sure her husband was being framed.

Under Aruban law, the men could be held for up to 116 days without being formally charged—but a lucky break prevented this from happening.

Four days after John's detention in cramped, cheerless Cell 20 of the Sint Nicolaas Police Station holding area, a new inmate arrived. He was delivered unseen to the adjacent stall, Cell 22. John welcomed the detainee's arrival. He had been held in all the trappings of solitary confinement for four days. Since the first twenty-four hours after his arrest, when he'd spoken to investigators twice, he had been completely alone.

Mickey was lying on the cement block bed meditating when he heard the clank of the cell door on the other side of the wall.

"My name is Bolo," he said, using his nickname.

"I'm Deepak."

"What are you in for, man?"

"I was picked up for the missing girl."

Mickey was a strong believer in good versus evil and he was convinced there was only one truth. Here in jail, he held fast to his faith, knowing the good suffer, but goodness always prevails. Somehow he felt relief from his suffering when the stranger arrived with a connection to the case.

The new inmate was Deepak Kalpoe.

That Thursday morning, June 9, two separate and simultaneous raids had taken place, one at the home of Joran van der Sloot and the other at the Kalpoe brothers' residence. At 5:30 A.M., police had arrived at the door of the Van der Sloots. Joran's mother hurried to the guesthouse to wake Joran. "Joran, the police are here to arrest you," Anita told her still groggy son.

Ironically, this was Joran's graduation day, liberation day for most teenagers. But there would be no pomp and circumstance, no ceremony. Joran's college plans, his entire future would have to be put on hold. Standing in the doorway behind his mother were five police officers and Aruba's attorney general, Karin Janssen. One of the officers had begun reciting his rights as a detainee. Unsure of what to do, Joran held his hands out in front of him, expecting to be handcuffed. He was told that he could brush his teeth and change his clothes before they put the cuffs on.

"You should put a towel over your head," an officer advised. "There's a lot of media outside."

"Don't worry, Mom, everything will be all right," Joran told his mother before emerging from the house with a blue-and-green-striped towel draped over his head.

Across the island in Hooiberg, officers were handcuffing Deepak and Satish Kalpoe. All three young men were brought to the central police station in Oranjestad. Joran did not remove the towel from his face during the twenty-minute ride in the back of the police car to the central booking facility in Oranjestad. The three-story, yellow-and-blue art deco building was on Wilhelmina Street, a narrow, one-way road with pink-and-white tile sidewalks about two blocks from City Hall. Deepak's silver Honda was impounded and computers and other evidence from both homes were seized.

Joran was led into the building in handcuffs through a back door and brought to a rear holding area with twelve empty cells. Officers removed his handcuffs and placed him in Cell 1, a small concrete cell with a hole in the floor for a toilet. On his way to what he thought was going to be an interrogation room, Joran passed his friend, Satish.

"Don't worry," he whispered to his Surinamese co-conspirator. "Just stick to your story and they will have to let us go in ten days." Joran was not interrogated that day. Instead he was transferred to another holding facility at the Noord Police Station, where security guard Abraham Jones was also being held.

Police opted to detain Deepak in the Sint Nicolaas facility. Perhaps they thought isolating him from the other two would encourage him to snitch. Whatever the reason, there he was, one cell wall away from Mickey.

Mickey John later claimed God had played a hand in the seemingly random cell assignment, giving him the opportunity to save himself. But on a human level, his ingenuity was pure brilliance. That afternoon, he launched his own private investigation of Deepak.

"Tell me the truth," John asked Deepak in a casual tone. "You saw the guys in the news."

John knew that he was one of the two "dark-skinned" security guards that the Van der Sloot-Kalpoe trio had implicated in Natalee's disappearance. He also knew that Deepak was unaware he was housed next to the man he had so cruelly implicated in Natalee's disappearance, and that they were now jail mates. Mickey John was at liberty to ask questions anonymously.

"You saw the guys in the news. Where do you think they are from?"

"I've heard one of them is from Grenada," Deepak responded.

John was from Grenada and knew Deepak was talking about him. He continued his probe. For the next couple of hours, John sang his favorite Rasta songs and spoke in a thick Caribbean accent, convincingly acting Jamaican. Deepak had no reason to withhold information from his new friend.

Deepak confessed that the story about dropping the girl at the Holiday Inn and leaving her talking with the black security guard was not true. He said that he, the Dutch guy, and the Dutch guy's father had concocted the story, believing that Natalee would resurface in a couple of days.

Deepak explained to John what *really* happened that night. They drove to the lighthouse, and he and his brother dropped

Joran and Natalee at the public, more deserted beach next to the Marriott Hotel and he and Satish went home. Deepak continued that when he got home, he went on his computer to chat with some friends. At some point, he received a cell phone message from Joran, saying that when he got home he would chat with him online.

From what Deepak was saying, the Dutch guy was the last person with Natalee Holloway that night. He also took notice that Deepak was strangely calm for someone who was being questioned in such a serious crime. He was so quiet that John was compelled to periodically check on his well-being. "Are you okay, Deepak?" he yelled to the man in the adjacent cell.

"I'm fine," was always his answer.

When he was confident that he had extracted all the important information from Deepak, John decided it was time for a proper introduction.

"Hey man, it's me," John said, smiling, pausing outside Deepak's cell on his way to a lawyer's meeting.

Deepak looked out at him through the bars.

"I am the security guard from Grenada," the black man in Cell 20 said with a wink.

For a moment, Deepak stood dumbfounded as he processed what he had just been told. The man he believed was from Jamaica was actually the innocent scapegoat of his false and callous incrimination.

"I'm sorry, man," Deepak pleaded. "You shouldn't be here. I lied and you are here because of my lie."

Months later, Mickey John still felt pain, referring to Deepak as an "evil man." "He did not tell the truth, and because of that I was arrested. He and his friends don't care about a poor black man," he lamented, referring to their ability to use and discard him. But, true to his faith, goodness had prevailed.

John immediately told the police detaining him what he had learned from his Surinamese jail mate. His clever interrogation had accomplished what police had been unable to do. Now, this new version of events pointed all suspicion to Joran van der Sloot.

Just after noon on June 11, Deepak Kalpoe sat down with
investigators at police headquarters in Oranjestad for the
fourth time since Natalee's disappearance. Faced with his
jailhouse admissions to Mickey John, Deepak acknowledged
that he had misled investigators from the start. What had
started out as a small lie, covering for a friend, had snow-
balled into a full-blown crime, interfering with a police investigation.

Still, he seemed to be relieved. Deepak Kalpoe and Mickey
John sat together in an interrogation room as Deepak disposed of his lie, admitting that the idea to point suspicion at a
security guard had been his idea. He had never seen John
before arriving at the Sint Nicolaas jail, he said, and signed a
statement to that effect. Once more, he apologized to him
directly for his trouble.

"I am now willing to make a statement that is in accor-
dance with the truth," Deepak told sergeants Burke and Kelly.
"Several details were missing from my last statement. I am
now going to tell you exactly what happened that night."

For the next several hours, Deepak revised his events of
May 30. Just a day earlier, he had provided police with an
alibi witness, a party boat disc jockey named Steve Croes,
who he claimed had witnessed the three young men dropping Natalee at the Holiday Inn in the early morning hours
of May 30. He had even provided police with a phone number for Croes, who he said was a customer of the Internet
café where he worked in downtown Oranjestad.

Now, just twenty-four hours later, Deepak was offering
detectives Burke and Kelly a radically different version of
the events of Monday, May 30. He confirmed that he and
Satish had, indeed, driven around the island with Joran and
Natalee in the backseat. But they had not dropped her off at
the Holiday Inn, as he had earlier insisted. He also confessed that Natalee was not as drunk as he and the others
had described her.

"She danced beautifully," Deepak recalled. "I lied in my

previous statement about her being unsteady on her feet when she stepped off the stage at Carlos'n Charlie's. The truth is, she had a steady walk, and in my opinion she was reasonably with it."

Once the three locals and Natalee were underway in Deepak's car, he said that Satish popped a pornographic movie into the DVD system. "The girl said in English, 'Oh my God, what's that?'" Turning to Joran, Deepak said in English, "Now she is going to think that we're perverts."

It was Joran who finally told Satish to turn off the video. "She's had enough of it," Joran said.

Deepak told the detectives that on the way to the lighthouse he pulled the car off the road so that he could relieve himself near Arashi Beach, before continuing north on L. G. Smith Boulevard. He had seen Joran and Natalee kissing, but admitted that he had lied in earlier statements about the rest. "I did not see Joran put his hand up the girl's skirt," he admitted.

Driving on a darkened stretch of L. G. Smith Boulevard near the Marriott Hotel, Deepak said he asked Joran if they should head back into town. Joran said no, to just let him out of the car there. Deepak pulled into a beach parking area and watched as Joran and Natalee got out together. He said he asked his friend how he was planning on getting home.

"I'll just walk," Joran replied, saying he and Natalee could stroll down the beach in the moonlight and he would drop her off at the Holiday Inn.

Deepak said that he and Satish saw Joran and Natalee walking in the direction of the beach holding hands. After that, they drove home. Satish went to bed immediately, but Deepak logged on to his MSN account and chatted with a friend. He told his chat mate that he had just dropped Joran and an American girl off at the beach and was waiting up to make sure Joran made it home okay. The group had a buddy system, and he was expecting Joran to call.

Around 3:00 A.M., Joran phoned and said he was still walking home. "You see, if you had stayed with me you could have gotten a ride home," Deepak said. He asked his friend if he'd hooked up with the girl.

"No, man, we just went into the water," Joran said, adding that Natalee fell asleep on the beach and he left her there.

"What do you mean you left her sleeping on the beach?" Deepak demanded. He told investigators that the idea of leaving a young woman alone and vulnerable on a darkened beach had made him angry.

"Yeah, well, I'm walking home barefoot," Joran continued. He told his friend that he had left his sneakers on the beach.

"You're not making any sense," Deepak said. The entire call was disturbing. Deepak thought this story sounded wrong. "I want you to call me as soon as you get home. I'm not going to sleep until I hear from you."

While he was in the bathroom, Deepak said, he received an online message from Joran saying he'd arrived home, thanks for waiting, and he'd see him tomorrow. At least he's home, Deepak had thought before climbing into bed.

The following evening around midnight, Deepak said he hooked up with Joran at the casino inside the Radisson Aruba Resort and Casino on Palm Beach. Joran was playing poker with two friends, Guido and Andre, when Deepak arrived. Not much of a player himself, Deepak took a chair and watched his friends play. Joran, he said, seemed pretty drunk, even belligerent.

At one point, Joran got into a heated argument with a tourist about cheating. The tourist thought Joran was working in concert with Deepak, Guido, and Andre to swindle him at the poker table. To avoid a full-blown fight, the three friends dragged Joran out of the casino. Guido and Andre went home, but Joran wanted to keep playing cards.

Deepak said the two climbed into his silver Honda and headed to the casino at the Wyndham Hotel to play some blackjack. While pulling into the parking lot of the Wyndham, Joran received the angry call from his father about the Americans camped out in front of the house.

"After the conversation, Joran said to me that it had been his father calling and that there were police at his house," Deepak recounted for the detectives.

Joran told him it was about Natalee. She was missing. Despite being told by his father to stay at the Wyndham, Joran and Deepak drove to the Van der Sloot home.

"'What the fuck is wrong with that bitch?'" Deepak related that Joran said, referring to Natalee. "Then he said to me that if police asked any questions we should say the following: That we left together with the girl when we departed Carlos'n Charlie's; that we drove around; that Joran had kissed and fingered her; that she fell asleep in the car; and that we had returned her to the hotel."

Joran realized he only had a few minutes to come up with a story, with Deepak and Satish as his alibi. Deepak admitted that Joran had heard his father when he told him to wait at the Wyndham, but had disregarded his instruction. He said he and Joran were still in the parking lot preparing to go into the casino when the call came. Joran insisted to Deepak they drive back to Montanja Street rather than wait for his father and the police. He didn't want the embarrassment of a confrontation in a public place. Also, he needed time to craft a story and make sure Deepak was on the same page prior to any questioning by police.

Deepak described Joran ordering "get your brother on the phone" as they pulled up to his house.

Deepak said that he then told Satish exactly what he was supposed to say if anyone tried to question him. The two men came up with the idea about directing suspicion toward a security guard *after* the confrontation in front of the Van der Sloot home.

"Be sure that Satish adds that piece to his story," Deepak recalled Joran telling him.

Investigators wanted to know why Deepak had perjured himself. If his new version of the events was true, then neither of the Kalpoes had done anything to Natalee. They had put themselves in harm's way for no reason at all. Before, they were innocent and now they were potential accomplices.

Deepak explained his two reasons for lying. His friend had asked him to lie and he was afraid of the police, foreseeing himself in terrible trouble if Natalee never reappeared.

The idea that Joran had killed or even harmed the young American had seemed ridiculous to him at the time. Deepak said that Joran had been "sociable" and not at all aggressive at Carlos'n Charlie's that night.

During the interview, police asked Deepak if there was anyone who could corroborate his story. He offered Freddy Zedan's name, Joran's neighbor, friend, and confidant. "Joran and Freddy have known each other for a long time and Joran trusts him. If you go and talk to Freddy, he will tell you the made-up story and maybe also the truth."

Deepak's new version of the events of May 30 was filled with other stunning admissions. Natalee had not made any racist comments as Joran had claimed. He also said that Joran's father, Paulus, believed their story, and had even found a lawyer for the Kalpoe brothers. "He told us that if we were to be arrested to remain calm and not come up with a different story," Deepak explained.

"What do you think happened to Natalee Holloway?" Sergeant Burke asked.

"I think that Joran raped her, but is afraid to admit it. I don't think he murdered her."

"What makes you think he raped her?" the officer prodded.

"I think that because he doesn't want to tell the truth."

Shortly before midnight, Detective Roland Tromp and Sergeant Shaniro Kelly loaded their prisoner, Deepak Kalpoe, into the back of a police car to return him to Cell 22 at the Sint Nicolaas Police Station. During the trip, the men attempted to pry a little more information out of Deepak. "The statement you just gave, was it the whole truth or did you have a plan B just in case what you guys had made up went wrong?"

Deepak told the officers that he had nothing to add to his statement and that there had been no plan B.

"Is it true that Paulus van der Sloot told you guys that if there was no body, the police had no case?"

Deepak told the officers that during one of his visits to the Van der Sloot home in the days after Natalee went missing, Joran's father had come into the room with a law book and explained what they needed to know in case they were arrested. According to Deepak, Paulus van der Sloot told them that authorities were required to advise them of their rights; that they would first be held for six hours; that they could be locked up after that; that they would have to be brought before a district attorney within two days; that the district attorney could decide to hold them for an additional eight days; that the judge commissioner could order them held for another eight days; that in total they could be held for 116 days; and that after that they could go home because, without a body, the police did not have a case.

Detective Tromp was stunned. "So Joran's father gave you guys some legal advice?"

"Yes," Deepak confirmed. "That's correct."

Paulus van der Sloot's supposed "no body, no case" statement to his son and the Kalpoe brothers prompted police to open an investigation into the elder Van der Sloot's possible involvement in the cover-up of a crime. Was this textbook legal advice or something more sinister? The media and police would read a great deal into this supposed statement. How would Paulus van der Sloot know that there wasn't a body unless he had inside information? There was even speculation that if Natalee had been murdered, Paulus had helped dispose of the body.

Over the next few days, Deepak described the admonishment that he and Joran had received from Paulus the night Beth Twitty's posse came to the Van der Sloot home to search for Natalee. After the reenactment at the Holiday Inn, where

Deepak and Joran had provided their blow-by-blow account of Natalee's farewell, Paulus and the two young men returned to the house, where he scolded and lectured them.

"Have you now learned your lesson?" Paulus implored.

Deepak said he answered, "Yes. Never give a ride to a stranger."

ELEVEN

When the video camera in Lima's Hotel Tac captured Joran van der Sloot exiting the hotel for the final time on the morning of May 30, he was wearing jeans and a short-sleeved red-and-white-striped polo shirt. His dark brown hair was military-style short.

Twelve hours later, a cosmetically altered Van der Sloot turned up more than 150 miles south of Lima in Ica, Peru, a bleak and downtrodden city of about 200,000 people. Ica was still recovering from the 7.5-magnitude earthquake that had rocked the region three years earlier, with many families still living in temporary housing. Despite the devastation, tourists and backpackers still made the five-hour trek from Lima, using Ica as a base for adventure—sand boarding on the dunes, visiting the magical oasis of Huacachina, or touring the vineyards that grow the famous Pisco white grape, picked and distilled into the liquor for the Pisco Sour, Peru's national drink.

Although no arrest warrant had yet been issued, Joran was a fugitive, trying to get out of Peru as quickly as possible.

After abandoning Stephany Flores's black Jeep on a side street near the Las Palmas Air Force Base, he had fled the area on foot. How he made the 150-mile journey south to Ica was unclear. Somewhere along the route, he had stopped long enough to shave his head and dye his remaining stubble an orange blond. He also changed his clothing, and was now sporting electric-blue Bermuda shorts, white sneakers, and a dark-colored T-shirt.

With a backpack slung over his shoulders and a beige duffel bag in one hand, he was perfectly disguised as a typical gringo on vacation as he walked Ica's downtown drag. It was a dusty stretch of road bordered by lean-to cabstands and run-down bus companies servicing long-distance travelers. His ruddy complexion and towering frame made it impossible for him to avoid attention, so he opted for the "tourist" character, a role he had perfected as a teenager in Aruba.

John Williams Pisconte, a taxi driver, was standing in front of his white minivan, waiting for a paying stranger to come along. He was sipping coffee and talking with his twin brother, John Oswaldo, when a rangy foreigner with a shaved head and bright blue shorts falling below his knees approached. Although Joran spoke only broken Spanish, he had no trouble communicating. He wanted to go to the Peruvian town of Nazca.

"No problem," said Pisconte, motioning him to climb into the minivan. The twins lived with their parents in Ica. Their small business made enough money to allow them a decent living, better than most people in the area. The two serviced the interprovincial route between Ica and Nazca, seventy-five miles southeast, rarely venturing outside their geographic comfort zone.

In Peru, Nazca was a hugely popular tourist destination. The Nazca Lines, hundreds of drawings intricately etched into the red desert plains surrounding the town, drew visitors from all over the world. They were an archeological wonder, akin to the pyramids on Mexico's Yucatán Peninsula. Scholars have attributed the elaborate geometric figures and depictions of plants and animals to an early Nazca culture, dating them to between 400 and 650 A.D. Their scale was so massive that once in Nazca, tourists bought tickets for small plane rides, at forty to fifty dollars a person, to view the six-hundred-foot monkey, the giant lizard, and other magnificent geoglyphs. In 1994, the Nazca Lines were designated a UNESCO World Heritage Site.

Ica was the staging area for Nazca. John Williams Pisconte and his brother earned about $350 a month shuttling passengers back and forth, filling the shared van to capacity before departing.

Joran van der Sloot appeared to be the first of another load of tourists as he got into the van. But after only a few minutes, he grew impatient. He didn't want to wait for the minivan to fill up with additional passengers. Irritated and anxious, he asked about the "express" service, saying he would pay a negotiated fare and have the van for himself.

He needed to get out of Peru as quickly as possible and had no time for this small-town way of doing business. After a short negotiation, the two settled on a one-way price of thirty dollars, the equivalent of six passengers.

John Williams smiled when he drove up beside the red Nissan station wagon owned by his twin brother, John Oswaldo. John Oswaldo was busy hustling customers into his transport. But John Williams was full, with only one passenger, and ready to embark.

The two men bore little physical resemblance to each other. John Williams had a long narrow face, dark skin, and close-cropped black hair. His brother John Oswaldo's features were round and fleshy.

"*Hasta pronto.* See you in Nazca," the thirty-one-year-old Ican native called, pulling away from the curb with Joran.

His passenger was a chain-smoker, he realized very soon after they were underway. Observing from his rearview mirror, he watched the foreigner finish one Marlboro, only to immediately light another. If he wasn't smoking, he was sleeping.

He seemed to prefer silence to making conversation. At first, he didn't answer simple questions like what he did for a living. Eventually, he became more talkative, telling the cabdriver that he was from Holland and had come to see the country. He said he had been to Cuzco, an ancient Incan town high in the Andes with centuries-old cobblestone streets and beautiful churches. Most tourists stop in Cuzco on their way to Machu Picchu, the Lost City of the Incas, so Joran's lie was appropriate.

"The girls in Peru are very pretty," Joran said, grinning.

"Where are you heading now?" Pisconte asked.

"Arica," Joran replied, referring to a small Chilean town about four hundred miles south, just on the other side of the Peruvian border. He explained that he was planning to tour the southern half of South America.

Around 11:40 P.M. that Sunday night, Pisconte dropped his passenger at the town's main roundabout, near the gas station. Nazca was a dangerous place, especially at night. Abject poverty and inattentive visitors mixed, making for a high likelihood of personal theft. Even locals avoided public transportation at night.

Here, at midnight, Joran found himself at the bus station, alone, a foreigner with a roll of money in his front pocket, a six-foot-four-inch-tall target. The Nazca terminal was dirty and lawless, surrounded by *pueblos jóvenes,* shantytowns. Despite his size and his seasoned-traveler expertise, he was worried.

Less than twenty minutes later, Joran was desperately seeking his cabbie. He found John Williams at the roundabout chatting with a group of other van drivers.

"Hey, did you bring me here?" Joran yelled.

"What happened?" Pisconte asked, noting the man was pale and nervous. "Did you leave something in the van?"

"No, I want you to take me to Tacna."

Pisconte was familiar with Tacna. The Peruvian border town was four hundred miles south on the Pan-American Highway. He also knew this well-paying customer was making his way to Chile. Joran had told him about a girlfriend there on the trip from Ica. However, the midnight hour and the distance made the trip close to impossible.

"There are buses over there," he said, pointing to the run-down cinderblock terminal. "Besides, I don't know the roads down there very well."

The ride from Nazca to Tacna along the Pan-American Highway was one lane in each direction with the Pacific Ocean on the right and the Andes on the left. During the day, the drive was breathtaking. But John Williams was exhausted, having spent the day driving back and forth on his usual route.

Joran was insistent and pleaded with the cabdriver to reconsider.

"Let me talk to my brother," he said, waving to John Oswaldo, who had just entered the roundabout in his red wagon.

After a few minutes, Pisconte snapped his fingers at Van der Sloot. "Okay, we'll do it for fifteen hundred nuevos soles!"

Five hundred dollars was more than either brother earned in a month. Joran agreed to the price, even though he knew he didn't have the money to pay the fare.

Because of the length of the trip, the brothers hired a third cabbie to help with the driving. For seven dollars, Carlos Euribe Pretil joined the journey. Pretil looked more like a lounge singer than a taxi driver, with his curly reddish locks combed into a pompadour. The thirty-eight-year-old Peruvian was unaware of the pay disparity, seven dollars for him, $493 for the twins, when he climbed into the back of the minivan with Joran.

They'd been driving south on the Pan-American Highway for several hours when John Oswaldo turned around to talk to their passenger, who had just awoken from a nap. "What's your name?"

"Van der Sloot."

Joran told the men he had had problems in Lima, but didn't elaborate. Instead, he reclined in his seat and closed his eyes again.

All three cabbies were startled at how their fare reacted

as they slowed at their first highway police checkpoint. The checkpoints were scattered along the length of the route to curb contraband, usually drugs. They were manned by heavily armed uniformed police in bulletproof vests, carrying automatic weapons. Sometimes a vehicle was pulled over to check papers and passports, and occasionally a random search was conducted.

Joran had no idea if the police were looking for him, or if Stephany's body had even been discovered. Nearly sixteen hours had passed since he'd walked out of the Hotel Tac alone. He assumed that her body had been found and that law enforcement had issued an Interpol alert.

Sitting erect in the back of the van, Joran lit a cigarette and watched nervously out the window of the minivan as they were slowed, then waved through, a procedure that repeated itself at least a half dozen times along the highway.

When he was awake, Joran was more talkative than he had been from Ica to Nazca. He told the trio he was from Aruba. Much had happened to him since he had first left the island five years earlier, including a residency in Thailand and the death of his father. These he kept secret. In response to questions about his employment, the pathological liar told the cabdrivers that he worked for his father at a civil engineering business. A few hours later, Joran elaborated, saying he had lived in Aruba for the past seventeen years, where his father owned a cement factory.

Methodically, every three hours, Joran asked the men how much longer it would be before they reached Tacna. He seemed anxious, and when he wasn't sleeping, he was lost in thought. Often, he was shivering, most likely because he was underdressed in his shorts and T-shirt. Although southern Peru is known to Peruvians as the "Land of the Sun," the desert nights could be frigid.

Six hours into the trip, about halfway, Joran asked the group if they could stop so that he could buy a Peruvian newspaper. He was told Moquegua would be their pit stop, about half an hour away. Around 7:00 A.M., they arrived in

Moquegua, a scorched, barren town with a wrought-iron fountain by Alexandre Gustave Eiffel embellishing the small central square.

The drivers were hungry and wanted to stop at a café on the square for breakfast. Joran, oddly, did not want to join them. "I'm not hungry. I'll just wait here," he said, reminding them about the newspaper.

Over breakfast, the three talked about their passenger. There was something suspicious about him. The consensus was that he was likely carrying drugs.

John Oswaldo picked up a copy of the newspaper *El Ojo* and handed it to Van der Sloot as he climbed back into the minivan.

"How much longer until we get there?" Joran asked.

"Three or four hours more, my friend."

Again underway, Joran began spinning a picaresque tale, saying he had stabbed a man with a lot of money. He was on his way to Santiago, Chile, where his girlfriend was waiting.

The taxi drivers were speechless. Perhaps the Aruban, with his rudimentary Spanish, had meant something else. Or, perhaps he was hinting that their part in his flight would be well rewarded, with a cut of the stolen money. Either way, they kept silent.

After passing through a police checkpoint in Tomasiri, Joran said he needed to urinate. The van pulled into a rest area and everyone but John Williams got out to use the bathroom.

John Williams had just been awoken from a nap break and he noticed Joran outside the van's window. He was shifting his laptop from his black backpack to his beige duffel bag.

Outside, his twin also detected Joran rearranging his luggage, removing some clothes from the duffel before dumping the rest of the contents into a garbage-strewn gulley beside the road. He also threw out a bag of marijuana before climbing back into the van.

Around noon, the men arrived in Tacna, another hectic

and dangerous outpost, despite its palm-lined avenues. This was the final stop, about twenty miles from the Chilean border. A visit to the Scotia Bank was in order. Joran had only advanced the men $175 of their $500, so he still owed the drivers the remaining $325.

He was good for it, he insisted. Nevertheless, John Oswaldo accompanied him to the bank machine and watched intently as Joran inserted a white bank card with the Maestro logo. The screen showed there was no balance.

"No worries," Joran said. He had another bank card from the Bank of Aruba. That account, he claimed, had a balance of 9,800 euros, almost U.S.$13,000, but he had to make his withdrawal from a bank-authorized ATM. If the men wanted to be paid, they would have to take him to Arica, Chile, where a Bank of Aruba automated teller awaited.

Arica was only thirty miles away, but going there involved crossing a border. The cabbies were extremely apprehensive. They had been driving all night, and still had the 475-mile return trip to Ica to make. They had heard this stranger bragging about assault and robbery with a knife and had watched him dump marijuana in the woods. No one knew what else he was carrying. Still, getting paid seemed worth the trouble of going to Arica.

None of the three had made the border crossing before, so they inquired at the taxi terminal as to what documents were necessary to proceed. The paperwork was straightforward. Only DNI cards, the standard Peruvian national identification cards, were required. Local cabbies told them a typical fare for this trip was twenty nuevos soles, about seven dollars.

Three hundred nuevos soles, $100, would get him to Chile, the cabdrivers told him. Joran did not make a counteroffer. He simply agreed.

At one-thirty that afternoon, the group, smelly, worn, dirty, and strained, fell into the van for the last leg. John Oswaldo was at the wheel when they departed for the Peruvian-Chilean border crossing in Santa Rosa.

But this twenty-mile finale was not without daunting obstacles. They still had the Atacama Desert and the Peru-Chile border control to navigate.

The Atacama Desert is a rust-colored, parched, other-worldly landscape that looks like the surface of Mars. Most of its six-hundred-mile stretch is on the Chilean side of the border, with only the Tacna region of the desert in southern Peru. It is the driest place on earth, inhospitable and remote, with no animal life, no vegetation, and no reports of rain in recorded history. Beneath the surface, hundreds of mines run tunnels to rich gold and copper deposits. In fact, the thirty-three Chilean miners, trapped a half mile underground for sixty-nine days in 2010, were in an Atacama mining operation.

In contrast, the border complex at Santa Rosa is a mammoth, glimmering, glass-and-metal structure rising out of the desert sandscape like the mirage of a spaceship. The sleek, modern facility looks more like a state-of-the-art airport than a provincial border checkpoint. Outside, security guards flank the roads and man the booths that stop the vehicular traffic. Inside, armed immigration officers take care of routine business and any travel or security problems.

Staring out the window of the minivan, Joran watched the complex grow bigger and more threatening as they approached. His heart was pounding, not knowing if Interpol had marked him as a fugitive and put out an alert.

However, only John Oswaldo was impeded in their border crossing. His DNI card was too damaged to allow him passage into Chile. Not wanting to scuttle the mission, he volunteered to wait in Peru while the others proceeded.

Just the three, John Williams Pisconte, Carlos Euribe Pretil, and Joran Andreas Petrus van der Sloot, exited the car and entered the blast of air-conditioning that chilled the final frontier. They registered with immigration control as required by Peruvian law for all international travelers. Joran, a master of concealing emotions, deliberately slowed his breathing and assumed the posture of a weary tourist. At the booth, the high-rolling Dutchman, the only one traveling with a passport, watched his document be approved and stamped, and the trio exited to the van.

At three that afternoon, John Williams took the wheel, replacing his brother. Carlos claimed the front passenger seat. Joran, relieved, melted into his backseat as the gates to the frontier checkpoint faded from view.

He had made it out of Peru and silently vowed to himself to never return.

TWELVE

In the two weeks since Natalee Holloway had gone missing, members of law enforcement and hundreds of local volunteers had conducted wide-scale land, air, and water searches, and five people had been taken into custody. Yet, no link could be made between the two dark-skinned security guards and the three young men who were last seen with Natalee.

There was no crime scene, no body, and sorting out the ever-changing mishmash of truths and lies offered by Joran, Deepak, and Satish was proving a maddening experience. If there was, indeed, a witness who could corroborate Deepak's newest version of the events—that he and his brother had left Joran and Natalee at the beach next to the Marriott and had not returned to pick him up—then detectives wanted to speak to this person immediately.

On June 12, officers followed up on Deepak's tip that Joran might have discussed his movements with his friend and confidant, Freddy Zedan. Freddy, a twenty-one-year-old Latino who called himself "Loco Man Pimp," was three years older than Joran, and spoke Papiamento. He was from

Venezuela, and lived with his parents a few houses away from the Van der Sloots in Noord.

Joran was fifteen when he first met Freddy at a tennis tournament at the Aruba Racquet Club. He idolized the light-skinned Hispanic man who wasted no time introducing Joran to Aruba's nightlife.

Freddy was charismatic, smooth, and utterly fearless. With a washboard stomach and perpetual tan, he was a hit with the young female vacationers. But his handicap was that he couldn't speak English. Their relationship, then, was a perfect complement—Freddy had the swagger and Joran had the language. Together, they combed the beaches and checked out the nightclubs for pretty female tourists.

Freddy appeared nervous when he sat down with detectives, but he wanted to tell the truth. He recounted Joran's visit to his home on Monday, May 30. He had returned home that afternoon to find his Dutch friend in the kitchen talking with his sister. The two went to his bedroom, where Joran told him about meeting an American girl at the casino, going to Carlos'n Charlie's, and dropping her off at the Holiday Inn. But the next day at the racquet club, Freddy recalled that Joran looked stressed and preoccupied.

Freddy said that he asked him what was bothering him and Joran confessed that he had lied to him the previous day and wanted to share a secret. He had not dropped Natalee at her hotel, as he and the Kalpoe brothers had told police. Instead, he and Deepak and Satish had driven with the young woman to the beach on the north side of the Marriott Hotel, where he said she collapsed several times. The last time, she did not wake up.

Unsure of what to do, the three panicked. "We left her on the beach and then Deepak and Satish drove me home," Freddy recalled him saying, repeating Joran's second version of the events.

After he talked to the police, Freddy felt obliged to visit Joran's parents. He was concerned about his friend and thought that Paulus and Anita van der Sloot needed to hear the truth. Aware that Joran's father was a judge in training, he believed he would likely know what to do. That afternoon, he telephoned the Van der Sloot home and spoke with Anita. He told her that he had just been interviewed by police, and asked if it would be okay if he came by the house. Freddy arrived wth his girlfriend that afternoon. The two joined Anita in the Van der Sloots' dining room, painted a cheerful shade of orange and filled with Anita's colorful paintings propped on easels in the corners. The three sat down at the long wood table.

"I need to tell you the truth," Freddy began.

Anita grew pale as she listened to the young man detail the confidential conversations he had had with her son, the ones he had just recounted for police. Paulus van der Sloot emerged from the kitchen to participate in the conversation.

Joran's parents believed Freddy's story. They knew how capable their son was of lying, of staring them in the eyes and spinning deceit. But those lies now seemed petty. He had stolen money, he had snuck out of the house, and he had run up minutes on his brother's cell phone. Now, with shame and horror, they began grasping that this lie was different, possibly involving murder, and almost certainly involving a cover-up.

Paulus had reluctantly accepted the story Joran and the Kalpoe brothers had first told him. But now faced with Freddy's revelations, Paulus's thoughts cycled through the potential legal ramifications. If Joran wasn't involved in Natalee's disappearance, then why had he created such an elaborate cover story? These certainly seemed like actions of someone guilty. But, this was his son.

Anita and Paulus intended to confront Joran with Freddy's account. Based on his version, it was more probable that Joran would need a full-blown legal defense with lawyers to support it. As hope for an innocent explanation crumbled, mental issues and psychiatric justifications were discussed. The possibilities were sickening.

Leaving the girl alone on the beach was bad judgment, but not criminal. Was there more to this nighmare than Joran had even confessed to Freddy?

On June 9, 2005, when Joran was first taken into custody and brought to the Noord Police Station, he was barred from any contact with his father. Joran's father had been with him at the casual meeting with police at the Bubali Police Station on June 1. Although Jan van der Straten had wanted the interviews with Detective Jacobs and Sergeant Kelly to be with Joran alone, Paulus had insisted on being present.

The police chief knew he had no choice. Joran was seventeen and still a minor. Dutch law allows minors to have parents present during police questioning.

But now, regardless of being a minor, Joran's status had changed from witness to suspect. Van der Straten, following a judge's orders, forbade communication with Paulus, granting permission only to Anita, his mother, for daily ten-minute visits.

Authorities understood the conflict. Paulus straddled the boundary between "father of a minor suspect" and "officer of the courts." Being a judge in training, and in a high position in the Dutch judiciary, he could easily give Joran insider legal advice if he had access to him. And as a lawyer, he could then have the right to lawyer-client confidentiality over their conversations.

The chief knew the danger of allowing Paulus visitation. But he knew the repercussions of *not* allowing it. He carried out the judge's ruling to keep the father and son apart. The elder Van der Sloot was incensed. He was sure that Dutch law had been violated, and he filed a complaint with the court.

The living conditions for Mickey John and Deepak Kalpoe at their police station were uncomfortable, but Sint Nicolaas at least offered a poured slab for a bed. At the Noord facility where Joran was housed, inmates were forced to sleep on the concrete floor. Joran casually emptied his pockets and removed the laces from his shoes, as directed by the police.

Officers led the handcuffed teen into the rear holding area. The air was oppressively hot. Most of the eight cells that he could see were occupied. When his jailors led him to a vacant Cell 6, his ambivalence turned to anxiety. The five-by-five-foot cage had a cement floor and metal bars. There was no bed, and the toilet was a hole in the floor. This was a far cry from the bachelor apartment he called home on Montanja Street. There would be no sneaking out of these quarters.

Joran wasn't able to make visual contact with the other inmates, so he listened attentively to their jailhouse banter. He quickly learned that the men were in custody for a variety of offenses, from stealing computers to drunk driving to possession of firearms.

"What are you in for, man?" someone asked him.

Joran told him he had been arrested in connection with the missing American girl.

"The guy in Cell 3 is in for the same thing," another inmate yelled.

Ever since Natalee's disappearance had become a news story, Joran had carefully followed the coverage. With the announcement that Cell 3 held someone connected to the case, Joran knew the man had to be one of the two black security guards, either Mickey John or Abraham Jones. He was surprised at how upbeat the man acted, noticing he spent a lot of time singing.

Joran, having been complicit in framing him, knew he was innocent. But how would Joran know how an innocent man behaved if he was not in such a position himself? Joran engaged the detainee in conversation, and when he learned that he had a wife and daughter, deduced that he was Abraham Jones. Joran confessed that he felt horrible for incriminating Jones, and he cried about it.

The empathy ended there. His overwhelming discomfort was his primary focus. He complained about the coffee being cold and the lack of dining utensils; all meals were eaten with only hands. He complained about the shower system, described as a pipe in the wall of his cell that streamed water two times a day, at 7:00 A.M. and 7:00 P.M., for exactly five minutes. He complained that he didn't have a pillow, and that he had to sleep on the floor. He complained that sleeping in the cell block's stifling heat was almost impossible, on or off the floor.

The first morning in custody, Joran awoke to the spray of lukewarm water pelting the floor of his cell. It was the 7:00 A.M. shower. He quickly shoved his clothes and towel between the bars, stripped down, and did his best to wash away the jailhouse grime.

As he was toweling off, two investigators appeared and told him he had to come with them. Joran was placed in handcuffs, and led past the other cells. Thinking furtively, he pulled his shirt up over his face in case there were camera crews waiting outside. He was put in the back of a patrol car and driven to the central police station in Oranjestad.

Detective Dennis Jacobs was waiting for him, and led him to a small interrogation room where a camera had been set up. His partner, Luigi Croes, joined them in the room.

"How are you doing?" Jacobs asked.

"Okay," Joran replied.

Jacobs explained that the interview would be recorded, and that he was not obligated to speak. In response to questions, Joran repeated the Holiday Inn story. He told the detectives that Deepak's car was clean, and that he usually sat up front because his legs were long.

"If you can barely fit in the backseat, how did you have room to finger Natalee as you had claimed?"

"Deepak and Satish pulled their seats forward because they aren't very tall."

At noon, Joran received his lunch in a holding area. His meal and water came with no utensils, exactly the same as at his cell. His bathroom break was unsuccessful—Joran was unable to urinate under the unblinking glare of Detective Jacobs in the doorway.

The afternoon brought more interrogation. Joran told detectives that he kept two pairs of boxing gloves in his apartment, and would sometimes stage bouts with his friends. He described Deepak as the weakest of the bunch. "Sometimes I allow my girlfriend and her sister to box." He smiled.

"How many girlfriends do you have?" Jacobs asked.

"I only have one girlfriend and her name is Florencia. Before I had Elaine and before that Carmen. At the moment she is my friend Freddy's girlfriend.

"I've had a girlfriend since I was fourteen. My first girlfriend now lives in the States. She and I were both enrolled at the International School of Aruba. I also had a girlfriend named Melody. I have had five serious girlfriends since I was fourteen."

"What about Deepak and Satish? Do either of them have a girlfriend?"

"They don't have girlfriends," Joran said. "Satish told me that he had a girlfriend in Surinam. I have thought about the fact that they don't have girlfriends, but not everybody needs to have a girlfriend."

The detectives wanted to know if Joran had access to a boat. "Do any of your friends have a boat?"

"My friend Koen's father has a boat, a speedboat. I don't know the name of the boat, but it is at Koen's house. I have never gone out on the speedboat. I get seasick. Koen doesn't have a boating license, but I assume he knows how to operate the boat."

"Are you currently under the treatment of a doctor?" Jacobs asked.

"I am not," Joran said. "I am being treated by a dentist because I have a toothache. I am also under the treatment of a psychologist because I felt bad about the fact that the girl had gone missing."

Joran explained that his parents had also taken him to a psychologist at the children's clinic in Oranjestad because he had stolen money from them.

"How do you get along with your brothers and your parents?"

"I get along fine with them," Joran said. "Usually I discuss my curfew with my mother because she is the one who makes the decisions. I always want to stay out later than she says."

"Who were you in contact with the day before you were arrested?"

"The day before we were arrested, Deepak, Satish, and I were at my house. We were on the Internet." Joran explained that they went on the Web site www.rhielworld.com because his picture had been posted on that site. He said that he and the brothers took down his Hotmail account and his profile on Tickle, a social networking site. Joran explained that his user name there had been "loverboy362."

"This is an account where you can leave pictures and you can meet with other people," Joran explained. "I then opened another e-mail account and sent an e-mail to rhielworld with the request to respect my privacy and remove my picture from their Web site. The man e-mailed me back and wrote that he would respect my privacy and remove my picture."

After the interview, Joran was moved back to a holding cell before being returned to the Noord Police Station at 9:00 P.M.

Joran's parents were waiting in the lobby. He was happy to see his father, although he was not permitted to speak with him. Only his mother was allowed in the interview area for her ten-minute unsupervised visit.

Anita van der Sloot confronted her son about her conversation with Freddy. Not one to hold back emotions, Anita expressed her fury that he had lied to everyone, and how disappointed she and her husband were with him.

Joran's reaction was calm and phlegmatic.

"Freddy always tells the truth," he said.

If Joran's mother had suspicions that her son was involved in a crime, she kept those thoughts to herself. In an interview with CBS's *Early Show* that aired on the morning of June 13, Anita van der Sloot showed support for Joran.

"I believe in my son," she said. "He is innocent, two hundred percent."

Anita said that her son had wanted to participate in the searches, but was advised against it. "It drove him crazy that he couldn't do anything," she said. "He still believes that Natalee is still alive and will turn up somewhere."

Two days after Deepak's stunning admissions, Aruba's

police chief, Jan van der Straten, sat down with Joran van der Sloot for an "informal chat." The brief conversation took place on June 13, at 1:00 P.M. at the police station in Oranjestad, where Joran was being detained.

Since being confronted with Deepak's version of the events, Joran had admitted that he lied to police about escorting the young woman back to her hotel. Van der Straten was a personal friend of Joran's father, Paulus, and unfounded rumors persisted that he was attempting to influence the outcome of the investigation. "Why did you lie to your father about dropping the girl at the Holiday Inn?" Van der Straten asked.

"I didn't want him to be disappointed in me," Joran explained, choking back tears. His father had raised him to be proper, and to not see a woman home would have been shameful, not the way a gentleman would have behaved. He maintained that he lied about dropping Natalee at the Holiday Inn because he had exercised poor judgment and he was embarrassed. But now that Deepak had broken ranks, he felt compelled to tell the truth.

Joran exhibited differing emotions during his brief exchange with the police chief, sometimes crying, sometimes answering in a matter-of-fact manner. He appeared distraught about how this ordeal was affecting his own family, especially his parents, but never showed concern for Natalee or the Holloway family.

He confirmed that he and Natalee had been dropped off at the public beach not far from the Marriott. He said that he had taken her to a spot near the Fisherman's Hut, a collection of concrete shacks built to withstand the elements where local fishermen store their equipment. The Hut was a ten-minute walk from the Holiday Inn, directly at the edge of the water. At high tide, the waves lapped at the doors of the small, pale blue shacks with their corrugated roofs. "Can you tell me what happened after the girl had fallen asleep on the beach near the Fisherman's Hut?"

"I called Deepak and he came with two dogs," Joran said.

Joran speculated that Deepak returned later that night, knowing that there was a girl passed out on the beach. "I think he raped the girl or did something to her."

Van der Straten bluffed, looking for a reaction. "Where was the girl buried, then?"

"I think she was buried next to the wall of the Fisherman's Hut."

"I suggest you answer only 'yes' or 'no' to the following question," Van der Straten coaxed. "Was the girl thrown into the sea?"

"No," Joran answered, but quickly revised his reply to, "I mean, I don't know."

Later that night, Joran was driven to the deserted stretch of beach next to the Marriott known to locals as "Lover's Lane," accompanied by four police officers. There, Joran pointed to an area next to the Fisherman's Hut.

"That's where he did it," Joran said, referring to his friend Deepak. "That's where he probably raped and murdered Natalee."

Unbeknownst to Joran, the area around the Fisherman's Hut had been searched earlier in the day. The police had drained a four- to six-foot-deep mangrove swamp located behind the Fisherman's Hut on Malmok Beach. Using fire engine pumps powered by a generator on a flatbed truck, they siphoned water from the pond. FBI agents and a search-and-rescue team from the Miami-Dade Police Department helped in the operation. Detective Alan Lowy and his cadaver canine, Bugg, performed a search of the Fisherman's Hut area, which was followed by a foot search by Aruban police detectives and uniformed officers.

The scene was too much for Beth Twitty, who had arrived in a police cruiser. This kind of search was a recovery, not a rescue. She had wanted to be there, but police needed to hold her elbows to keep her from collapsing on the sand.

The search turned up no sign of Natalee.

On June 14, Joran sat down with detectives Dennis Jacobs and Luigi Croes at police headquarters in Oranjestad to detail his latest story. The interview began at 10:00 A.M. Joran admitted that he had lied about dropping Natalee at the Holiday Inn, claiming he was scared of his father's reaction to learning that he had left a girl asleep on the beach. He was also worried about the reaction of his girlfriend, whom he didn't want to know about the rendezvous.

"One thing my father definitely told me was to tell the truth. My father was right. I should have done that," he lied.

Now he was saying that Deepak and Satish had dropped him and Natalee at the beach next to the Marriott just before 2:00 A.M. He described their hour and a half together, beginning with Natalee and him strolling the beach hand in hand.

"While we were walking, I noticed there was sand in my shoes. So I took off my shoes and socks, tucked my socks into my shoes, and held them in my hand as we walked down the beach. Natalee and I stood for a time at the water's edge and kissed. She told me that she liked Aruba."

Joran said the two talked for a bit and then walked in the direction of the Holiday Inn. "On the way there Natalee told me that she didn't want to go back to the hotel, she wanted to walk in the other direction.

"We sat down on the beach in front of the Marriott, close to the water. There, I placed my shoes on the sand and we started French kissing and talking. At some point, Natalee told me she wanted to keep walking down the beach. We stayed about five minutes in front of the Marriott, then we stood up and walked hand in hand in the direction of the Fisherman's Hut. We French kissed each other but that wasn't easy because we were walking."

Joran said Natalee still wanted to see the sharks on the north coast, but he told her it was too far and he wasn't walking there with her.

"When we got to the first building of the Fisherman's Hut, she told me that we should sit on the beach. We sat in the sand next to each other and then lay on top of each other. We had dry sex."

"I was lying on the sand and she was sitting on me and pretending like we were having sex. I told Natalee that I didn't have any condoms on me. She said that it was better that we didn't have sex.

"After that, Natalee put her hand down my pants and masturbated me.

"I opened my trousers so that my penis could come out and make it easier. While she was masturbating me, she told me to tell her before I came so that I wouldn't come on her because she didn't want that to happen. Before I came, I told her so. When I came, I came into my own hands.

"I stood up and washed my hands in the ocean. I then walked back to Natalee and we continued to French kiss. I started feeling her breasts and continued to finger her with two fingers. I believe I fingered Natalee for about fifteen minutes.

"At some point, I thought that I had been fingering her for long enough. I stopped doing it, and I told Natalee that we should go back to her hotel.

"I also told her that I had school in the morning," Joran claimed. "I asked her to walk with me back to the Holiday Inn. She said she didn't want to. I offered to escort her, thinking that she would agree. But Natalee refused, saying she didn't want to go back to her hotel. She said she wanted to stay there on the beach."

Joran admitted to the officers that he grew frustrated, and at one point, picked Natalee up and began walking with her in his arms toward the hotel. "Natalee told me to put her down," he said. "I put her down, and I thought to myself, That's it! And I called Deepak."

Joran claimed it was 3:00 A.M. when he dialed his Surinamese friend from his cell phone. "I asked Deepak what he was doing. He said he was chatting online. I told him the girl wouldn't listen and she was sleeping on the beach. I asked him if he would come and pick me up."

Joran claimed that Deepak said he would head right over. Their conversation lasted only a few minutes. "I then walked back to Natalee. She was still sleeping and I lay down next to her."

Natalee Holloway as a member of the Dorians dance team. In this photo, the team marches in the Mountain Brook High School homecoming parade, November 5, 2004, in Birmingham, Alabama.

(Courtesy of Dana Mixer/ Getty Images)

The Holiday Inn SunSpree Resort on Palm Beach, where Natalee Holloway and her classmates stayed on their senior trip to Aruba in May 2005. *(Courtesy of Veronique Louis)*

The Fisherman's Hut, where Joran claimed he spent several hours with Natalee Holloway on the night she disappeared. *(Courtesy of Veronique Louis)*

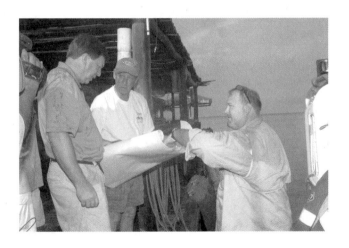

Natalee's father, Dave Holloway (left), speaks with Tim Miller and his team of divers from Texas EquuSearch before a search for Natalee's body. *(Courtesy of Veronique Louis)*

Tim Miller preparing for a water search, prompted by a tip concerning the location of Natalee's body in the waters off Palm Beach. *(Courtesy of Veronique Louis)*

Joran van der Sloot sits in a car with his father, Paulus, after being released from Aruban custody for a third time on December 7, 2007. *(Courtesy of Associated Press/ Pedro Famous Diaz)*

Peruvian murder victim Stephany Flores in an undated photo.
(Courtesy of Splash News)

A series of surveillance stills of Joran and Stephany at the Hotel Tac: 1. The two entering the hotel lobby around 5:30 A.M. on May 30, 2010; 2. Entering Room 309; 3. Joran leaving Room 309 alone around 8:00 A.M.; 4. Joran returning from his coffee run, carrying two cups—at which point, police believe, Stephany was already dead.

(Courtesy of Peruvian National Police)

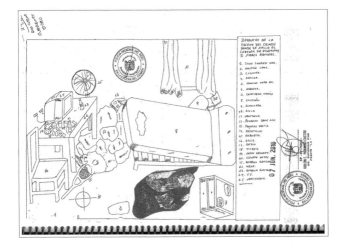

Crime-scene sketch of Room 309 of Lima's Hotel Tac, where Stephany Flores's body was found.

(Courtesy of Peruvian National Police)

The bloody shirt police believe Joran used to smother Stephany Flores. Joran was captured on video wearing the shirt when he entered Room 309 with Stephany on the morning of May 30, 2010. *(Courtesy of Peruvian National Police)*

Peruvian Homicide Team 2 assigned to the murder investigation of Stephany Flores. Left to right: Detective Miguel Tong, Detective Jose Castro, Captain Juan Callan, Detective Macedonio Ugarte, and team driver Rivera Herrera (not pictured: Detective Frank Gonzalez).   *(Courtesy of Cole Thompson)*

Personal effects of Stephany Flores found by police in Room 309. Among them Stephany's Nextel phone and her "flower power" wallet, which police found emptied of cash and credit cards.   *(Courtesy of Peruvian National Police)*

Joran's personal effects, returned to police by the taxi drivers who unwittingly assisted him in his flight across the Peruvian border to Chile. Among the items is the shirt Joran was wearing when he fled the Hotel Tac.

(Courtesy of Peruvian National Police)

Stephany's parents, Mariaelena and Ricardo Flores, walk with their daughter-in-law, Carolina Flores (left), during Stephany's funeral on Thursday, June 3, 2010. Stephany's mother clutches her daughter's favorite stuffed animal, a pink Minnie Mouse.   *(Courtesy of Associated Press/Karel Navarro)*

Chilean police officers escort Joran van der Sloot to an airplane to be flown back to the Peruvian border. The photo was taken in Santiago, Chile, on Friday, June 4, 2010.

(Courtesy of Associated Press/Roberto Candia)

A high school senior, disappeared in Aruba during a class trip, May 30, 2005.

Beth Holloway, Natalee's mother, speaks at the opening of the Natalee Holloway Resource Center at the National Museum of Crime & Punishment in Washington, D.C., on Tuesday, June 8, 2010. *(Courtesy of Associated Press/Pablo Martinez Monsivais)*

A makeshift memorial to Natalee Holloway on an isolated strip of beach near the Fisherman's Hut, where Joran claimed to have taken Natalee on the night she disappeared *(Courtesy of Veronique Louis)*, and Stephany Flores's grave at the Jardines de la Paz cemetery in Lima, Peru.

(Courtesy of Cole Thompson)

According to Joran, it was around 3:30 A.M. when Deepak came in the silver lowrider to get him. On the way to drop him at his apartment, he said he told Deepak that he had left the girl on the beach and that she was being annoying because she didn't want to go back to her hotel.

"Deepak asked if I had fucked her. I told him that I hadn't because I didn't have a condom. I even told him that I'd lifted her up and tried to carry her, but she didn't want to go back to the Holiday Inn."

" 'Fuck that bitch,' " Joran said Deepak had exclaimed.

In the car, Joran said he told Deepak about the sneakers, a pair of white-and-blue K-Swiss, size fourteen, that he had left on the sand. Unlike Joran, who needed to wake up for school in the morning, Deepak told him he didn't have work the next day.

According to Joran, at 3:45 A.M., Deepak dropped him at his house and told him that he was going home to log on to his computer. "I asked Deepak if he could pick up my sneakers. He told me that he would go and get them immediately and then he drove off," Joran said.

Joran was creating a scenario that left open the possibility that his friend Deepak, knowing that Natalee was lying passed out on the sand, had returned to the site of their rendezvous, where he raped and murdered her.

Joran said that the next day he took the bus to school, returning around 4:00 P.M. His mother was still in Holland. After finishing his homework, his father gave him a ride to the Aruba Racquet Club for his daily tennis lesson. But he wasn't in the mood to play tennis; he wanted to gamble. He had lied to his tennis instructor, excusing himself from his lesson because he was exhausted. He told the instructor the elaborate story of the night out with the American girl.

So, with his tennis lesson canceled, Joran went for a swim with a seventeen-year-old Dutch-Argentinean girl he had been dating, as well. Then, he called his friends Guido and Andre to arrange to meet up with them later that evening at the casino at the Radisson Resort.

Joran said he walked along the beach from the racquet club to the Palm Beach hotel strip, stopping in front of the Marriott to look for his missing sneakers. The beach was crowded, and he didn't find them. He said he did not go to the Fisherman's Hut to see if Natalee was still there. He figured she would have woken up by then. At that moment, he was more worried about the shoes he'd left behind, because he was not aware that Natalee was missing.

Joran said he played at the gaming tables of the casino inside the Radisson until 1:00 A.M., when Deepak arrived. He told the investigators he was on a roll and wanted to remain at the poker table for another hour.

Joran never mentioned the fight that Deepak claimed, in his police interrogation, had occurred between Joran and a tourist, who had accused the Dutch teen of cheating at the tables. He simply said that Deepak wanted to go to the Wyndham, so the two climbed into the gray Honda and set off on J. E. Irausquin Boulevard. They were just pulling into the Wyndham parking lot when Joran's father called him on his cell.

"He told me the police were at the house and they were looking for a missing girl." Joran said he immediately told Deepak a girl had gone missing, and without hesitation, his friend said, "It must be that girl from last night."

Joran said he thought about the American girl he had left on the beach. He hoped Deepak hadn't hurt her. Deepak was the one who had crafted the story about driving Natalee to the Holiday Inn, flagrantly implicating his friend.

Although Jacobs and Croes had not personally taken Deepak's most recent statement, they were familiar with what the Surinamese man had told police. Joran's version of the night and Deepak's description were different in several seemingly minor details. However, someone was lying, and determining who was the liar was critical.

Joran continued implicating Deepak, telling the detectives that he had called his friend on the way to the Bubali Police Station with his father the day after Natalee disappeared. "I told Deepak I was en route to the police station to make a statement about the missing girl. Deepak's answer to this was 'Shit!' Deepak reminded me to stick to the story that we had dropped the girl off at the Holiday Inn."

Joran said that after that night at the Radisson casino and the Wyndham parking lot, he and Deepak only had telephone contact. He had called the elder Kalpoe to warn him about his father's concern that the FBI might tap their phones and monitor their online chats.

While most people would have taken this advice, and stayed away from phones and chat rooms, Joran said he deliberately did the exact opposite. He suggested to Deepak that they speak as often as possible, repeating the same lie. That way, the fabrication would seem like the truth to any surreptitious listeners.

He also confessed to detectives that he had told his friend Freddy Zedan and both his parents about his suspicion that Deepak may have gone back to the beach and raped the girl. He claimed that Freddy had told him if that were the case, he would be in serious trouble since he was the last person to be seen with her.

Sitting before the detectives that Tuesday afternoon, Joran was confident about his newest version of the events of May 30. He was sure he had outsmarted the officers with his theory about Deepak.

But holding up a computer printout, Jacobs and Croes called his bluff. Leaning forward in his chair, the heavy-set Jacobs asked, "Isn't it true that on May 30 at approximately 3:15 A.M., you sent Deepak a text message saying: 'Hey Buddy, I'm back home and will see you tomorrow,' to which Deepak replied, 'OK.'"

Jacobs saw a flash of anger in Joran's eyes. He was caught. Why would he send Deepak a message telling him that he was safe at home, if Deepak had been the one to drop him off? Joran mentally grabbed at any answer that might work but found nothing. "Yes, it's true," he finally muttered, aggravated and disarmed. He looked down at the table. "I did send Deepak that message."

He was cornered. He didn't want to talk anymore. "If you have more questions, I am willing to answer them tomorrow," he said.

By then, detectives were confident they had their man. Now, they had to locate Natalee.

THIRTEEN

The two security guards, who had been pulled from their beds, handcuffed, and paraded before the cameras ten days earlier, were quietly released from jail under the cover of darkness.

Shortly after 11:00 P.M., Mickey John walked out of the police station. Ninety minutes later, Abraham Jones was released. A small crowd of well-wishers, mainly other blacks, stood outside the blue-and-white police station in Sint Nicolaas to greet them. The Aruban government had intended to have their liberations go unnoticed, as if the men's detentions had been minor inconveniences. However, news crews had been alerted and, despite the late hour, captured their release on camera and broadcast it to audiences in the United States.

Now freed, the security guards became players in the media frenzy. Mickey John appeared on Greta Van Susteren's Fox TV show *On the Record* to say, "The justice system, the detectives, they're all fools."

Even though the pair was no longer behind bars, they

were not officially cleared as suspects. Their association with the case continued to hold them in a never-ending nightmare. With the black mark of suspicion hanging over them, they couldn't find employment on this small island where everyone knew everyone else's business.

"Since the incident, I can't get work," John grieved more than four months after his release. "My lawyer said that after three months, the charges would be expunged. But it's now October and there has still been no clearance. I can't fill out a job application and honestly say that I have never been arrested because the prosecutor will not clear the file," John lamented.

More red herrings and bizarre leads were soon pulled from the sea. Steve Croes's arrest was his own fault. He was the man whose name Deepak had offered as an alibi witness early in the investigation. He was a disc jockey on a party boat, the *Tattoo*, that ferried groups from the hotel strip for off-shore sunset cruises with effusive drinking and dancing. Despite early rumors that Natalee and some of her friends had cruised on the *Tattoo,* and thereby encountered Croes, this was unfounded. Croes's real connection to the case was his acquaintance with Deepak.

The twenty-six-year-old divorced father was a customer at the Internet café where Deepak worked. According to Deepak, Croes approached him in the days after Natalee went missing claiming he had seen Deepak and his friends dropping the American teen at the Holiday Inn. The claim was impossible, but Deepak seized the opportunity to have an alibi and passed Croes's name to police.

Croes's ten-day detention was the result of his bizarre self-involvement. In custody, he admitted that he had not seen them drop the girl at the Holiday Inn. He had only overheard Deepak tell the story to someone else at the café and voluntarily stepped forward. By now, Joran and the Kalpoe brothers had already changed their stories. Croes's motive for sacrificing himself as an alibi witness remains a mystery, although one could surmise that he sought money or fame. His nautical experience aboard the *Tattoo* certainly piqued the interest of investigators, who were actively pursuing a theory that the teen had been discarded at sea. He was now facing felony charges of conspiracy and obstruction of justice. As for his arrest, however, he was completely useless in the effort to find Natalee.

On the afternoon of June 15, police officers again descended on the Van der Sloots' orange stucco home. While some conducted a room-to-room search, others stood guard at the edge of the property. Two vehicles, Anita's blue Hyundai Tucson and Paulus's red Suzuki Samurai, were towed away from the scene and processed for blood, fibers, and other forensic evidence.

Special agents from the FBI performed forensic testing on the vehicles four days after they had been impounded to determine if either car had been used to transport a body. Using a luminol-like product called Starlight Bloodhound that is commercially available and used by hunters to track wounded game at night, agents received positive responses on the steering wheel, stick shift, the key hole/ignition area, and the interior driver's door pull of Anita's Hyundai. But more specific tests using Hemident, a more sensitive forensic tool that could detect trace amounts of blood as little as one part per million, were negative. Similar tests performed on Deepak Kalpoe's silver Honda tested negative, as well.

During the execution of the search warrant, police carried other evidence from the Van der Sloot home in paper bags. Later that same day, more investigators arrived to aid officers already on the scene.

A Dutch forensic team, led by senior homicide forensic investigator Paul van der Hoven, performed a search of Joran's apartment. The apartment was also scanned by Miami-Dade police detective Alan Lowy and his canine, Bugg, assisted by special agents from the FBI.

Bugg and his handler also performed searches of a vacant lot adjacent to the Van der Sloot residence, and a rear garden. But there were no hits.

A few days later, police questioned Paulus van der Sloot.

He agreed to sit down with Detective Tromp and Sergeant Burke to answer questions related to his son's detainment.

On the evening of June 18, Paulus told the officers that he had wholly believed the story his son and his friends had told him about dropping Natalee at the Holiday Inn.

"After that, Freddy came by to see us with another story," he said dryly. "My wife and I were very upset with Joran that he had not told the truth from the beginning."

Freddy came back to the Van der Sloots that evening with his parents. He had been reluctant, having an exam the next day that needed his attention, but Paulus had retained a lawyer, Antonio Carlo, for Joran. He wanted Freddy to talk to him.

Paulus admitted that in the days after Natalee's disappearance, he spoke with Joran and the Kalpoe brothers on a regular basis. "The girl remained missing, and that preyed on their minds," he explained. "Satish and Deepak's mother called us, and we spoke to her at the house. She was also concerned and wanted to share those concerns.

"Joran completed his exams and attended school as normal. My wife took him to and fro since she is a teacher at his school. Once, there was an incident at the International School Joran attends when family members of the missing girl hung up posters with her picture on them and the text: 'Kidnapped: Ask Joran van der Sloot.'

"The headmaster banned these people from the school grounds."

Joran's father explained that he did speak with Joran and his friends about what to expect if they were indeed arrested. He explained to them basic interrogation procedures, as well as how long they could be detained. "If they didn't find the girl, then I knew there was a possibility that the boys would become suspects again.

"I found it strange that they were not questioned any further, and concluded from this that they had evidence that the girl had been seen after the boys dropped her off."

He emphasized that the girl had disappeared on May 30, but after taking their initial witness statements, the police had seemingly lost interest in them. Nine days passed between their initial statements and their arrests and subsequent interrogations on June 9.

"Have you spoken to any of your friends about this?"

"We most likely did speak about all this with the friends who'd been stopping by. It was on everyone's mind. A few of our friends are members of the 'Friends of Aruba,' a social network for newcomers to the island, and were closely involved in the search for the girl."

Paulus expressed other concerns about his son's gambling and cheating. He seemed more preoccupied that Joran had been gambling for money than he was about Natalee's disappearance or her family's unbearable pain. He was completely frustrated that his son had disobeyed his house rules.

"I allow Joran to play in the free tournaments, but he's not allowed to play in the casinos for real money," he explained.

Three days later, Paulus was arrested.

FOURTEEN

Having successfully negotiated the Peruvian border crossing, Joran van der Sloot was confident he would pass through the Chilean customs several hundred yards ahead with similar ease. At 3:00 P.M. that Monday, a Chilean border patrol officer, seated at a window inside the modest brick building, stamped his passport. Minutes later, another officer waved the white minivan driven by taxi driver John Williams through the highway security booths.

Carlos kept his front passenger seat, and Joran was in back as the three proceeded south on the Pan-American Highway. En route, Joran switched his clothes. He exchanged the gaudy blue shorts and short-sleeved T-shirt with beige shorts and a black turtleneck.

The van encountered its first Chilean army checkpoint within ten minutes of finally being underway. These guard posts were insufferable for Joran. But the poker face he had managed throughout these brief delays in Peru served him well again. The three were stopped, checked, and waved through with satisfaction.

Finally the outskirts of Arica loomed. Clusters of rectangular warehouses rose from the cactus scrub, their parking areas brimming with eighteen-wheelers. Arica was an important port city on the Pacific Ocean, and the semi-trucks were either delivering cargo to the container ships or picking up freight for destinations all over South America.

Arica was the "City of Eternal Spring." Surfers seeking an endless summer swarmed to its renowned "El Gringo" pipeline. High-end and budget travelers loved the Pacific Ocean locale, its casino, and its myriad hotels, bars, and restaurants. Shoppers found the two beautiful pedestrian malls, Plaza Colón and Vicuña Mackenna, abundant with duty-free shops and outdoor restaurants. However, the one and only point of interest for John Williams and Carlos Euribe was a bank, hopefully one with accessible money for Joran van der Sloot.

John Williams found a parking place near the El Morro de Arica, a huge outcropping of burnt-sienna rock that dominated the skyline and was the site of a monumental battle between Peru and Chile one hundred and thirty years earlier.

Today, the salty air was thick with the aroma of bougainvillea and steaks cooking over wood-fired grills as Joran and his two escorts started off on foot in this foreign town. At 4:30 P.M., the banks had all closed, but ATMs were available outside four or five bank buildings.

Joran tried his card at them all, but he was denied. He needed a human teller, he lamented.

Waiting until the next day was out of the question. John Oswaldo was stuck at the border and John Williams had been traveling with this scoundrel longer than any passenger in his livery career.

Joran fumbled through various pockets and found a wad of 288 nuevos soles, about U.S.$100. He promised to wire the driver the outstanding balance in the morning.

John Williams was furious. This payment, plus promissory note, was unacceptable. Voluntarily or compelled by force, Joran added his Ferrari-brand watch, worth more than

$7,000 by his account, to the settlement. In fact, he unloaded most of his possessions faster than a hot-fingered hood at a pawnshop. He gave them a digital camera without a battery; a blue Nokia cell phone that was missing its SIM card; two cell phone chargers; a paperback biography of Prohibition-era gangster, Al Capone entitled *Al Capone, Chicago's King of Crime,* by Nate Hendley; a bottle of Arrow-brand cologne; a metal tin of Prickly Heat foot powder; a brown leather portfolio case from the Wyndham Hotel marked "The Right Way. The Wyndham Way"; and a Nicorette inhaler.

Joran even threw in the red, white, and black striped short-sleeved polo shirt that he had been wearing when he left the Hotel Tac for the last time on the morning of May 30.

With a shove and a curse, John Williams and Carlos Euribe slammed the van doors and left Joran behind still with his stories and lies, but without his watch. They retrieved John Oswaldo at the border at 6:00 P.M. They stopped in Santa Rosa for dinner, and divided up the loot.

John Oswaldo took the Ferrari watch and the digital camera. Carlos Euribe got the red, white, and black striped shirt, the cell phone, the foot powder, and the Al Capone biography. John Williams kept the box of Ben Wa balls, believing Joran's overblown worth of the ten-dollar trinkets. Joran had described them as jade, valued at a few hundred dollars. John Williams called them "the Chinese game inside of which are two small balls that shine." The police identified them as "a small box lined in green fabric inside of which are two green balls with a symbol in black and white that make musical sounds." In any fashion, for the moment, they were his.

Twelve hours later, back in Ica on the morning of June 1, the brothers, bone tired and underbathed, were delighted to be home to business as usual. Even though they had been swindled, they had inflated their fare enough to at least have extracted an acceptable profit.

The following morning, a Channel 4 news segment playing in their living room interrupted their relaxed mood. The story was about the murder of a twenty-one-year-old woman,

Stephany Flores, in Lima, 150 miles away. And the face of their rogue passenger stared back at them in a photo on the television screen.

He was the prime suspect, the news announced, calling him a presumed murderer. The story detailed the murder of the daughter of a famous race-car driver, and how the suspect had fled, leaving her lifeless body in a hotel room. He was also implicated in the disappearance of a young American woman on vacation in the Caribbean five years earlier, assumed to be murdered, as well.

The Piscontes were dumbstruck. It was at that moment, they claimed, that they realized they had aided a fugitive, a murderer, in escaping Peru. As they flipped the channels the story was everywhere. There was even an American newscast discussing the case. They began to comprehend that they had become part of an international incident. They had just spent the last twenty-four hours with him in extremely close quarters—first in Ica giving the stranger a solitary ride; then haggling and handshaking in Nazca; then storytelling, even joking and laughing, en route to Arica. The odyssey had ended in a spit and a curse.

Across town, Carlos Pretil had heard the news over the radio and immediately called the Pisconte home to speak with the brothers. But the line was busy. Moments later, his friend, John Oswaldo, called him back. Oswaldo sounded nervous. He confirmed that from news reports it appeared that Joran, the Dutch citizen they had just driven to Chile, was the prime suspect in the murder of Stephany Flores back in Lima.

"I've got to get off the phone," John Oswaldo announced, his voice shaky and tinged with fear. "The police and the media just arrived at our house."

The taxi drivers had not been hard to locate. Immigration officials had entered their DNI numbers into a logbook at the border crossing. The three men were scared and initially gave police conflicting accounts of their ride to Chile. But after hearing investigators rattle off a long list of possible criminal charges, including crime against the administration of justice, crime against jurisidictional function, material concealment, and omission of reporting to police, they were more forthcoming.

"What was your passenger's demeanor during the trip? Was he nervous, as if he were running away?" police in Ica asked John Pisconte.

"He acted normally. He didn't seem nervous, he smoked and he slept. In a space of thirty minutes he would light up a cigarette, finish it and light up again, and having smoked a whole pack, he went on smoking a cigarette every half hour."

"Did you have any knowledge that Joran had murdered Stephany inside the Tac Hotel?"

"I heard through the newscast on Wednesday, June 2, 2010, that they made reference to me and that I was the driver of the vehicle that took him to Arica."

"Did you call the police and if not, why not, when you learned that Joran, who you had transported, had likely killed Miss Stephany Flores?"

The taxi driver paused before answering. "I didn't call the police because I got scared," he admitted. "I did think about it. But around noon on June 2, Commander Caparo of the DIRINCRI from Ica arrived at my home and he interrogated me about the case and I said that 'Yes, in effect, I had transported Joran to Arica.'"

By agreeing to give a stranger a ride, the three Peruvian taxi drivers had unwittingly become key witnesses in one of the most high-profile murder cases Peru had ever seen.

FIFTEEN

The June morning had brought the usual baking heat, mitigated by the prevailing easterly breezes. Anita and Paulus van der Sloot had just left the Korrectie Instituut Aruba in Sint Nicolaas (KIA), Joran's latest place of confinement, when Anita's cell phone rang with important news.

A sprawling correctional center, the Korrectie Instituut Aruba was perched on a bluff overlooking the Caribbean Sea, at the northernmost tip of the island. It was the most secure of Aruba's detention facilities, surrounded by a dual perimeter, a chain-link fence topped by barbed wire and a high cement wall with watch towers on each of the four corners. It rarely reached its maximum capacity of three hundred prisoners, the vast majority of whom were facing charges relating to drug trafficking. Herds of goats grazed the scrub that grew between the prison and the bluff.

Joran and the Kalpoe brothers had arrived separately the day before, June 22. Joran was isolated in the juvenile wing. Under Aruban law, they could be detained there for one hundred days without being formally charged, and then they would have to be either charged or released.

That Thursday, Anita had spent almost forty minutes visiting with Joran. Although Paulus had accompanied her, he was barred from contact as per the judge's order so he remained in a waiting room.

The Van der Sloots were on their way home when Anita answered a call from her excited neighbor. He was calling to inform them that uniformed police officers were outside their house.

Concerned, Anita immediately dialed Chief Jan van der Straten to find out what was happening. She was told that she and Paulus should go directly to the Noord Police Station.

The police chief had not elaborated, and the couple, wondering and worrying, pulled up to the Warda di Polis. The building looked more like a La Quinta Inn with its faux Spanish façade than a police headquarters, but at 2:00 P.M., the couple parked and hurried inside. The police officers waiting in the lobby area promptly arrested the elder Van der Sloot for his suspected involvement in Natalee Holloway's disappearance. Paulus was furious.

"To answer your question as to what I have to say about my arrest for charges of accessory to murder, manslaughter, and kidnapping resulting in death, I can state this: I find it ridiculous and absurd!" Paulus sniped at Detective Roland Tromp and Sergeant Clyde Burke. "To answer your question to the degree of ridiculousness, I can say this: I think that my arrest reaches the highest level of ridiculousness and absurdity."

Although Paulus agreed to participate in the interrogation, which was conducted in Dutch, his request to have his lawyer present was denied. Even without a lawyer, the precision of his language was undeniably lawyerly and calculated.

Detectives began dissecting Paulus's time line. In all his official statements to police, he said he had picked up Joran at the McDonald's on Palm Beach at 11:00 P.M. on May 29.

But Natalee's mother, Beth Twitty, remembered a different story. The night that they had all gathered in the Van der Sloots' driveway, Paulus had told the group he had retrieved Joran sometime around 4:00 A.M. on May 30.

"Can you explain the discrepancy?" Burke asked.

"I have previously stated that I picked up Joran on Sunday May 29 in front of McDonald's at approximately 11:00 P.M. Then I woke up at approximately 5:45 A.M. on that Monday morning. During the time in between, I was sleeping and didn't hear that Joran had gone out or come back either; 5:45 A.M. is when my alarm always goes off and when I wake up. I wake the children at around 6:00 A.M.

"I woke up Valentijn, Sebastian, and Joran."

"Was Joran difficult to wake up that Monday morning?"

"Joran is always hard to wake up. It didn't seem any harder than usual to get him to wake up. Nothing seemed out of the ordinary."

Paulus van der Sloot was vague, seemingly forgetful, and spoke in generalities. When police had first talked to him, he had been very precise. Now, his memory was deficient. He couldn't remember if Joran had gone to school that Monday or if he had or hadn't picked him up at school during the period of May 30 to June 9. He couldn't remember the exact dates of his wife's trip to Holland.

Detectives also focused on the gym bag that Joran claimed to have left behind the bar at the racquet club the day after Natalee went missing. Something about the sneakers that Joran claimed to have lost on the beach seemed suspect. If Paulus had helped dispose of any evidence that could link Joran to a homicide, they wanted to know about it.

"I don't recall whether or not I returned to the racquet club to pick up the bag Joran had left there. I don't think I returned to the club after I dropped off Joran. I can't be completely sure."

The police wanted to know exactly what Paulus had discussed with Joran and the Kalpoe brothers. "I don't recall if I had a conversation with Joran, Deepak, and Satish about the missing girl on June 1, 2005," Paulus recounted. "I did speak extensively to Deepak, Satish, and Joran from the time that they were questioned to the time they were arrested. We read the papers, saw the news and spoke about it.

"I was in touch almost every day with Jan van der Straten. At no time did I doubt the boys' story. When we spoke of the girl, it was about what the consequences would be if she didn't show up somewhere. I was under the impression that the boys assumed that the girl would turn up sooner or later.

"Naturally we spoke of the possibility that she would not show up. I based my hope on scanty information provided by Jan van der Straten that the girl had been seen again after they dropped her off at the Holiday Inn. He didn't say so in so many words, but I made the assumption seeing that the boys were not questioned again."

"Weren't you suspicious when the boys asked a lot of questions about the consequences if the girl didn't show up?"

"My recollection is that the boys didn't even bring it up. I was the one who initiated the conversations about the girl."

"Why did you do so?" Detective Tromp pressed.

"I kept bringing it up in conversation because I was concerned. I was concerned for her and for the boys, due to the fact that if they were the last ones to be seen with her, the investigation would turn back to them. I had no doubts as to the validity of their statements."

Paulus had been in the hot seat for more than five hours. Aruban law allowed police to interrogate a suspect for no more than six hours unless they believed the suspect had more information vital to a criminal investigation. At that point, the prosecutor's office could request an additional forty-eight-hour hold.

At just after 8:00 P.M., the elder Van der Sloot was informed that he would be taken into custody and held overnight in a cell at the Noord Police Station.

"This is completely ridiculous and absurd," Paulus objected. "I consider it to be malicious in intent if the purpose of my detention is to bring my son to make false statements."

Paulus told police he was more than happy to tell them everything he remembered, if it would help in clearing up the case of the missing girl. But he felt that he could better serve this purpose as a witness rather than a suspect.

After learning that he would be detained, Paulus continued to answer questions for another hour. Police wanted to know why he arranged legal representation for the boys if he thought they were innocent.

"At a certain point, I realized that I needed to face the fact that they might be considered suspects in the future. I wanted to allow that process to run more smoothly and facilitate their release from custody. Again, I believed their story to be true.

"If they already had an attorney at their disposal, then the whole process would move along more quickly, their statements could be taken and no time would be lost. It was meant purely to facilitate the process."

Sergeant Burke jotted a note on the pad in front of him. "Why did you make these arrangements even though you were convinced they were telling the truth?" the officer asked.

"Because the boys could have been the last to see the girl before she disappeared, was enough to make them suspects, I reasoned. As I said, I wanted to facilitate the process.

"Moreover, I didn't want the boys to panic due to pure lack of knowledge about the procedure they would be subjected to. I wanted the truth to prevail and not get clouded with half-truths. The situation as it was and its subjectivity to police and justice department pressures for results could have resulted in such buckling to these pressures."

"Why were you so concerned that the boys would buckle under the police questioning if you were so convinced of the truthfulness of their statements?"

"I have said that I believed the boys' statements. I was more concerned that the pressure put on the police to produce evidence would influence the amount of undue pressure put on the boys. I was afraid that the boys might be influenced into making false statements.

"I told them repeatedly that they are lucky that there were three of them and that their interrogations would not be difficult since they were just telling the truth."

"Mr. Van der Sloot, isn't it true that Joran has lied in the past?"

"Yes, Joran has lied in the past," Paulus affirmed. "He lied about money he had stolen from us. We discussed it as a family extensively and there was also guidance from a youth psychologist with whom he had several talks while going through puberty. I was under the impression that he had turned over a new leaf. I did not assume that I would have to question everything he said to me."

Anita van der Sloot was frantic when she left the Noord Police Station that Thursday afternoon, alone. She had not missed a day of work since returning from Holland on June 1, when she learned from her husband that Joran and his two friends, Deepak and Satish Kalpoe, were the last people seen with Natalee Holloway.

Over the weeks, the situation had intensified, but she and Paulus had each other for support. Now, both her son and her husband were suspects in a potential murder investigation. She had been told that they were both facing life in prison and she was terrified.

Anita believed in a karmic order to life. She could believe in her son's innocence and grieve for Natalee at the same time. Even though the lives of these teens had intersected, she hoped that their encounter could emerge from this current shroud of tragedy with Natalee safe and Joran exonerated.

Since coming back from Holland, she had gone into a Christmas storage box to retrieve an angel. With the angel, a lit candle, and a photo of Natalee, she created her personal shrine to the missing American teen, praying for her well-being and return.

Still, Joran's recounting of his grueling ten-hour interrogations was heart-wrenching. He said the detectives had placed him under extreme pressure, calling him a psychopath and a murderer, and demanding that he reveal where he buried Natalee. He also told her that the interrogators were withholding food and threatening him with acts of physical violence.

Anita was devoted to her three teenage sons, and her two younger ones still needed her at home. She wanted to conceal her grief when she arrived home that Thursday afternoon without her husband, but the anguish on her face was unmistakable. She wasn't even able to get inside to embrace them without navigating the reporters camped outside her orange ranch house.

Needing to be the spokesperson for her family, she invited the group onto her enclosed back patio. Dressed casually in a short-sleeved pink top and dark purple slacks, she summoned her courage and called her husband's arrest "ridiculous."

"My husband has done everything that authorities have asked of him," Anita said, choking back tears. "It hurts because my husband gave fifteen years of his integrity to this island, and that this could happen is so bizarre. He is the most honest, beautiful man that you can think of," she proclaimed. When she spoke about her husband, Anita's face was filled with soulful admiration.

Forty-nine-year-old Anita was convinced that Aruban justice had been hijacked by the American media. "This is not about Natalee anymore. It's about enormous pressure from the States and the media.

"I'm very angry," she explained. "But, I will hold up. I have to because I believe in my husband. I believe in my son. It will be fine."

Anita and Beth Twitty had met for the first time earlier in the week. Beth, accompanied by news anchor Greta Van Susteren and a Fox news crew, was in the Van der Sloots' neighborhood passing out flyers and prayer cards.

Paulus was outside when the group showed up on Montanja Street. After he and Beth talked briefly over the fence, Paulus invited her inside to her complete surprise. News anchor Greta Van Susteren was invited to accompany her, but all cameras were to remain outside.

The visit lasted ninety minutes. Beth, dressed in blue jeans and a white tank top, her red hair pulled up in a ponytail, tried to stay upbeat. She presented Joran's parents with the "Hope for Natalee" bracelets she had been handing out to everyone.

Natalee's friends back in Mountain Brook had made thousands of the three-thread yarn bracelets as a project to keep Natalee's search filled with hope. The wristbands were being distributed throughout Alabama, and many more had been shipped to Beth in Aruba to hand out on the island.

The Mountain Brook community was deeply invested in finding Natalee and helping the Holloways and the Twittys in their efforts. Daily prayer vigils were held at the Mountain Brook Community Church, and members tied yellow ribbons to mailboxes, storefronts, fences, and lampposts throughout Birmingham.

Although the face-to-face meeting with the Van der Sloots had ended with Beth and Anita in an embrace, Natalee's mother left that Tuesday convinced that Joran's father knew more than he was revealing. She noticed that Paulus had been sweating profusely and his hands had been trembling, so when news of his arrest that Thursday afternoon broke, she was elated.

"We are very pleased that the investigation is progressing," Twitty told reporters. "We feel like this will lead to more information to give us the answers we need for finding Natalee."

Joran had only been at the KIA prison in Sint Nicolaas for two days when his father was taken into custody. Since arriving at the facility, the teen had been struggling to manage his anger. Already, he had gotten into a scuffle with the police officers who had transported him there.

The men had been compelled to use force to subdue him.

Aruban prison director Fred Maduro wasn't surprised at Van der Sloot's level of aggression. Maduro was a fair-skinned man who shaved his gray hair down to the stubble. He had worked with Paulus van der Sloot in the past, and knew Joran from his youth. He had noticed even then that Joran had an explosive temper when he didn't get his way.

On the afternoon of June 24, detectives arrived to transport Joran back to Oranjestad for more questioning. But Joran refused to go.

In an arrogant tone, he announced he was not cooperating. He would only go if his father was released from jail. Advised by his mother and his attorney, Antonio Carlo, he said he was no longer giving statements, instead invoking his right to silence. His father was being represented by Antonio Carlo, as well, and a second attorney, Rudy Oomen, was helping in their defense out of friendship, Joran explained. He, himself, would not speak again until clearance came from either lawyer. If he stayed silent, following legal advice, his father would be released in two days.

"I realize that by making another statement, I could get my father into more trouble," Joran explained. "My father has a poor memory and that's why our statements don't match. He can't even remember what clothing he had on yesterday."

Joran took the position that his father's detention was centered on the McDonald's time line, the time Paulus said he had picked up his son at the McDonald's on Palm Beach on the night Natalee went missing. His father had said "middle of the night, May 30" and Joran had described, "11:00 P.M., May 29." But Beth Twitty had remembered a different time. Natalee's mother had claimed to have heard Paulus say that it was 4:00 A.M. on May 30. Joran thought this was absurd. He wanted the police to leave his friends and family alone. He would take new questions only, and only then with his lawyer present.

Furthermore, he was not going anywhere that afternoon because he was expecting a visit from his mother at 2:00 P.M. He needed her to brief him about how the lawyers wanted to proceed. "Only if my father's lawyer advises me in the meantime to give a statement, will I do so," Joran announced. "I'm waiting to see my father's statement before giving another one myself."

In spite of Joran's many objections, he was transported to police headquarters in Oranjestad that day anyway. Two investigators began a line of questioning completely unrelated to Natalee Holloway. They wanted to know about a different sexual assault on another young woman.

For six hours, Joran was interrogated about his interactions with a girl we'll call Bridgette. He denied the allegations presented to him and said the sex was consensual.

"I know the girl Bridgette, but I don't know her last name," Joran told the detectives. "I had sexual relations with her, but I can't remember exactly when."

"Did the sexual relations take place during Carnival this year?" Detective Jacobs asked, referring to the country's annual celebration in downtown Oranjestad.

Joran nodded in the affirmative, recalling that when he first saw Bridgette that past January she was dancing with his friend Jaime "Beto" near the bridge of the Renaissance Hotel. "I suspected that Bridgette had been drinking." Joran explained that after the festivities, Bridgette joined him and his friends Jaime, Freddy, and Koen at Carlos'n Charlie's. "Inside Carlos'n Charlie's, Bridgette and I walked upstairs and started French kissing."

Joran recalled that he and Bridgette then went for a walk along the pier in the harbor, where he asked that she give him a "blow job." "I can't remember if I was standing up or lying down on the ground when she gave me the blow job. I wanted to have sex with her, but I didn't have a condom."

Joran said his friend Freddy called him on his cell phone while he was out on the pier with Bridgette and asked him if he needed a ride home. Joran, Bridgette, and Freddy caught a ride home with a Mexican friend, Chato. During the car ride, Joran and Bridgette sat in the backseat, where Joran claimed that she performed oral sex on him for a second time. The four returned to Joran's apartment behind his family's house, where Joran and Bridgette lay on a sofa and began fooling around under a blanket. Bridgette had been drinking whiskey from a flask with Chato.

Chato asked if he could join them in a threesome, but Joran said that Bridgette declined. Joran said that after his friends left, he put on a condom and he and Bridgette engaged in intercourse. Joran swore to the officers that the sex had been consensual.

Police implied that Bridgette indicated that Joran had taken advantage of her drunken state and had forced himself on her. "I can't tell you what condition Bridgette was in when I had sex with her," Joran said, explaining that he had also been drinking whiskey from his friend Chato's flask.

In response to the detectives' questions, Joran said that he had sex with Bridgette on three separate occasions, including a recent encounter during which she spent the night at his apartment. "I had told my mother that Bridgette would be staying for the night," Joran claimed.

During the questioning, detectives introduced the names of three other young girls, one as young as twelve, who had also come forward with claims against him.

Joran denied having sex with any of them. He claimed that one of the young women had had sex with his friend Freddy Zedan in the back of Freddy's Honda, while he and another friend sat in the car drinking alcohol. "I gave Freddy a condom before he had sex with her," Joran recalled.

Joran said the third girl police mentioned had been a girlfriend. "But we didn't have a sexual relationship with each other," Joran explained. "We had, perhaps, French kissed, but nothing further. She was only twelve years old. Her parents caught wind of the relationship and put a stop to it."

Although the three young women had come forward with allegations of date rape, no formal charges were ever filed.

Helen LeJuez, an attorney for Beth Twitty, said the girls' mothers would not permit the three to proceed with any criminal complaint for fear their daughters would become entangled in the media maelstrom now surrounding Natalee's disappearance. Lacking parental consent, the authorities could not compel the young girls to testify.

At 10:00 P.M., Joran, in handcuffs, was escorted outside to

a waiting police vehicle for the return trip to KIA. To his surprise, Deepak and Satish Kalpoe, his coconspirators, were also loaded into the same blue-and-white SUV.

For more than two weeks, the young men had been isolated from each other. Now, the police had purposely arranged for the three to travel together back to the Korrectie Instituut Aruba in Sint Nicolaas. They were going to be able to speak freely with each other and police planned to listen to every word.

The verbal hostility exploded. Joran accosted Deepak first, accusing him and Satish of being responsible for the sexual assault allegations Bridgette had lodged against him. In a venomous rant, Joran threatened to blame Satish for Natalee's assault, and added that he was going to tell police that Deepak had paid Steve Croes, the party boat disc jockey, to lie about being a witness.

"How does it feel?" Deepak asked, taunting his Dutch friend about the arrest of Joran's father.

Joran shot back, blaming the brothers for implicating his father during their interrogations.

"You can fix this in one fell swoop," Deepak insisted. "You know you can."

"Tell me what you mean, how can I fix it?" Joran asked.

"You just need to tell the truth," Deepak repeated. "Tomorrow I complete the last of my eight days, and then I go home."

"That's what you think," Joran retorted.

"I'm going home," Deepak insisted.

"Just wait 'til I tell them stuff about you guys. Then we'll see if you go home." Joran snickered.

"I guarantee it," Deepak said with a smile.

The back-and-forth continued with each side accusing the other of telling lies.

Joran threw out a veiled threat. "The police just told me, like, if you guys go after me, then I'll go after you," he said.

"Ha ha ha ha ha ha," the brothers chuckled.

"We aren't putting you in harm's way," Satish told Joran. "We're just telling the truth."

"You should try and keep your mouth shut!" Joran scolded the elder Kalpoe. "It's your fault that my father is in jail."

Joran blamed Deepak for getting his father arrested by telling police it was Paulus van der Sloot who had advised them "no body, no case." "My father was only trying to help you guys and this is how you repay him?"

Joran also blamed the brothers for the arrests of the two black security guards. He relished telling them, "One of those guys is going to kill you because of that."

Next, he accused Satish of cowardice, describing him as weak because he claimed to have seen the ghost of Natalee in his jail cell.

"I should beat the crap out of you for what you've done!" Joran said, returning to Deepak. "I'm not afraid to be locked up in jail. I swear, I'm gonna kill you!"

Deepak shot back. He told Joran that the police were keenly aware that he and Satish had nothing to do with Natalee's disappearance and that he had read Joran's statements and knew about the lie he had told police about him, that Joran had accused Deepak of burying the girl by the Fisherman's Hut.

"You don't give a shit about your family," Deepak snapped. "You only care about yourself." Deepak advised that threatening to kill him while in the company of two police officers was not wise. "Satish and I will only be in custody for eight more days, but you'll be getting fifteen years!"

For the rest of the ride, Joran was silent. The two brothers exchanged small talk. Deepak's reference to the police officers in the car had brought the fireworks to a fizzle. Weeks earlier, Joran's father had advised the three that by telling the same story, everything would be all right. Sitting in the back of the police truck, Joran realized this pact was officially over.

It was every man for himself.

SIXTEEN

In Chile, June was a winter month. The Casablanca Valley, in which Joran now found himself in a cab heading toward Santiago, was always temperate, however. By midday, the cooling low-lying clouds trapped each night by the snow-capped Andes to the east and the coastal range to the west had burned off, and the temperature was a pleasant 73°F. The taxi was nearing the toll plaza east of Curacaví, a small hillside town in central Chile known for its wine and chocolate.

Joran had been in the coastal town of Viña del Mar when he hired the cab. He was familiar with Viña del Mar. It was renowned for its nightlife and gambling, and was supposed to have been the final stop on the Latin American Poker Tour, before the powerful 8.8-magnitude earthquake that past February had compelled the organizers to relocate the event to Peru. Viña del Mar was an immaculate resort town with a climate similar to the Mediterranean, gorgeous palm-lined boulevards, high-end hotels, and casinos, including the historic Casino del Mar, the first and largest in Chile. It had been spared catastrophic damage from the quake and was, for the most part, back in business.

Three days had passed since Joran had bilked the Peruvian taxi drivers back in Arica. Since then, he had traveled nearly 1,200 miles down the Chilean coast to Viña del Mar. The morning fog hovered over the town as he climbed into the backseat of a private taxi he had hired to take him to the capital city of Santiago de Chile, about eighty-five miles southeast on Highway 68. Despite what he had told the cab-drivers, he somehow still had access to funds. Getting to Viña del Mar was easy. It was only five miles from the historic port city of Valparaíso. From there, a one-hour drive on a modern four-lane highway cutting through the magnificent Chilean Coastal Range mountains ended in Santiago, 2,100 feet above sea level.

Joran was filled with anxiety that morning. He had seen his picture in the newspaper, and he knew he was a wanted man. Still, he was determined to get to Santiago, hoping he could "disappear" among the five million people that called the city home. From there, he would be able to pursue escape options to either Aruba or Holland.

The cab sped through the vineyards and wineries of the Casablanca Valley. It passed tour buses of day-trippers out to enjoy a taste of a premium Sauvignon Blanc. Like northern California's wine country, the rows of vines stretched from the highway's edge clear to the mountain bases in the distance, fading from sight into the horizon. The wine produced by these grapes was enjoyed worldwide. Joran's thirst, however, was trumped by his misery. Just before 12:30 P.M., the taxi entered the Zapata Tunnel, a one-mile-long mountain pass just west of Curacaví. On the other side, the highway widens into multiple feeder lanes as it approaches the massive toll plaza bisecting the road. Spotting the booths ahead, Joran crouched down in the backseat, trying to make himself invisible as the taxi driver slowed to pay the toll. But his height made hiding impossible and his odd behavior drew the attention of the toll collector.

All tollbooth attendants had been placed on high alert

since Chilean authorities had notified them of a suspected murderer on the run from Peru the previous day. This passenger seemed to resemble the description that had been provided, and an alert witness contacted the highway authority. Within moments, blue-and-white police vehicles converged on the scene and Joran's fugitive status came to an abrupt halt.

Officers didn't know what to expect when they ordered Van der Sloot out of the vehicle. Many were surprised by his indifference. He looked almost relieved that this flight had come to an end and did not resist in any way.

TV news crews were waiting at the Borgoño police barracks in the Independencia district in the northern part of Santiago, fifteen miles from the toll plaza. Journalists had been tipped off that Stephany Flores's alleged killer had been captured on Highway 68 outside of Curacaví.

Just before 3:00 P.M., reporters got their first look at "El Holandés," the name given to Van der Sloot by the Peruvian press who had a hard time pronouncing his Dutch surname. Joran looked agitated as he climbed out of the black unmarked police vehicle and into the custody of three Chilean detectives. The officers were dressed in navy-blue windbreakers with the acronym "PDI" written in yellow block letters on the back and had police-issue nine-millimeter pistols holstered on their belts.

Reporters used to working the crime beat were surprised that Joran, a man suspected of a brutal murder, was not in handcuffs. He had also lost the country club good looks he had flaunted in photos from the previous five years. Joran looked like a street tough now, with an angry scowl. His head was shaved and he had dyed the remaining stubble a garish orange. At six feet four, he dwarfed the stocky Chilean officers leading him into the headquarters. Joran's once slender frame had filled out, and he appeared muscular and fit in his khaki slacks and black hooded sweatshirt covered in colorful geometric designs, the brand name CIRCA written across its front in celestial-blue lettering.

A phalanx of media and curious bystanders watched through the black wrought-iron fence surrounding the sprawling police barracks.

"Joran! Joran!" a photographer yelled out, hoping to get the suspect to turn in his direction.

Joran didn't try to hide his face from the cameras, as he had in Aruba. He looked confident and walked across the asphalt parking lot with a swagger.

Photographers lined the steps of the headquarters, snapping pictures like the paparazzi after a reclusive superstar. Joran, sandwiched between two officers, finally disappeared behind the barracks' red wood door.

For more than five years, the Dutchman had endured the cameras, the microphones, and the questions. Today, he had nothing to gain, no financial upside to speaking to the press.

Since Natalee's disappearance, Joran had cashed in on his supposed role in her tragedy. Although most news outlets wouldn't pay him outright for these one-on-one interviews, they often paid him for any photo or video he was able to provide. The calculating side of Joran knew that the media outlets had no real interest in the pictures he offered. Paying for these souvenirs was the equivalent of paying him for his camera time, without blatant violations of propriety. His standard licensing fees for the materials was $25,000, including a titillating—and believable—story.

For the past five years, he had "confessed" to various versions of the truth about what had actually happened the night Natalee went missing: he had sold her into sexual slavery for $10,000; she had snorted cocaine and fallen off a hotel balcony and was disposed of in a swampy lake; and that his father was an accomplice to his silence.

None of his claims had ever been substantiated.

Inside police headquarters, Chilean investigators sat down with Joran to take some basic information. They had no plans to interrogate him, merely to process him before expelling him from the country.

The Chileans had decided to forgo an extradition proceeding, which can be a tedious, technical legal process involving international cooperation. They chose to handle the situation as a straightforward immigration matter.

All foreigners entering Chile were required to fill out basic paperwork, addressing two issues: What is the purpose of the visit? And what is the local domicile of the visitor? Joran had lied on both counts, claiming he had entered the country as a tourist, which he clearly wasn't, and had provided no valid hotel reservations.

As far as Chilean immigration was concerned, he was an undesirable whose only real purpose for entering the country was to escape murder charges in Peru. Despite being informed that he was under no obligation to speak, Joran announced to the investigators that he wanted to make a statement, in English, so there would be no misunderstanding.

He was innocent, he insisted, and wanted authorities to know what had really happened in Lima. Just after 9:00 P.M. that Thursday evening, Joran sat down with Chilean detectives. For the next several hours, he spun a fantastic tale about meeting Stephany Flores and how the two had fallen victim to a pair of con artists posing as members of the Peruvian National Police.

"I am a professional poker player," Joran said. He explained that he gambled mostly online, but had participated in tournaments around the world. "It was going to be my first time in the Latin American Poker Tournament in Lima and I did not get to play."

Joran told the officers that his reason for the journey from Aruba to Peru on May 12 was for the tournament.

Unfortunately for Joran, investigators examining his worn, brown Dutch passport noted the Peruvian entry visa was actually dated on May 14. The date was the first of his many lies.

Calmly, Joran explained to his interpreter that after flying into Lima he had checked into the Hotel Tac, which he described as a three-star hotel, in Miraflores, not far from the

Atlantic City Casino. "My room was number 309 and it was fifty soles a day. I paid in cash and in advance. I stayed there for two weeks."

Chilean detectives kept closemouthed about what they already knew. Captain Juan Callan, the Harley-Davidson-riding homicide detective in Peru, had updated them with the latest developments in Lima. He had given them the witness statements from staff at the Hotel Tac, confirming that Joran had entered Room 309 with Stephany Flores in the early morning hours. He had likely committed an act of premeditated murder before fleeing the scene in the victim's SUV. Callan had also included a brutal blow-by-blow account of the injuries the young woman had sustained. He had apprised them of Joran's known movements during the previous five years, including his suspected involvement in the disappearance of American teenager Natalee Holloway in Aruba.

Joran told detectives that he had not had any problems with immigration or airport security when he had flown into Peru, even though he claimed to be carrying $25,000 on his person when he stepped off the Avianca flight at Lima's Jorge Chávez International Airport. "That's the typical amount I carry with me when I go to participate in a poker tournament," he claimed.

"I stayed almost all nights in the casino, sleeping during the day, eating at a restaurant and mostly playing poker. This is where I met this girl, Stephany. She sat at the table and right away she started talking to me. She wanted me to teach her to play. She told me her father had money, and that she was studying, and that she was not interested in guys."

Joran said he could not remember Stephany's exact age, but estimated she was between twenty and twenty-two years old. "We mostly spoke about poker."

He was vague about where and when he had met her but had a clear memory of a terrifying incident in which he and Stephany were brutalized by Peruvian cops. He claimed that the two were on their way to a casino in Miraflores when they were stopped by two men traveling in a white car. The men were wearing police uniforms and badges, and both Joran and Stephany had assumed they were cops.

Stephany pulled over to the side of the road and the two assailants demanded money, Joran recalled. "They said, 'Give us the cash, or else!'

"I offered them $1,000 and they laughed. I then offered $4,000 and they agreed. Then one of them told me to give him something as a souvenir, so I gave him one of my bracelets that I brought from Thailand and they let us go."

Joran described the men as "dark skinned," and said they spoke only Spanish. "It is hard for me to provide an exact description of their uniforms.

"One of the men was younger than the other," he added.

Most tourists reported assaults and robberies to their embassies, but Joran claimed that at such an early hour the office would have been closed. His only desire was to find a cup of coffee and go to his hotel room with Stephany, forgetting about the assault.

He said he purchased some coffee at a place called Holly's Coffee, around the corner from his hotel, then headed up to his room with Stephany to play some poker online.

"I can't say what time it was, but the sun was rising and we entered the hotel through the lobby. We took the elevator to the third floor where my room was."

Joran told the Chilean investigators that he and Stephany weren't even safe once they were inside Room 309. "A man came out of the bathroom, holding a knife in his hand, and blocked the exit. Another man with a pistol in his belt was on the bed.

"The man with the knife told me to 'Shut up,' but Stephany yelled out and the man with the knife punched her in the face, causing her nose to bleed. Then the man with the gun said that they only wanted money."

Joran described how he had scanned the room and realized the intruders had already rifled through his luggage. Clothing was strewn everywhere. They had clearly been looking for money. "I told them that I had no money, but that I could go to an ATM to get some.

"Stephany kept asking 'Why is this happening?'" Joran recalled. "Her nose continued to bleed. When I offered to pick up the money, they agreed, but the man with the pistol said that I should remember that they had Stephany."

Joran said he was certain the man with the pistol was one of the police assailants who had robbed them on the roadside. He was also sure that the one with the gun was in charge because he did all of the talking, while his partner stood holding up the knife.

"I left the room, went downstairs and exited the hotel without speaking to anybody. I did not want to go to the authorities because of my previous experience with the police.

"I went to Stephany's car and thought about fleeing, but then I decided to come back."

Joran admitted that he had lied to the dirty cops who were holding Stephany hostage about needing to find an ATM. "I did not need to go to the ATM machine because I was carrying $20,000," he claimed. After being robbed of $4,000, that was all the money he had left.

When he returned to the Hotel Tac from his ATM run, Joran said he realized he had left his room key upstairs. Stopping by the reception, he tried to remain composed, asking the uniformed man at the front desk for a spare. The man was a member of the housekeeping staff. He agreed to escort Joran to the third floor, where he handed him the key and walked away.

Joran described how he knocked on the hotel room door several times. No one answered so he let himself in using the key he had just been given by the hotel employee.

"The man with the pistol was very angry with Stephany and was covering her mouth with his hand," Joran continued. "And he was angry with me for coming back into the room without giving him a warning."

Unsure of where this frightening experience was heading, Joran said he handed the crooked policeman a wad of cash. "I gave him $10,000 and hoped that would have closed the deal."

Joran had assumed that he and Stephany would be released.

But the men demanded more money. "I told them that I could get more money so I went downstairs again, but the woman at the front desk told me I needed to move Stephany's car."

Stephany had left her black Jeep parked in front of the hotel lobby, and Joran's dilemma intensified. He did not want to leave her car to get towed or ticketed, but to move her car he would need her keys, and they were back in Room 309.

Back upstairs he went to borrow the keys. But Stephany's captors were now furious. Why had he come back empty-handed? He hadn't brought the money.

Joran said the men began shouting at Stephany in Spanish, but they were speaking so quickly he could not make out what they were saying. "They told me to gather my things and go. Go back to my country and speak to no one!"

He shoved his personal belongings into two bags. In his haste, he had to leave a lot of things behind, mostly clothing. But he had to follow the armed thugs' directive. He closed the door and fled, leaving his abandoned property, his two assailants, and Stephany in the room.

Before departing, Joran said that Stephany handed him the keys to her Jeep. He wanted to park her car safely. He described driving around for several minutes before realizing he didn't know his way around the city and abandoned the Jeep several blocks from the hotel. He then flagged down a cab and headed for the airport. Joran said he didn't call the police because the assailants were members of law enforcement and he was scared.

The events of Room 309 that May morning were recounted in Joran's words and presented by him voluntarily. Chilean authorities were not interested in interrogating him, only getting him out of their country. Maybe he thought this would be his best chance for a sympathetic audience; nonetheless, he had thoroughly mastered the art of spinning himself as a victim. In his rendition, he himself had barely escaped with his life. When he minimized his role in Stephany's brutal murder by "confessing" to telling the captors a lie—that he had needed an ATM to withdraw the ransom when in "truth" he had thousands in concealed cash—the story became absurd.

His tale of woe continued. Although he had purchased a roundtrip ticket from Aruba, he wanted to change the reservation and book a flight to Argentina instead. Unfortunately, he claimed, when he arrived at the airport a reservation agent told him he couldn't book a seat on a flight until the following day.

Frustrated, he left the terminal, flagged down a taxi driver and asked him to drive him to Chile, some nine hundred miles away. The driver had politely declined and instead drove him to the bus terminal.

"When I arrived, there were no express busses to Chile, but only local busses." He then walked outside where another cabbie agreed to take him to Ica, Peru, for $500.

Never mentioning the Pisconte twins or Carlos Euribe, Joran told Chilean investigators that in Ica he was able to arrange private taxi service with another driver to the Chilean border for an additional $500.

After crossing the border in Santa Rosa, Joran said he stayed in a small hotel in Arica. "I do not remember its name or location, only that it was a five-minute walk from McDonald's."

He claimed that after spending the night in Arica, he took a bus to Antofagasta, a mining town more than eight hundred miles north of the Chilean capital of Santiago. From there, he caught a flight on PAL Airlines, arriving in Santiago on June 2.

After landing in Santiago, Joran said he reached out to a poker buddy to let him know he was in town. "I don't remember his name. He told me I could stay in his home and after we had a couple of drinks I spent the night, but first I did a little sightseeing in Santiago."

Despite being a friend, Joran claimed his host had taken advantage of his situation. "The man charged me for the night," he complained.

The following morning, Joran wanted to do a little gambling in Santiago before he went to Viña del Mar by public bus. He took a taxi from his friend's house to the Monticello Grand Casino, a 700,000-square-foot property with a hotel, seven restaurants, and one hundred table games. But the casino was closed, having sustained considerable damage in the big quake.

Before leaving for Viña del Mar for a one-night gambling stand, he logged on to his laptop and learned about Stephany's fate.

"In the morning, after checking my e-mail, I learned what had happened to Stephany. I got in touch with my mother and she told me to speak with the authorities to resolve this matter."

Joran's arrogance was mind-blowing. Authorities had captured him crouching in the back of a cab with as substantial a makeover as he could manage on the run, and now he was claiming to have turned himself in voluntarily on the advice of his mother.

True, Joran had phoned his mother the previous day while on the run in Chile. Anita was already beside herself when her son called. He had telephoned her several days earlier from Peru claiming to have been the victim of a police kidnapping. Joran had sounded scared, almost manic. He described meeting a young woman in Lima and claimed they had been kidnapped and robbed by two Peruvian men who were posing as police officers. The assailants had shown them a photograph of Natalee Holloway during the terrifying ordeal.

Over the years, Anita had grown accustomed to her son's fantastic tales and bouts of paranoia. This wasn't the first time he had called home with such an incredible story. Joran could be sweet and loving. But more often the impetus for his phone calls was money. He was always broke. And he always had a tale of woe: his wallet was stolen; someone had broken into his apartment; he had a gambling debt and there were people after him. The stories were endless. Anita was never sure when he was telling the truth.

When Joran called her back on June 2, he claimed that he was in a taxi traveling south to Chile. He sounded scared. By then, Anita had heard the news broadcasts about the dead woman found in his hotel room. The story was unbelievable. The young woman had been murdered on May 30, the five-year anniversary of Natalee Holloway's disappearance. Anita was in disbelief. To have such a coincidence seemed impossible. Someone was trying to frame her son.

"Joran, there is an international warrant out for your arrest," Anita said. "A girl has died."

There was a long silence.

"A girl dead?" Joran repeated. "It's not Stephany, is it? No, not Stephany!"

Anita had urged her son to go to the nearest police station and surrender.

Now, sitting before the Chilean police officers, Joran was insisting that he had been trying to follow his mother's instructions and was en route to a police station when he was apprehended at the toll plaza in Curacaví.

"I said to a cabdriver that I wanted to go to the police and I explained the problem. He said that he had a relative who was a police officer. It was through him that I arrived here after he met us at the tollbooth on the way back to Santiago," Joran explained.

"Is this your first time in trouble with the law?" one of the officers asked.

"I have had problems with the authorities since a 2005 case in Aruba, but after being detained for three months I was released without charges. Since then I have not had problems in Aruba, but I did in the Netherlands, where they tried to make it appear as if I was involved in prostitution with young girls in Thailand, but the story was not true."

Having taken the investigators through his version of events, Joran was convinced that they would see that he was innocent. He had not murdered Stephany Flores. She had been alive when he last saw her in the company of the rogue Peruvian police officers.

With an air of confidence, he announced that he simply

wanted to go home to Aruba. Should the Chilean government decide to expel him from the country, he wanted to be sure he wasn't returned to Peru. His life was in danger there.

Chilean immigration officials informed Joran that on the following day he was going to be expelled at the Santa Rosa border crossing, the place where he had entered the country three days earlier.

Joran, defiant and hostile, refused to sign his statement.

SEVENTEEN

Natalee Holloway had been missing for nearly a month when search-and-rescue expert Tim Miller stepped off the plane at Aruba's Queen Beatrix International Airport on June 23. Miller understood the Holloways' anguish and flew to Aruba when he received a request from the family to assist in the search for their daughter.

Tim's empathy for the Holloways came from a place of personal experience. More than twenty years earlier, his sixteen-year-old daughter, Laura, had been murdered by a serial killer. Tim's wife had been running late for work one afternoon and had left the high school sophomore talking on a pay phone at a convenience store not far from their home in League City, Texas. The family had just moved into a new house and their phone had not yet been connected. When Laura's call continued longer than her mother was able to wait, Laura assured her mother she would be fine and would walk the half mile home when the call was done.

When Laura failed to return home that night, her worried

parents searched the neighborhood. The next morning, they filed a missing persons report at the police station.

Tim and his wife were told that Laura, a slight brunette with long feathered hair, had likely run away, the same prediction Dave Holloway had been given.

The couple was frantic. Their daughter suffered from seizures and needed medication. She would never have run away. Tim had been shocked that the police were not taking his daughter's disappearance more seriously.

He became so desperate he began to do his own investigating. He discovered that another young woman had been found murdered six months earlier. The victim lived only a few blocks from the Millers.

Unwilling to sit doing nothing, Tim begged police to tell him exactly where the girl's remains had been found, convinced a serial killer was operating in the area. He wanted to search this location for his missing daughter. But the police refused to tell him.

A year and a half later, Tim checked himself into a hospital. The stress of his missing daughter had destroyed his marriage. He had lost his job and had been drinking heavily. He even entertained thoughts of suicide.

One morning while he was in the hospital, he was reading a newspaper and learned the dreadful circumstances of Laura's death. Police had found three sets of human remains in an abandoned oil field. One set was identified as Laura Miller. She had been shot in the head.

The bones were discovered in the location Tim had begged the police to disclose to him. Police later theorized that the oil field, within the city limits of League City, was the dumping ground of a deranged serial killer.

In 2000, Tim founded Texas EquuSearch, a nonprofit volunteer search-and-rescue operation dedicated to finding missing persons. He had participated in nearly five hundred searches and had reunited nearly one hundred people with their families by the time he became involved in the Holloway case.

Texas EquuSearch was based in Houston and its volunteers usually conducted their searches on horseback. Their means of transportation would have to be modified for the unique terrain of the Caribbean island. In Aruba, they would have to rely on all-terrain vehicles, boats with side-scan sonar, and scuba diving and canine search teams.

Tim brought a team of twenty-four people, many either current or former law enforcement personnel. He had initially agreed to stay on the island for a minimum of five days. But Tim was dogged to the point of obsessed in helping families find closure. Anyone who knew Tim Miller knew that if his work was not finished in five days he would stay until he was no longer needed.

Before beginning the search, Tim met with Chief Jan van der Straten to discuss how to proceed. The meeting was tense, with Van der Straten hesitant to have an outside team involved. But the two parties reached an agreement. Tim was allowed to commence his search on the condition that he would share any findings with the police before speaking to the media.

Since Natalee's disappearance, other American search missions had provided their efforts. Special agents from the FBI had been dispatched, first from Miami and then from Alabama. They joined the thousands of unspecialized volunteer searchers who provided boots on the ground and support.

The federal agents had participated in the search of a cement plant and several ponds near the Kalpoes' home in Hooiberg; a large area south and east of the Aruba Racquet Club; and west of the Fisherman's Hut.

Tim Miller and his team set off on Saturday, June 25, beginning with searches of wetlands on the northern tip of the island and areas around the California Lighthouse. They weren't so much searching new areas as re-searching old ones. Eight rescue divers and four cadaver dogs with their handlers added their expertise.

For the water search, the team used a borrowed boat fitted

with the side-scanning sonar equipment they had brought from Texas. Side-scan sonar was special equipment used for capturing images on the ocean floor.

The land search was equally difficult. The heat was unbearable and the terrain was grueling. The dogs had to wear specially designed booties to protect their paws from the cactus-strewn landscape.

When Tim Miller and his team began their search, five suspects were in custody, Joran van der Sloot, Deepak and Satish Kalpoe, Steve Croes, and Paulus van der Sloot. But two of the suspects, Paulus van der Sloot and Steve Croes, were going to be released the following day.

On Sunday, June 26, a hearing was held to determine if police had enough evidence to hold the men. Given that Paulus was a judge in training, a magistrate was flown in from the neighboring island of Curaçao to preside over the hearing to avoid any appearance of judicial impropriety. After listening to the public prosecutor's argument for an extension on the forty-eight-hour detention of Paulus, the judge found insufficient evidence and ordered that he be released.

Aruba's public prosecutor, Karin Janssen, cited two reasons for why her office believed Paulus should remain in custody.

The first was a discrepancy in his time line, specifically when he picked up Joran at the McDonald's. Two witnesses, Beth Twitty and another person in the posse, insisted that Paulus had told the group in his driveway that he had picked up his son at 4:00 A.M. on May 30. Later he had said he'd picked Joran up at 11:00 P.M. on May 29. This inconsistency was so glaring that it could not be dismissed, written off as a foggy-headed man's poor memory.

The second reason was the witness claim about a "no body, no case" discussion between Paulus and his son and the Kalpoe brothers. Paulus had explained to them that there could be no conviction without a corpse, and as such, Janssen believed that he had attempted to influence the outcome of the case.

During the hearing, Paulus stressed he had nothing to

hide. He had been completely cooperative while in custody and was willing to testify in the event the case went to trial. Under Aruban law, parents have the right to refuse to testify against their children so Paulus's promised willingness was supposed to shore up his apparent innocence.

Outside the courthouse, Paulus told a reporter from the Dutch television program *Nova* that he had been misunderstood. He said he had simply explained the procedures to the three young men so that they would not panic. "That was sufficient for the prosecutor to suspect that I was an accomplice," he said.

Paulus raised questions about the prosecutor's decision to include witness statements from two people who were "in the back of the crowd" that first night on his driveway and not the testimony of the female police officer, "to whom I was talking."

Party boat disc jockey Steve Croes was also ordered released by the judge that Sunday after spending ten days in custody for his bizarre false alibi. Croes's mother had been an emotional wreck since her son had been arrested. She was outside the courthouse when she learned the judge's ruling that her son was free to return home, and overwhelmed with emotion, she collapsed on the sidewalk.

Anita was delighted she would be taking her husband home, but her son was not so fortunate. The judge ruled that Joran and the Kalpoe brothers would be held in detention for another eight days.

Joran was relieved that his father was out of jail. But the assurance from Paulus that there was safety in numbers was collapsing. When the elder Van der Sloot had given that advice, he had assumed that the three boys had been telling the truth about their movements on the night of May 29 into May 30.

However, now Freddy Zedan had come forward to inform the police and Joran's parents that Joran and Natalee had been dropped off at the beach by the Marriott. Joran could no longer rely on him to keep their story straight.

Perhaps it was a police tactic, but detectives did not

question Joran or the Kalpoe brothers for three days after Paulus van der Sloot was released from custody. The brief reprieve gave Joran time to craft an explanation for any discrepancies in his story.

On June 29, detectives Johnny Melvis Erasmus and Zoraida Magaly de Cuba resumed their questioning at police headquarters in Oranjestad, beginning with Joran's cell phone use. In particular, they wanted to discuss the eight-and-a-half-minute phone call he had made to Deepak at 2:26 A.M. on the night of Natalee Holloway's disappearance.

While his friend Deepak had told police that the connection was terrible and that he could barely hear his Dutch friend, Joran claimed that he had had decent cell phone reception and could hear Deepak perfectly.

"When I called, I was with Natalee, the missing girl," Joran recounted. "I spoke with him in Dutch and Papiamento to be certain that she wouldn't understand what I was saying.

"I told Deepak that I was with the girl on the beach by the Fisherman's Hut and that after we'd been dropped off there, the girl didn't want to go back to her hotel, but rather walk in the northern direction. I told Deepak that I was on the beach close by the Fisherman's Hut.

"Deepak said I always get lucky and always get the girls. I laughed.

"I asked Deepak if he could pick me up at the Fisherman's Hut at the second group of trees, not the first. He said okay.

"Deepak told me during our conversation that he was talking to a Surinamese girl on the computer, in other words, he was chatting.

"Not long after our conversation, Satish, *not* Deepak, pulled up in the gray Honda."

Detective Erasmus shifted further upright in his chair and shot his partner a look of disbelief. Instead of admitting that he had been caught in a lie, Joran was creating another story. Confronted with the hard evidence that Deepak had been at home on his computer and couldn't possibly have picked him up at the beach that night, Joran offered up the younger Kalpoe.

Unlike Deepak, Satish had gone straight to sleep that night and had left no digital footprint. He had made no cell phone calls, and had not logged on to his computer. Aside from his brother, an exposed liar, no one could verify his whereabouts.

Joran was proud of his new version of events and continued to plug the other holes in his story. Putting Satish behind the wheel of the Honda explained his "thank-you" text message to Deepak.

"After I got back home, I sent Deepak a text message. The message was: 'Hey, thanks. I'm home now. Can you go online?'"

Joran again confirmed that it had been his idea to make up the Holiday Inn story, and that Deepak had added the detail about the "dark-skinned" security guard.

He wanted to clarify another point about the route they drove that night. "Natalee did say that she wanted to see sharks, but never mentioned the lighthouse and we never went to the lighthouse."

"Why did you lie to Natalee's parents when they came to your house that night?" Detective Erasmus asked.

"First of all, I didn't realize at the time that they were Natalee's parents. I was told that they were FBI agents. Secondly, I was afraid that something bad had happened to her."

Even though Joran had changed his story and was now claiming that it was Satish who had picked him up at the beach that night, he stopped short of suggesting that Satish had harmed the Alabama teen and insisted that the police officers take a closer look at Deepak.

"I have my suspicions regarding Deepak and whether or not he went back to the girl on the beach. I know how he thinks. . . .

"Satish . . ." Joran paused. "I don't know."

Joran ended the six-hour interview with contrived optimism. "I'm starting to believe more and more that the girl is alive, otherwise she'd have long since been found."

While Joran was providing investigators with a new angle, Deepak Kalpoe was asserting his innocence in another interrogation in the same headquarters.

Since his arrest, Deepak had been interrogated more than ten times, and he was frustrated and angry. When Sergeant Clyde Burke asked him about his salary at the Cyberzone Internet Café, he became indignant.

"I am of the opinion that my wage has nothing to do with this case. I am not going to answer questions about how much I make. I am angry. I have already agreed with my lawyer that I would no longer make any statements. I know I am innocent."

Deepak made it clear that he only wanted to stick to the facts that he considered relevant to the case. He confirmed that he was at Joran's apartment when his Dutch friend told the Holiday Inn story to his good friend Freddy Zedan. He also responded to questions about the route the men drove and confirmed that Joran had told him about leaving his sneakers behind at the beach during their 2:30 A.M. phone call.

"Didn't you find it strange that Joran left his shoes on the beach?" the detective asked.

"I did find it strange, but they were his shoes, so not my problem."

"Didn't you buy sneakers for someone at the Athlete's Foot?"

"I bought sports shoes before the girl went missing. Can you tell me when it became a crime to buy sneakers?"

During the interrogation, detectives pointed to an online chat that Deepak had had with a friend after dropping Joran and Natalee at the beach on May 30. During the chat, Deepak told his friend that Natalee had put her hands down his pants. But that admission had never been repeated in any of his interviews with police and detectives wanted to know why.

"I did this to mess up the investigation," Deepak claimed. "I wanted the police to focus on me and Joran because we were worried Satish would screw up the details regarding the Holiday Inn story. At that time, I was pretty sure that our telephone conversations were being recorded and that my computer was being monitored as well.

"Although this never happened, the story about the girl putting her hands down my pants, I'd like to know since when is this a crime? I repeat, this never happened, but my question to the district attorney is how is this considered a crime?"

"You've had Joran's back from the beginning," Burke said. "You agreed to go along with him on the story about dropping Natalee at the Holiday Inn. What do you have to say about all the lies that Joran is now telling us about you and Satish?"

Deepak explained that he had been willing to go along with the Holiday Inn story because Joran was his friend. But after learning that Joran was trying to implicate his brother and him, he changed his mind and decided to tell the truth.

"What do you think Joran meant when he said that he had left Natalee passed out on the beach?"

"I took it to mean that she had fallen asleep," Deepak explained.

Officers next focused on the 3:45 A.M. text message Joran had sent to Deepak that night saying that he was at home.

"What do you think Joran meant when he said, 'thanks for waiting'?"

"He wanted to thank me for waiting online," Deepak said. The group had a buddy system and checked in on each other to make sure they had made it home safely.

After reading the statement he had just given to police, Deepak refused to sign it, citing that his attorney wasn't present as he had been in previous interviews.

The following day, detective Dennis Jacobs and his partner, Haydee Nadal, sat down with Deepak's brother Satish at Oranjestad headquarters.

Satish had been implicated by Joran in his last statement to police. But as he sat in his chair at the interrogation table, he was unaware of his friend's recent betrayal.

In his previous statement, Satish had expressed frustration

with Joran. He hadn't known that Freddy Zedan had been told that the Holiday Inn story had been revised.

He, Deepak, and Joran had formed a secret pact, and Joran had deviated from the plan when he told Freddy that the brothers had dropped Natalee and him at the beach next to the Marriot.

"I thought that stunk because I was not aware that Freddy was told the beach tale," Satish said.

The younger Kalpoe admitted that even in the early days he thought Joran was lying about leaving Natalee sleeping on the beach. "He acted nervous when talking about it," Satish recalled. "He kept avoiding eye contact and changing the subject back to the Holiday Inn cover story."

Now, Satish regretted his decision to cover for a friend. "We had lied in the interest of Joran and now I sit locked up," he said. "I have lied at the request of Joran and Deepak."

"What do you think happened to Natalee Holloway?" Detective Jacobs asked.

Satish theorized, "I think Joran left her too close to the beach and she drowned."

That same afternoon, detectives Erasmus and De Cuba interviewed Joran. This would be the Dutch teen's thirteenth statement to police. The questioning got underway with a discussion about Joran's schooling.

"I just finished my senior year at the International School," Joran told the officers. "I have never failed any of my subjects. My last exam day was the day before my arrest and I passed everything. The police at the Noord station showed me my diploma.

"During the last school year, I have completed about thirty projects that were school related. The most recent reports were on government, economics and advanced placement English and calculus. Government and economics were about politics and the economy worldwide. Advanced placement English was about a book I had to read. Calculus is mathematics, for me the most difficult subject.

"On May 29, 2005, when Deepak and Satish stopped by my house, I was printing out my homework for school. It was a report about the book *Life of Pi*. Pi is a boy lost at sea on a boat with a lion, monkey, and a zebra. Pi's father works in a zoo. The boy must learn to save himself.

"That same evening I was working on government and economics.

"I complete most of the work on my own. I search for information via the Internet, library, and just things I already know by heart. The Internet info I usually find through Google or otherwise Ask Jeeves or the MSN.

"I use the computer quite a bit. At home we have a computer and a laptop. The laptop is usually in my brother's room. My dad never helps me. His English isn't too good. I am very self-reliant.

"My mother wants to string me along, but my dad just lets me figure it out. I think it's because he's from a family of ten children and had to figure it out for himself, too.

"My mother helps when it comes to arts and crafts.

"That Monday, May 30, I did go to school. I had testified before that I'd run late and that my dad had dropped me off near the Drive Inn so I could make the rest of the trip with the school bus. However, I was mistaken: that was on a Thursday, the day after my mother had gone to the Netherlands.

"Monday, May 30, about 6:45 A.M., I took the bus to school. I talked about this with my dad today and we're a hundred percent certain that that is how it went. At 3:45 P.M. the school bus brought me home."

Joran was next asked about a condom that Rita, the family's housekeeper of eight years, had supposedly found in the pocket of his pants. The officers did not indicate when the condom was found, but Joran acknowledged that Rita worked for the family and very well could have found a condom in his pants pocket while doing the family's laundry.

"Rita is not a liar," Joran said, "so it is entirely possible that she did."

During the interview, Joran indicated that he had made a request to speak with a mental health professional. "While at the KIA prison, I asked if I could speak to a psychologist because I didn't feel well," he explained. "I have spoken to one in the past because I had lied so much."

"Did you have anything to do with the disappearance of Natalee Holloway?" Detective Erasmus asked.

"The only thing I have to do with the disappearance of Natalee Holloway is that Deepak, Satish, and I were the last people to be with her, as far as I know, before she disappeared. Other than that, I have nothing to do with her disappearance."

Joran went on to detail a dream he had while sleeping in his cell in the Noord Police Sation. "I dreamt that I was driving with her in a car to Las Vegas. We were laughing. She was laughing so hard."

"Have you ever used drugs?"

"I have never used hard drugs before. By hard drugs I mean: cocaine, heroin, base, PCP."

"Did you leave Natalee unconscious on the beach that night?"

"I didn't leave the girl behind while she was unconscious. I had even lifted her up. Before leaving her behind at the beach, I lifted her up to carry her back to the hotel. She said she didn't want to and asked me to stay with her. I just left her behind and didn't look back to see whether or not she was sleeping."

"Do you have any regrets about leaving Natalee on the beach?" one of the officers asked.

"At first I didn't feel guilty about leaving her behind . . . I just assumed everything would be fine. She wasn't yet missing. Now I regret having left her behind alone. If I had known this would happen, I never would have left her alone."

"You've said in the past that you believe it's possible that Deepak or Satish could have gone back for Natalee that night."

"I don't want to talk about that anymore. Before I had said that Deepak had said that he wanted to rape a girl. He was taking screen shots of a girl as she was talking to her boyfriend at the Internet café. I was angry with him that day, and walked out of the café angry. That's why my thoughts went the way of thinking he might have gone back for her," Joran claimed.

"Let's get this straight: can you tell us who picked you up from the beach that night? Was it Deepak or Satish?"

"Satish is the one who picked me up," Joran insisted.

On July 3, detectives Jacobs and Nadal sat down again with Satish. Police had again taken the younger Kalpoe to the beach by the Marriott so that he could retrace his and his brother's steps on the night they supposedly dropped off Joran and Natalee. A police photographer documented Satish's reconstruction.

Once back at police headquarters, the officers informed the younger Kalpoe that three new witnesses had come forward, three night fishermen, who were on the beach at the time that he and Deepak claimed to have dropped Joran and Natalee there.

"They did not see your brother's silver Honda. Can you explain that?" Detective Jacobs posed.

"That's because we parked Deepak's car on the north side of the Marriott Hotel," Satish asserted. "Joran and the missing girl immediately got out of the car and walked towards the beach. The three men couldn't have seen Deepak and me because we didn't go on the beach."

"The fishermen said they didn't see Joran and Natalee, either. How do you explain that?"

"I can't tell you if Joran walked off in another direction after getting out of the car because Deepak and I drove away immediately."

That afternoon, Satish's brother, Deepak, was also questioned. Police wanted to know everything, each detail of dropping Joran and Natalee at the beach, what the weather was like, if his engine was still running, even the exact location where he claimed to have pulled off the road to take a leak. Investigators also asked if he had seen anyone else on the beach that night. Deepak said he hadn't seen anyone.

Police also confronted Joran van der Sloot that day.

"You have informed me that you have various questions you'd like me to answer. I am going to exercise my right to silence," he told detectives Erasmus and De Cuba that Sunday afternoon.

"Joran, we just need you to confirm a few things we have already discussed," Detective De Cuba explained.

Joran and the two officers had just returned from a walk-through of the beach area where Joran claimed he had taken Natalee in the early morning hours of May 30.

The on-site tour had been an uncomfortable experience for Joran. Police had taken him onto a crowded beach in full daylight and forced him to walk between tourists as he performed his reenactment of his night with Natalee. One woman who had been sunning herself in a beach chair jumped up and ran away at the sight of him. Joran assumed she had been frightened because of his infamy. He was mortified when she returned a few minutes later with a camera and began snapping pictures of him. Other tourists on the beach were gawking and whispering, "Hey, there's the guy who killed Natalee."

Joran had been humiliated. He had been handcuffed, displayed, and mocked. He felt like a marionette on a string. He was furious that the police hadn't done the walk-through in the evening when the beaches were empty. He was a public spectacle and convinced that the midday event had been orchestrated for the benefit of the American public to show that officials were taking Natalee's disappearance seriously.

Deepak and Satish Kalpoe were also taken to the beach that Sunday afternoon. Their reenactment was carefully studied to compare it with Joran's.

When Joran returned to the police station that afternoon, he was vindictive. He invoked his right to silence, except for answering the policemen's questions with regard to the time line of May 29 into May 30.

"Natalee and I walked on the beach in the direction of the Holiday Inn, but we laid down on the beach in front of the Marriott Hotel. After that, we walked in the northern direction, with our feet in the water, towards the Fisherman's Hut.

I had left my shoes at the Marriott. We laid down in the sand behind the first cement hut of the Fisherman's Hut.

"You ask if we engaged in sex there. Yes, a hand job and fingering. I stood behind the Hut to call Deepak. Because of the wind, I stood there in order to make myself audible. Deepak had said that he was having a hard time understanding me, that's why I stood behind the hut. Natalee remained lying in the sand. I was able to see her.

"The time of the conversation with Deepak was 2:26 A.M. I know this because I was confronted with the information during my detention. The conversation lasted eight minutes.

"After the phone call, Satish came and picked me up. That happened within a half hour after the call.

"I heard Deepak's gray Honda approaching from a distance, so I walked out to the asphalt road. At the car, I realized it was Satish driving.

"The night of May 29 to 30, 2005, was clear and unclouded. The stars were visible. There was wind, but nothing out of the ordinary. I didn't pay attention to the direction of the wind, or whether or not it was especially hard or soft.

"In front of the Marriott were various couples. On our way to the Fisherman's Hut, Natalee and I encountered one other couple. Where Natalee and I were, there was no one else.

"Natalee and I were there from 1:50 A.M. to about an hour later. Satish picked me up before 2:50 A.M."

"Joran, we have three witnesses who claim to have been fishing where you say you brought Natalee that night," Detective Erasmus divulged. "They said they didn't see you there. Can you explain this?"

"They are lying," Joran said. "I've got a better one for you. From now on, I'm exercising my right to silence."

Joran refused to sign his statement that day. He told the officers he had already given several statements and was done cooperating. He informed them he was not willing to participate in any more field trips with investigators.

"It's enough!" Joran exclaimed.

On July 4, Joran, Deepak, and Satish were transported to

the courthouse in Oranjestad to go before a judge. Their most recent eight-day detention had expired and prosecutors were asking to hold all three men for another sixty days.

Judge Rick Smid was brought from Curaçao to preside over the closed hearing that Monday. After listening to the prosecution's arguments, the judge ruled that there wasn't sufficient evidence to hold Deepak and Satish Kalpoe any longer and ordered their release from jail. No travel restrictions were placed on the brothers.

Beth Twitty was irate. At a news conference later that day, Natalee's mother told reporters, "My greatest fear is that they will leave Aruba. These criminals are now free to walk among the tourists of Aruba while I have not seen my beautiful daughter in thirty-six days. I am asking all nations not to offer them a safe haven."

While the Kalpoe brothers were free to go home, the judge ruled that Joran, who was seemingly the last person to see Natalee alive, could be held for another sixty days while police continued their investigation.

Back in his cell at the Korrectie Instituut Aruba, Joran was given writing materials and began keeping a journal. "I'm tired, sad, upset and angry all at the same time," he began. He complained about time passing. "I can't grasp how they cannot find Natalee, dead or alive." He was heartened that he had a lawyer. Joran wrote that he was pleased that he could no longer be questioned without his lawyer to relieve some of the pressure. "Sometimes the pressure is unbearable and you just want to tell them whatever they want so you can go back to your cell and sleep."

He wrote about his promise to his parents to remain silent with the interrogators, noting that: "I have given fifteen statements, and I have told the same story more than ten times. All they are trying to do is trick me into saying something that isn't true."

When someone stole the milk and orange juice from his cell, he tried to calm himself down with a cigarette. "It really worked," he wrote.

He outlined his life in jail by his daily schedule:

6:00 P.M.–6:00 A.M.: cells are locked.

6:00 A.M.–10:00 A.M.: cells are open, and there is a big hall for ping-pong, dominoes, or chess.

10:00 A.M.–10:50 A.M.: outside is available to play soccer or relax.

11:00 A.M.–12:00 P.M.: back in cells for lunch.

12:00 P.M.–3:00 P.M.: the hall is open again.

3:00 P.M.–4:00 P.M.: cells are locked to change guards.

4:00 P.M.–4:50 P.M.: outside again.

4:50 P.M.–6:00 P.M.: hall open for the last time. At 6:00 P.M. back in cells "and the process repeats itself the next day."

For the time being, Joran finally had structure, something his parents and psychologist had wanted for him. Meanwhile, Tim Miller and his team were panning the chaos of the hard, hostile Aruban landscape in the hopes of finding justice for Natalee.

EIGHTEEN

JUNE 2, 2010
LIMA, PERU

The afternoon air in Lima was thick with humidity. Heavy gray clouds blanketed the city as Richie Flores steered his BMW along Cangallo Street en route to the central morgue in the gritty downtown neighborhood of Santos. This was the second time in less than twenty-four hours that he had been asked to identify his baby sister's corpse.

Earlier that morning, he had made the informal identification of Stephany's body in Room 309 of the Hotel Tac. Now, a member of the family was required to come to the morgue to make the official identification, and again Stephany's eldest brother had stepped forward.

Richie was exhausted. He had not slept in two days, and was in shock over his sister's brutal murder. His father and Mariaelena were in mourning, and he and his younger brother, Enrique, had been busy making funeral arrangements and calling family members, relatives, and friends.

Mariaelena had lovingly packed a bag of clothing that she wanted her only daughter to wear before she was lain in the coffin.

Upon arriving at the Morgue Central de Lima, a colonial-style two-story building, Richie was led to a viewing area. The bag of clothing under his arm, he affirmed that the battered body lying on the steel gurney was Stephany's. He related his stepmother's request that his sister be buried in the clothes he had brought with him. But to his horror, her body was so bloated that the garments didn't fit. Lab assistants at the morgue sympathetically dressed his sister in a hospital tunic for transport.

Shortly after 1:00 P.M. that Wednesday, Dr. Juan Martin Villalobos signed off on the autopsy, and released Stephany's remains to her family. His examination had concluded that the vibrant college senior had suffered a violent and protracted death. She had been choked, beaten, and finally smothered. These were details no family wanted to hear about a loved one.

"We are very sorry for your loss," staff members told Richie, as he made his final departure from the morgue.

The family had planned a wake for later that evening at the Santísimo Nombre de Jesús, a Catholic church in the Floreses' neighborhood of Chacarilla. The church was a beautiful concrete structure with a modern arched roof and glass façade on Calle Los Picaflores.

Mariaelena had told her husband that she was too distraught to attend the wake, so Ricardo had made arrangements with the funeral home to have the casket brought to the house. He wanted his wife to have an opportunity to say good-bye to their daughter.

The sun was beginning to set over Lima when the black hearse pulled into the family's driveway. Ricardo was inside preparing some of Stephany's belongings to take to the funeral home. He directed the driver to pull the hearse into the garage, wanting privacy. His wife needed to be able to lay her hands on her daughter's casket and have a few minutes alone with her.

At the sight of her daughter's coffin, Mariaelena was so overcome with emotion that she fainted. When she regained consciousness, she was more composed. To the surprise of everyone, she announced that she wanted to accompany Ricardo to the wake. Being in Stephany's presence had given her renewed strength.

Ricardo was relieved and comforted. He hadn't wanted to go to the wake without her. Still, he beseeched family and friends not to approach her with condolences during the service.

Hundreds of mourners lined up outside the church to pay their respects to the Flores family. Despite the darkness, Mariaelena emerged from the limousine wearing a pair of gold-framed sunglasses to conceal her red and swollen eyes. Ricardo Flores, dressed in a black suit, also hid behind dark sunglasses. He helped Mariaelena out of the car. She was visibly distressed and wobbly with grief. Her two sons, Ricardo Jr. and Bobby, supported her as they navigated through the crowd.

Ricardo remained on the street amid the crowd of mourners and photographers to supervise the removal of his daughter's coffin from the hearse. The cherrywood casket bore copies of two color photos of Stephany taped to the top. In the photos, Stephany was a radiant and beautiful young lady, wearing a pink halter dress. She was holding two oversize stuffed animals, a huge white teddy bear in a red bib, and a brown bunny with a red velvet coat and a red bow. Her smile and her twinkling eyes were breathtaking.

The mourners included friends and classmates of Stephany as well as friends of Ricardo, powerful people in Lima's political and social circles. Lima's mayor, Luis Castañeda, and Peru's minister of defense, Rafael Rey, were there, as well as Peruvian race-car rally legend, Henry Bradley.

The young woman so brutally murdered had touched the hearts of the Peruvian people. Like Natalee Holloway five years earlier, she had become everybody's daughter and her funeral belonged to everyone.

The following morning, Stephany's body was brought to the Jardines de la Paz for a graveside mass. The cemetery was in La Molina, one of Lima's more upscale neighborhoods. The Jardines de la Paz cemetery spread over fifty acres in a pastoral location at the foothills of the Andes. Its grounds were carefully planted and manicured, an oasis of green in an otherwise barren landscape.

Stephany's brothers accounted for four of the six pall-bearers who pulled the casket from the hearse and rested it on their shoulders. The mood was as gloomy as the winter weather, gray and chilled, when suddenly, beams of sunlight broke through like a gentle gesture from heaven. The brothers carried the casket to its final resting place through a sea of mourners gathered for the event.

As she had for the wake, Mariaelena found the courage to accompany Ricardo to the burial. The couple relied on each other and had been inseparable since the tragedy. As difficult as it was going to be to see her daughter lowered into the earth, she would at least have Ricardo at her side.

News reporters were among the crowd, capturing the procession.

Lawn chairs had been set up around the burial site, and Ricardo and Mariaelena sat silently in the front row. Their expressions reflected unbearable pain. Mariaelena, distraught, sat clutching her daughter's favorite stuffed animal, a Minnie Mouse.

During the service, her husband stood to lay two white roses on their daughter's coffin. Stephany's father had to remove his sunglasses to wipe away tears.

When the service was finished, Ricardo embraced Mariaelena and almost carried her to a car waiting nearby, ensconcing her in the backseat, and snapping his fingers at reporters to keep their distance. He returned to the burial site and stood with Richie, his eldest son, until cemetery workers had shoveled the last bit of dirt onto his daughter's grave.

The idea of leaving before the end was out of the question. Stephany had been his best friend, his navigator, and his spiritual compass since the day she was born. His face was slicked with tears, his pain unfathomable.

"I love you, Stephany," he whispered, brushing away tears.

In the middle of the burial mass, Ricardo was informed

that Joran van der Sloot, his daughter's alleged killer, had been apprehended in Chile. Those with faith in the Lord were confident He had played a role in bringing Joran into custody just as Stephany was being returned to the earth. Even nonbelievers rejoiced in this small miracle in an otherwise anguished day.

Members of the press had also learned about the arrest in Chile and wanted a reaction from the family. Ricardo was grateful for the press, knowing it had expedited the suspect's capture. Throughout the course of events related to Stephany's murder, the ranks of the press had seemed to multiply. Having to grieve so publicly had certainly been difficult, especially having so many cameras at the Jardines de la Paz.

Bolstered by the arrest, Ricardo tamped his grief enough to address the cameras. He poignantly used Stephany's freshly filled grave as his backdrop. He thanked law enforcement for their professionalism throughout his family's ordeal. He also begged political leaders on both sides of the border not to delay in returning Joran van der Sloot to Lima.

"The Peruvian authorities are doing everything they can to have this killer brought back to Peru," Ricardo stated. "I don't think they will extradite him because this will take too long.

"Since he is wanted in Peru, I am sure that the Ministry of Interior will send a delegation to see that he is brought back immediately."

Choking back tears, the elder Flores closed his brief statement with thoughts of Natalee Holloway's family. "At long last this girl from Aruba is going to rest in peace," he declared. "She was brutally assassinated just like my daughter was."

Ricardo vowed not to sleep until Stephany's alleged killer was back on Peruvian soil and signed off with a slight nod.

Security guards protected him as he left the impromptu news conference and slid into the backseat of the limousine beside Mariaelena. He cradled his wife, who was still shocked in grief, as she clutched the pink Minnie Mouse.

He offered her water from a plastic bottle and gently stroked her arm.

The limousine pulled away from the remaining mourners and reporters as Mariaelena was burying her face in Ricardo's chest.

The Flores family had buried their daughter, Stephany, but the Holloways were still searching for Natalee. Five years had passed since her disappearance and they were making no progress.

NINETEEN

Meanwhile, Beth Twitty's road to justice for Natalee was giving her no traction. Leads generated by the tremendous publicity were going nowhere. The day before, a judge had ordered the release of two more detainees, the Kalpoe brothers, on the grounds that the evidence against them was not enough to keep them in jail.

Beth Twitty held a two-minute news brief to express her outrage. "The two suspects who were released yesterday were involved in a violent crime against my daughter," Beth decried, choking back tears. Referring to the two young men as "criminals," she lamented that they were not only free to walk among the tourists and citizens of Aruba, but that the judge had imposed no travel restrictions, meaning they were also free to leave the island and travel to any destination in the world.

Her criticism of the ruling sparked an angry backlash among the Arubans, the majority of whom had been expressively sympathetic. In downtown Oranjestad, more than two hundred people protested at the yellow colonial-style courthouse, many carrying placards with messages of "INNO-CENT UNTIL PROVEN GUILTY" and "RESPECT OUR DUTCH LAW OR GO HOME."

The Holloway story had created a very public negative image of Aruba, a usually quiet, distant Caribbean island overlooked by the crowds. Tourism had been badly affected, with bookings down significantly. Many Arubans thought the media was presenting the island as a backward banana republic, despite its having a low crime rate and a well-educated population, many of whom were able to speak four or five languages.

Elgin Zeppenfeldt, a lawyer for Satish Kalpoe, called Beth's comments "inflammatory, libelous and totally outrageous," and threatened legal action against Natalee's mother. "A criminal is a person who has been tried and found guilty in a court of law, while a suspect is a person who is under investigation by corresponding authorities," Zeppenfeldt said in a statement his office released that Wednesday. "Mr. Kalpoe is the latter. The statement made by Mrs. Twitty, calling Mr. Kalpoe a criminal, is uncalled for, especially since my client is maintaining his innocence."

Later that week, Beth issued an apology, saying that her comments were the result of frustration and despair. She went on to thank the people of Aruba for their continued efforts in helping to locate her daughter.

The Arubans understood Beth Twitty's desperation. They also were invested in finding her daughter and arresting her murderer, but they needed Beth to temper her criticism of their homeland and justice system.

Murder on Aruba was a highly unusual crime. On the average, there were between four and five murders a year, usually connected to a domestic dispute or drug-related violence. Murders of tourists were virtually unheard of.

A high-profile disappearance and likely murder such as the Natalee Holloway case was unprecedented.

The timing of her criticism had potentially devastating effects on the Aruban economy. Tourism was fundamental to sustain the island's relatively affluent state for a Caribbean

nation. Nightly coverage focusing on murder and drugs per-
petuated fear, when in fact Aruba had one of the Caribbean's
lowest crime rates. So, just when Americans and Europeans
were planning their winter vacations, Aruba's appeal had
vanished along with Natalee.

The number of people helping search for Natalee had
been in the thousands, made up of tourists and locals alike.
Uncountable volunteer hours were supplemented with dona-
tions of money and supplies of food and equipment for those
out looking in the harsh conditions. Arubans had lovingly
tacked up posters of the missing teen over the island's seventy-
five square miles.

Dutch Marines had been dispatched from the Netherlands to assist those already on the ground and engaged in
the massive search effort. Three F-16 jets had also been de-
ployed from Holland and sent to the neighboring island of
Curaçao, which they would use as a staging area to conduct
flyovers of Aruba's terrain and surrounding waters. The F-16
fighter jets, also known as Fighting Falcons, were rigged
with special infrared sensors to aid in the searches.

Beth's criticism of the Kalpoes' release seemed to pro-
mote a sense that Aruban justice officials were equal to the
Keystone Kops.

It bears noting, however, that the methods of Dutch and
American investigations differ in several ways. One difference: Dutch detectives do not speak to journalists on or off
the record, as is common practice in many countries. In the
Holloway case, the American press filled this "information
vacuum," first with suspicions of incompetence, and then
with a slew of rumors and speculations. Another difference:
plea-bargaining does not exist in the Dutch judiciary. Therefore, arresting all three suspects and hoping one will squeal
isn't an option in Aruba.

Nonetheless, anything connected with the Natalee Holloway case was a media event, and Deepak and Satish Kalpoe's release from jail was no exception. Cameras captured
them coming out of the prison like hobos with their posses-
sions packed in black, plastic garbage bags. They kept their

heads down and climbed into a waiting SUV without speaking to reporters and were quickly driven away.

Joran van der Sloot was now the only suspect still in custody. The ruling to detain him for an additional sixty days had come as a surprise. He had thought the presentation by his attorneys at the hearing had been strong and persuasive. Nonetheless, the evidence was sufficiently compelling and his detention was extended.

At the hearing, Joran did win the right to have legal representation during police interrogations, something he had been denied. Having an attorney was a victory for the defense, but it also safeguarded the prosecutors. Joran had been complaining to his mother about the bullying tactics used by detectives. Having a lawyer present on his behalf would eliminate this issue.

Prior to the hearings, his father had advised him to remain silent during an inquiry, advice he had rejected. Each time Joran spoke, he changed his story and multiplied his problems. Now that the judge had extended his detention, Joran vowed he would no longer cooperate.

Whatever mess Joran had made by speaking until now, at least his father had been freed. In sixty days, he would also be released unless new evidence was discovered. He promised to make them sixty silent days.

On July 9, Joran was taken to police headquarters in Oranjestad for his sixteenth round of interrogation, this one the first to be audio recorded. Previously, they had been attested to by sworn statements.

Detectives Haydee Nadal and Marlon Gumbs began the questioning to a blank stare. Joran had his lawyer present and seemed emboldened and defiant; calm and disinterested.

"Did you see anyone else at the beach during the time you were there with Natalee?" Detective Nadal asked.

Joran glanced at his attorney, then back at the detective. For several minutes, he sat silently, with his narrow, brown eyes fixed on his interrogator.

"What was the last thing you said to Natalee that night?" the detective prodded. "What was the conversation?"

Joran said nothing.

"In a previous statement, you told us that you had seen someone on the beach that night. Was it a couple or a homeless person?"

Joran blankly announced he had nothing to say and refused to sign the sworn statement.

When the interview was officially over, Joran explained his new conviction that the police were responding to intense pressure from the media. High-profile cases necessitated quick arrests, and his situation was an example.

"You just want someone to hang," he declared, suggesting they had the wrong man.

Nine days later, Joran and police staged a second reenactment at the beach recorded by a technical team. When they returned to headquarters, Joran refused to answer questions about it.

He also refused a request to provide DNA. "I am not prepared to voluntarily give DNA samples of myself," he dismissively announced to Detective Jacobs.

The questioning continued. "Is it true the parents of Natalee Holloway wanted to speak with you? And have you spoken to them?"

"In regard to your question," Joran announced, "I can answer in the following way." He then proceeded to stare at Jacobs, giving no answer at all.

Aggravated, Jacobs's partner, Eric Louis Soemers, turned to the lawyer to see if there were any acceptable questions.

"That may be possible at a later date," the attorney replied.

When the interview was over, Joran reviewed the transcript, including the details of his decisions to invoke his right to silence. He declared the statement was accurate but refused to sign it. When asked why, he remained defiantly silent.

Natalee's father, Dave Holloway, had been in Aruba for more than six weeks. He had participated in dozens of searches:

digging in the cactus scrub brush with Tim Miller's cadaver dogs; searching the water from one of the boats outfitted with side-scan sonar; standing with teams draining swamps and sifting through landfills. But he had not met Joran van der Sloot.

On Saturday, July 16, Dave Holloway climbed into his rental car and drove to the Korrectie Instituut Aruba in Sint Nicolaas, where Joran was being detained. He parked and approached the entrance gate just as Anita and Paulus van der Sloot were coming out from Anita's daily ten-minute visit.

Dave recognized them from the media coverage. He extended his hand to Paulus, introducing himself as Natalee's father. Paulus pulled back, but Dave only tightened his grip. Dave needed to explain the purpose of his visit before they escaped to their car.

He wanted to speak to Joran, he said. Anita liked the idea, saying Joran had even mentioned interest in a meeting. Paulus disagreed. He didn't think a meeting was prudent until the police had finished their investigation.

Dave pulled two photographs of Natalee with her two sisters from a pocket, and activated a tape recorder hidden in another pocket.

For nearly forty minutes, Dave and the Van der Sloots stood in the parking lot exchanging stories about their families. Paulus and Anita confided that Joran had been tormented by his decision to leave Natalee alone on the beach, but he had not harmed her. He was only guilty of leaving her so vulnerable.

Dave, in turn, told them about Natalee and her three siblings back in Alabama and Mississippi, who loved and missed her. He had accepted the possibility that his daughter was dead, but he needed to know what had happened to her.

Paulus was the guardian of his *own* family. He hoped Dave would find resolution in his search for Natalee, but as far as his son was concerned, Paulus was compelled to believe him and protect him.

Dave had brought three spiritual books with him, hoping to give them to Joran in jail. Instead, he presented them to Paulus.

Paulus accepted two, but declined the third, the Bible. Joran had a copy already and had been reading it since his incarceration.

The men embraced before returning to their cars. Dave had decided to postpone facing Joran. He had come no closer to answers about Natalee, but he still came away feeling like he had communicated with the Van der Sloots on a compassionate level.

On July 25, Beth Twitty announced a reward of $1 million for information leading to the safe return of her daughter. Generous friends had come forward to pledge the enormous reward.

A separate reward of $100,000 was offered for information vital to solving the case. Tips began to stream in—odd activities at landfills; submerged barrels; and shallow graves. They were all actively investigated.

One person claimed to have seen a man dumping a bag at a landfill in the middle of the night. Another witness said he had been jogging two days after Natalee had vanished and had seen several men discarding a woman's body at the same landfill.

The landfill on the southern part of the island had already been searched by the police and the FBI. Still, Natalee's father wanted to search again. "If we find the haystack, we can find the needle," Dave told members of the press. "But where is the haystack?"

Over the weekend of July 30, searchers scoured through debris in the stultifying heat. Their heavy equipment, including a backhoe and a bulldozer, was supported by K-9 teams. Between the heat and the amount of trash, the task was monumental.

The landfill supervisor directed the group to an area of the landfill where the garbage from early June would have been dumped. Dates on old newspapers confirmed they were in the right spot. Ebby, a border collie in the canine unit, became excited several times but soon lost interest. The scent arousing her curiosity was most likely medical waste mixed with hotel and residential trash.

For the human searchers, the stench emanating from the heap in the searing heat was unbearable, despite a series of upgrades in face masks.

They labored for hours, digging five- to six-foot holes about fifty yards apart, which were then scanned by the K-9 units. Ultimately, the landfill held no new clues.

Another tip came from a tourist who had spotted a barrel under water just off shore, half-buried in sand. After locating it, Tim Miller, his team, and dozens of volunteers tethered it with ropes and wrestled it onto the beach. It was filled with construction debris, illegally dumped but insignificant to the Holloway case.

The Arikok National Park was the setting of another tip. The park on the northeastern part of the island was eight thousand acres of dunes, limestone caves, craggy shores, and inlets. It was there that someone had noticed what appeared to be a shallow grave in the sand.

The Miller team was stunned but confident when they saw the sight in a remote area of the park. Within the cactus scraggle, the impression in the sand was six-feet long, four-feet deep, and edged with dirt piled on one side. It was clearly man-made and freshly dug, but it was empty.

The searchers discussed the possibility that this had been a temporary grave for Natalee, who had since been moved. They conducted an exhaustive search of the area but could not uncover any trace evidence supporting a human grave, not a fiber nor a hair. Cadaver dogs brought to the location showed no interest in the hole, either.

It was finally identified as a drop site for illegal drug runners. The area was so remote that traffickers could come and go by boat, bury an illegal cache, and have it recovered on land later. But it was not Natalee's grave.

Another discovery on the northeast coast looked promising as a lead. A piece of duct tape with several strands of hair, both blond and dark, was found by a park ranger, Mario

Rasmijn. He had been picking up litter in Boca Tortuga, a craggy inlet pocked by small caves, when he discovered it.

Samples of the hairs were divided between a crime lab in the Netherlands and an FBI lab in Quantico, Virginia. Both labs concluded the hairs were not Natalee Holloway's.

A trained search team scavenged the old Atlantis Hotel, an abandoned and derelict beachfront property not far from the Marriott. Several hours of searching turned up nothing but a dead cat shrouded in a garbage bag.

Tim Miller personally attempted to gain permission to search the Van der Sloots' property. Investigators had already searched it, but Miller was curious about an abandoned well and newly poured concrete around the pool. He intended to use ground penetrating radar equipment to probe these locations.

Paulus van der Sloot was outraged. He listened to Miller's case—"There could be something back there that you don't know about. And if you cooperate, it's gonna kind of clear your name," Tim reasoned. But Van der Sloot refused them entry.

Meanwhile, Aruban investigators and local firefighters were draining a pond near the Marriott Hotel. The pond had become a location of interest after a local gardener, Carlos Penata Ramos, had come forward to claim he had seen Deepak's car near there the night in question.

Unable to sleep in his sweltering apartment, Ramos said he had gotten up in the middle of the night to go to the home of a friend who had air-conditioning. Ramos, a twenty-six-year-old Colombian, was a gardener for Eric Mansur, a powerful family on Aruba. Eric's cousin, Jossy Mansur, was the owner of *El Diario,* the Papiamento-language newspaper.

Ramos decided to travel across the Mansur property to a guest cottage with air-conditioning. He looked at his watch; it was 2:30 A.M. He climbed into his van, and took his shortcut, a dirt road.

That was when he spotted Deepak's silver Honda near the Aruba Racquet Club. It was parked between two mounds of sand and brush, as if it were trying to be hidden from view.

He claimed he saw three men inside the vehicle. The two in the front seats tried to obscure their faces behind their hands, while the one in the back ducked down out of sight. Ramos claimed the man sitting in the driver's seat was Joran van der Sloot, whom he was able to identify only after newspaper photographs emerged.

Ramos gave his witness account on July 26 at the Bubali police headquarters, but curiously, he refused to sign his statement and said he would no longer cooperate. Still, based on the tip about the gray Honda being near there, police began the massive undertaking of draining the pond like they had drained the swamp four weeks earlier.

Searchlights aided the fire department in this nighttime effort. Despite the fire engines being able to pump 3,600 gallons an hour, the pond wasn't sufficiently emptied until the following day.

Like all previous searches, no clues as to Natalee's whereabouts were discovered.

Ramos appeared to be the first eyewitness to events that had occurred late that night. The fishermen had made statements to what they had *not* seen. But Carlos had claimed to have actually seen the three prime suspects. However, after his initial interview, three weeks and a warrant were needed to persuade him to reveal more. When he finally came in to talk, Ramos told police that he had been away on a fishing trip with his boss and several of his boss's friends.

On August 15, Ramos was brought to police headquarters to give a deposition in the presence of the lawyers for Joran van der Sloot, Deepak Kalpoe, and Satish Kalpoe. He explained his reluctance to discuss his eyewitness account was because of the false arrests of the security guards. Since his first interview, he had been unaware that he was being sought. But he would talk now.

The attorneys grilled him. "How were you able to see the vehicle if it was late at night and the road was not lit?" his attorney asked.

"When I encountered the car in question, it was on a dirt road," the gardener explained. "I had to brake and drive slowly to pass it. The headlights of my van shone on the car. The person in the passenger seat covered his face with his hand. I saw how the driver slid backwards a little."

Deepak's attorney wanted to know how Ramos could have seen inside the vehicle from the driver's seat of his van.

"In the curve, I had to pass over a sand hill which caused my van to tilt over a little bit," the witness said. "That's why I could see inside the car. I recognized the car from the rims and transparent screens."

Ramos was able to identify Joran, Deepak, and Satish from the mug shot lineup shown to him by police.

Throughout the investigation of the new leads, Joran's interrogations were continuing. Earlier in the month, two special agents from the Netherlands, sergeants Antoon Ronald de Ruiter and Clemens Johannes Maria Burgwal of the Utrecht region, arrived in Aruba to participate in the case. They met the Dutch teen for the first time on August 2, joining senior police officer Jaqueline Josette de Windt of the Aruba Police Corps.

The four gathered at the Oranjestad headquarters, De Windt and De Ruiter sitting with Joran in the interrogation room and Sergeant Burgwal following the proceedings by video system. Joran's attorney, Antonio Carlo, was also present, as had been permitted by the judge.

"How was your drive from the KIA prison to the police station this morning?" Officer De Windt began. "Did the media presence bother you?"

The media had swarmed the police vehicle carrying Joran from the correctional facility that morning, yelling his name and shouting questions.

"I don't care what the media says about me," Joran said, shrugging his shoulders. "I don't read the papers anyway."

A series of questions followed, to which Joran invoked his right to silence.

"What is remaining silent going to do for you?" Sergeant De Ruiter asked.

"I am being accused of something I didn't do, which is why I can answer some questions and not others."

"How do you think that remaining silent is going to help you if it comes out that you have been lying from day one?"

Joran did not reply.

"How do you think the people of Aruba will look at you, and the people of the U.S.A.? And how do you think your parents' lives will be affected by your silence?"

"Can I have a glass of water?" Joran asked. His request was granted.

Sergeant de Ruiter asked Joran to imagine how the world would look upon him should he be released.

He gave no reaction.

"Do you understand everything? Do you have any questions?"

Joran was silent. About an hour into the interview, Joran indicated that he was cold and asked that the air-conditioning be adjusted. The officer on duty complied.

Next, the interviewers confronted Joran with statements made earlier by him and the Kalpoe brothers. "What do you think about those statements now, since they appear to be fabricated stories?"

Joran gave no response.

At 11:20 A.M., the teen asked for a break, saying that he was tired. This time his request was denied.

Joran was then told about the existence of a tape of the conversation between the Kalpoes and him when they were being transported between Oranjestad and the KIA prison.

Again, Joran did not react. Forty more minutes passed with Joran in silence.

At noon, the group recessed for an hour for lunch. Joran got a hot meal, sandwiches, coffee, and water. His bathroom escort afforded him privacy, and Joran took advantage, indulging in a smoke from a secreted pack of cigarettes.

At 1:00 P.M., the interview resumed. "How was your meal?" was the first question asked. Joran responded that he had enjoyed it. When asked next what his reaction was to so many witnesses retracting or amending statements, Joran said nothing.

Next he was asked for a reaction to the fact that reward

money causes people to tell untruths and to perpetuate them for a long time.

Still, Joran said nothing.

"How do you feel about the international press swarming outside the police station, waiting to interview you?"

Joran shrugged his shoulders.

Returning directly to his own statements, he was questioned about discrepancies he had made, specifically about the event when he and Natalee had separated. Was the girl no longer able to walk, passed out on the sand, or was she through with him and walked off in the other direction? He had attested to both scenarios.

Joran sat stone-faced.

"It doesn't make sense to leave a pair of new, expensive shoes behind on the beach and not to go back and look for them," De Ruiter stated. The Dutch investigator then added that Joran's K-Swiss sneakers had not been recovered by the beach cleaning service or taken to a hotel lost and found.

De Ruiter pointed out there was now a $100,000 reward being offered for any clue that could help solve this case. If indeed Joran had left his sneakers behind then someone would have surely turned them in by now to collect the reward money.

Joran stared at the police sergeant but said nothing.

At 3:40 P.M. the interview was halted for the day. Only when it was over did Joran tell Sergeant De Ruiter that he would have answered some questions with simple answers, but his parents and his lawyers had advised against it.

On August 6, Joran celebrated his eighteenth birthday in jail.

Two days later, his interrogation began again, after well wishes for a happy birthday and the reading of his rights.

Joran gave the officers a half-hearted grin.

He was informed that the chief prosecutor of Aruba had filed a petition with the court to extend his detention until September 4. Joran seemed unconcerned.

He was asked why his legal team had been making misleading statements to the press, such as claiming it had been

denied access to him or that his eighteenth birthday had
been spent in an interrogation room.

Joran remained impassive.

Police showed him a statement he had made claiming that
he and Natalee had gone for a walk on the beach. "We now
have a statement from someone who saw Deepak's car at a
location several hundred yards from the Fisherman's Hut,"
De Ruiter announced. He said the witness had seen the car
with three people in it, the Kalpoe brothers and him, and it
was on a dirt road near the Marriott. He asked him if he had
an explanation.

Joran maintained his poker face.

He was confronted with the statements of several of his
close friends about his character. Many said he had lied and
one had described how he had cheated with a friend's girlfriend.

"These guys say that you are constantly playing them.
Can you comment on that?" the sergeant asked.

When Joran did not respond, De Ruiter confronted him
with the statement of the teenage girl who had come forward
claiming that he had molested her. "The girl said that she
was offered a drink during sex that made her lips tingle. Can
you tell us about that?"

Joran sat across the table staring at the interrogators.

"Can you take off your shoes, please?" Sergeant De Ruiter
instructed.

Joran stared at the officer in confusion. He then looked at
his attorney, who didn't coach him on how to respond.

"Your shoes, please," the interrogator repeated.

Reaching down, Joran pulled off one of his shoes and
slammed it down on the table. The noise startled his lawyer,
and he looked up to see Sergeant De Ruiter inspecting his
client's shoe.

"Why did you say you were wearing K-Swiss shoes, size
fourteen, on the day in question and you are now wearing
size ten and a half shoes?" De Ruiter demanded. Throughout multiple investigations, Joran had insisted the sneakers
he had left on the beach were size fourteen.

Joran did not respond.

Sergeant De Ruiter waited until the teen had put his shoe back on, then bent down and pressed his finger on the toecap to feel where Joran's toes were in the shoe. He noted that the shoe was a perfect fit.

Joran did not respond.

The following day, Joran returned to police headquarters. Sergeant De Ruiter informed him that it was possible that authorities in the United States might attempt to extradite him regarding the disappearance of Natalee Holloway.

Joran laughed.

The sergeant next explained that the charges against him might be divided into separate charges, one a charge of murder with a possible life sentence, and another, a charge of vice for sexual misconduct. "How does that make you feel?"

Joran stared ahead as if he had not heard a word.

Once the recorded interview was done, Joran again had things to discuss.

Sergeant De Ruiter forewarned him that even unofficially his remarks would be entered into the record. The officer's transcription of their conversation, which later became part of the official Aruban police file, was remarkably candid and devoid of Joran's usual stonewalling.

Joran complimented the sergeant on his professional interviewing techniques and insisted that had both he and Deepak been interviewed in this fashion from the start, "the truth" would have been revealed sooner.

During the conversation, Joran also told De Ruiter:

- that moving forward he expected to be harassed and possibly even the target of physical violence because of his connection to the Holloway case.
- that he had been open to speaking to people about his connection to the case—even though his mother and lawyer were against it.
- that Natalee could still be alive, but had gone into hiding because of all the media surrounding the case.

- that it was easy for a girl to dye her hair and not be recognized anymore.
- that no one could prove him guilty of a crime that hadn't even been proven to have taken place.
- that was also the reason why he expected to not have his arrest prolonged by the magistrate.
- that his father was now looking at his career options, but had accepted that he'd never work as a judge.
- that his mother would, after the summer break, go back to work at school.
- that his lawyers had not once panicked regarding the new interrogation techniques and that he placed his full trust in their advice.
- that his lawyers had never leaked anything to the press and everything that was presented to the press was done so with consulting him first.
- that he knew there would be people who rejected him, but that he wasn't interested in people like that.
- that he did, in fact, enjoy the company of American girls.
- that it should be made clear that though he enjoyed hanging out with American girls, it didn't fit his personality to murder a girl.
- that he had no secrets and that police could even listen in on the conversations he'd had with his parents.
- that he knew that he has gotten himself into trouble by lying, just as Deepak and Satish had.
- that he had gotten himself into trouble by manipulating the wiretaps on his phones.
- that he had only come up with the Holiday Inn story in the car with Deepak on the way to his house, and not before.
- that at that time Satish knew nothing of the concocted plan.
- that Natalee's parents didn't first come by to find out

where she was, but were aggressive right away and accusing and called him an asshole.

And so concluded Joran's off-the-record record.

Joran was the only one remaining in custody, but the police were still busy with a short list of characters, some familiar, some new. They still had the Kalpoe brothers under surveillance. The gardener, Carlos Ramos, had raised questions that needed attention.

On August 16, in a strange phone call to the Natalee tip line in Alabama, a woman identified herself as an ex-girlfriend of Deepak Kalpoe. The connection was bad and the caller was nervous.

She claimed that Deepak had sent her a text message, asking that she tell authorities that he was with her the night Natalee Holloway disappeared. She also claimed he told her "the gardener was lying."

She had only managed that much information when someone entered her room and she deliberately disconnected. She called back and disconnected several more times, but eventually provided the operator with a cell phone number. The operator passed the information to the FBI field office in Birmingham. But as was so often the case, this lead was another dead end.

On August 26, Deepak and Satish were rearrested, along with Joran's good friend, Freddy Zedan. Although there was wild speculation that there had finally been a break in the Holloway case, the allegations against the three turned out to be unrelated to Natalee's disappearance. The arrests were sparked by a complaint that the four young men had taken advantage of an underage girl sometime prior to Natalee's arrival on Aruba.

According to Freddy Zedan's lawyer, Diana Emerencia, her client was being accused of taking photos of a young girl in "tempting poses" and showing those photos to other people. Emerencia said Zedan was also suspected of having unspecified "physical contact" with the girl. Emerencia said that her client had denied all the charges, but had admitted he had been there when the photos were taken.

Joran's mother, Anita, also confirmed that her son and his friends were present at the time the photos were taken, but denied that the snapshots had sexual undertones.

"They are lovely pictures of a young girl in a bikini," she told reporters. She called the charges a desperate attempt to get the boys to talk, although there was nothing to talk about. She called the whole thing nonsense.

Joran's lawyer, Antonio Carlo, said that during the hearing prosecutors introduced two allegations of a "sexual nature" against his client. But he stopped short of specifying what those allegations were.

Prosecutors were asking that the Kalpoe brothers be detained for another eight days, and Joran be held for another thirty days.

But the prosecutor's pleas were to no avail. Under gloriously sunny skies, a smiling Joran van der Sloot emerged from the Korrectie Instituut Aruba on Saturday, September 3. A judge had ruled at a hearing two days earlier that there was insufficient evidence to hold the eighteen-year-old and ordered his release on the condition that he remain in Dutch territory. The judge also ordered the conditional release of Deepak and Satish Kalpoe, stipulating they remain in Aruba because of their visa requirements.

Despite the enormously extensive coverage devoted to the Holloway case, the release of the three young men barely made headlines in the United States. Hurricane Katrina had made landfall in New Orleans two days before the hearing, and the city was devastated; 80 percent of it was under water. Eighteen hundred people had lost their lives. News crews everywhere had been redeployed to a press staging area, as close to ground zero as safety concerns would allow. The largest natural disaster in the United States in a hundred years usurped any interest in the newfound freedom of three young suspects in Aruba, 1,763 miles away.

Beth Twitty was devastated by their release, however. She accused the Aruban government of cowardice. "They have chosen to hide underneath the cloak of Hurricane Katrina," she fumed. Beth believed that if the investigation had been handled properly from the beginning "the world would not have witnessed and experienced the pain and suffering my family and I have endured."

That Sunday, Beth boarded a plane for Alabama, but vowed to make frequent trips back to Aruba to continue her fight for justice for Natalee.

Anita shared Beth's sentiment that the investigation was botched from the beginning, but for different reasons. Her concern was that Joran and the entire Van der Sloot family had been scapegoats in a witchhunt.

"His life has been turned upside down," she told reporters on the day of his release. "We were the victims of slander based on rumor and gossip. It is easy to destroy the lives of people, especially through the press."

Anita van der Sloot believed police were looking in the wrong direction. Despite Joran having perjured himself, she knew in her heart that he was not capable of murder. She felt police should focus on Natalee's home life; perhaps she was unhappy and had maybe run away. Joran's mother also believed that investigators should widen their search to include Venezuela.

Nearly every inch of the island and its surrounding waters had been searched, but nothing had been discovered. As much as the police hated to admit it, Paulus's rumored advice to Joran and his friends, "no body, no case," had proved to be an accurate assessment of the situation.

Investigators were at a loss to explain how a seventeen-year-old could have murdered a young woman and disposed of her body during the brief window of time between 1:00 A.M., when Joran and Natalee left Carlos'n Charlie's, and 3:45 A.M., when Joran logged on to his home computer to send Deepak the thank-you message.

If Natalee had died on the beach that night, where was her body? If Joran had tossed it into the waters right off the beach, it would have surely washed back ashore. He would have needed access to a boat, and time to weigh the body down properly to ensure that it would not float up to the surface. But Joran didn't own a boat, which meant he would have needed an accomplice. How would he have been able to find an accomplice willing to participate in such an unsavory mission at that hour, who was loyal enough to keep the secret? Was his father involved? And if so, again, where was the body? Was it possible that the last time Joran saw Natalee she was alive, but asleep or passed out, and someone besides him was involved? If an accidental death had occurred, an alcohol overdose or a fatal fall, why did Joran not offer or seek help?

The answers to these questions were no closer to being resolved, but Joran was free to resume his life regardless.

TWENTY

Four days after Joran regained his freedom, he and his father flew to Holland to attempt a new start there. The teen had withdrawn his matriculation into the American university, Saint Leo's, because of his notoriety and travel restrictions imposed by the judge. The promising young "sporter" was now back in Arnhem, the city where he had been born.

His mother was comforted by the fact that he would be with family while he was so far from Aruba. The legal fees had broken the family financially so at least in Holland he had a safe place to live and access to a free education. He moved in with his mother's sister. His maternal grandmother lived only ten minutes away. He enrolled as a commuter student at the Hogeschool van Arnhem en Nijmegen, where he planned to study international business management.

By this time, his notoriety was international. Even in Holland, strangers pointed and gawked. On his first day of classes at the Hogeschool, Joran stood in front of his fellow classmates, introduced himself, and detailed his version of the events in Aruba. He was neither arrogant nor humble, but he had certainly made a bold impression.

The chance to reinvent himself in Holland was fleeting. Arnhem was near the Dutch town of Nijmegen, an ancient Roman stronghold four miles west of the German border. By number of casinos alone, Nijmegen was ranked number six out of ninety-one cities in the Netherlands with legalized gambling.

These world-class operations made Joran's Aruban haunts seem like bingo parlors. The nightlife outside the casinos was also pulsating with bars, cafés, and dance clubs, all featuring booze and legalized drugs.

Joran had barely begun his studies when he slipped into his old habits. He moved out of his aunt's house and shared an apartment with several other students, becoming lost in a fog of whiskey Cokes and marijuana smoke. While he was sleeping late into the afternoons, he was skipping classes and failing. Signs of depression were obscured by drinking. His waking hours were spent gambling and avoiding the press, who seemed unnervingly obsessed with him.

The obsession with news about him or, better, *from him,* was the perfect partner to his gambling addiction. News outlets paid him money for a story; money allowed him to gamble; gambling made him happy until he needed more money. And the media had deep pockets. He would tell 90 percent of his Natalee story exactly the same, but change up the last 10 percent to keep the public interested.

Joran was so shrewd he once bragged that he was offered $1 million to go on the record saying he had murdered the Alabama teen. As appealing as the offer was, he declined, saying prison life was not an experience he wanted to repeat.

Sometimes Joran's careful media scheming backfired. In February 2006, he traveled to New York to sit down for an interview with ABC's Chris Cuomo. Upon landing at John F. Kennedy International Airport, Joran was served with a civil lawsuit that had been filed in New York by Natalee's parents, Beth and Dave. Unbeknownst to Joran, the process server was sitting three rows in front of him during the flight, so was able to serve him with the complaint while the plane taxied to the gate.

Joran's father had arrived in New York earlier than his son and was waiting at the Lucerne Hotel when he was also served with legal papers. The lawsuit, filed in the Supreme Court of the State of New York, accused Joran of "malicious, wanton and willful disregard of the rights, safety and well-being of the plaintiffs and their daughter, Natalee Holloway."

The sixteen-page filing described Joran as "The Predator," and alleged that his parents, Anita and Paulus, had allowed him to spend his free time gambling, drinking, and "trawling for victims." The suit also accused Paulus of creating a "permissive environment" for Joran that "knowingly facilitated" his own son's "predatory" behavior toward Natalee.

Later that summer, the case was dismissed on jurisdictional grounds. But Joran had learned the danger of traveling to the U.S.

Still, he brazenly continued to reap the profits from his "side" of the Natalee story. In April 2007, the arrogant nineteen-year-old published his autobiography, *De Zaak Natalee Holloway* (*The Case of Natalee Holloway*). He promised to be "open and honest about everything that happened, for anyone who wants to read it." The book was published in Dutch, but never translated into English. The author and everything he represented had become so loathsome in Holland that even the name Joran, a once-popular name for a newborn boy, was shunned.

The book's publisher never released sales figures for the book. The ghostwriter, Zvezdana Vukojevic, described her experience working with Joran in an article titled "The Madness of Joran" published in 2010 in a Dutch magazine, *Review*. The assignment had turned out to be a nightmare.

Vukojevic first met the teen to discuss the project in 2006, shortly after he had enrolled in the Hogeschool. He was haughty and entitled. He referred to his girlfriend at the time as "a groupie," a joking reference to the perks of fame.

Success of the joint venture depended on Joran's accessibility. After the teen promised his ghostwriter that he would happily and readily comply, Vukojevic began drafting Joran's chronicles.

The writing sessions, however, were surreal. The meetings were on Joran's terms and he would not accept being inconvenienced. Vukojevic complained of hours spent standing at the apartment door while Joran was asleep inside. A roommate would eventually answer the knock and Vukojevic would enter a pigsty reeking of beer and marijuana.

Sometimes Joran met with her for an hour, claiming his plans for the evening prevented him from staying longer. Other times, he created excuses to cancel altogether: he had dropped the phone in the tub; he had fallen at the train station and may have a broken leg; he had no more minutes left on his phone card. Once, he canceled out of paranoia. "They're after me," he cried.

His paranoia was well founded. Peter de Vries, a Dutch investigative reporter, had become Joran's nemesis. The silver-haired De Vries and his television crew were relentless in their determination to see Joran behind bars.

Eventually, the book project was finished, with Vukojevic having toured Joran's mother's dining room in Aruba with its Natalee shrine, and having picked up Texas hold 'em tips from the self-described master of card games himself.

Joran's publishing career was already short-lived when legal problems took precedence. In 2007, Joran was arrested in Arnhem on an Aruban warrant, with prosecutors citing "new incriminating evidence" in connection with Natalee's disappearance. The Kalpoes were rearrested in Aruba the same day.

The new evidence came from computer and online chat records that had taken place between the three young men. Using technology that was not available to them in 2005, police uncovered a chat in which the three men had discussed "picking up American girls and what they planned to do with them."

Again, all three suspects, on advice of their counsel, refused to discuss the evidence. Ultimately, the judge hearing the case ruled that the recorded chat, while damaging, was not evidence enough to justify further detention and Joran, Deepak, and Satish were once again released.

Soon, Joran returned to the Netherlands and the casinos of Nijmegen. His father suggested a stint of missionary work in Africa, thinking such altruism would help his image as well as curb his sense of entitlement, but the idea was not pursued. Joran was cocky and confident after his latest legal victory. A chance encounter with a true self-styled "gangster" named Patrick Paul van der Eem was affirmation of his winning ways.

Patrick Paul van der Eem was a thirty-five-year-old native of Curaçao who had two drug convictions and carried himself like a brute from a *Dick Tracy* comic book. He looked like a rogue the mob would send to "have a talk" with a gambler who had welshed on a large bet. Van der Eem was muscular, stocky, and had a large scar that extended from the side of his mouth up through his left cheek. In criminal circles, the scar is called a "smiley," the mark of a snitch. He bragged that he had gotten his *boca grande* (big mouth) years earlier for talking too much, but didn't elaborate. He wore it like a badge of honor.

"Hey, *matón*," Van der Eem said, using the Papiamento word for "murderer," when he spotted Joran in a casino in Nijmegen in the fall of 2007.

Joran smiled. The guy was a ruffian *and* he spoke in Papiamento. Despite the derogatory reference, the former Papiamento pimp liked him immediately and they became quick friends.

Or, rather, they were two Dutch Caribbean compadres with similar interests, outcast gamblers in the Old World, speaking Papiamento on the side. Van der Eem later claimed he knew that he was going to befriend Joran the moment he saw him. He recognized him from his infamy. However, he befriended him for justice.

For seven months, Van der Eem and Van der Sloot spent hours together and built a trust. They partied, gambled, hung out, shared stories, and on occasion, they shared drugs. Van der Eem wanted Joran to trust him enough to confess what had happened to Natalee, motivated by no particular agenda of his own.

When the opportunity seemed right, he contacted Peter de Vries, the television reporter and Joran's bane. He had a proposition. He knew De Vries from his coverage of the Holloway case, and he offered himself as a double agent in the "confession" plot.

The Dutch reporter was thrilled to be in on the undercover scheme. Joran hanging himself with his own words would finally lead to justice for Natalee.

Together, he and Van der Eem rigged the gangster's Range Rover with an array of hidden cameras and microphones. On a night when Joran and his Papiamento pal were out cruising the town and sharing a joint, the plan was activated and the tapes and cameras started to record.

Joran told his scar-faced friend what many believe to be his honest confession of what had happened the night Natalee disappeared. Joran said that he and Natalee had been having sex on the beach when Natalee suddenly suffered a seizure. She was unconscious and when she didn't come around, he panicked, Joran said.

His attempts to revive Natalee failed. "I tried to shake her, I was shaking the bitch. I was like 'What is wrong with you, man?' I almost wanted to cry," Joran told Van der Eem. "Why does this shit have to happen to me?"

Joran claimed that Natalee died in his arms. Instead of calling for help, however, Joran said he found a pay phone on the beach and summoned a friend with a boat. Natalee's body, he claimed, had been dumped at sea.

"How do you know she was dead, Joran?"

Joran shrugged his shoulders, and said he just knew. "Patrick, I had absolutely no bad feelings about it. I have not lost one night of sleep over it.

"I think that I am incredibly lucky that she has never

been found because if she had been found I would be in deep shit."

Van der Eem gave the recordings to Peter de Vries and on February 3, 2008, De Vries aired them to more than seven million viewers, the highest-rated news broadcast in Dutch television history. The footage was stunning, Joran completely unaware he was being recorded, sitting in the passenger seat comfortably toking a joint. His confession was chilling, methodical, emotionless, and shockingly succinct.

De Vries's broadcast was recognized for its brilliance with the International Emmy Award for Best Current Affairs Program. (In September 2008, Natalee's mother joined De Vries in Manhattan to attend the awards ceremony, where he dedicated the Emmy to the memory of Natalee Holloway.)

Prosecutors in Aruba added the secretly recorded confession to their growing case against Joran van der Sloot. Unfortunately, however disturbing, the tape in and of itself was not enough to warrant another arrest. It was not a sworn confession, it might not be admissible in a court proceeding, and none of the claims that Joran had specified could be verified.

Police couldn't confirm the call Joran had supposedly made from a pay phone or the boat driver that he claimed to have found on short notice in the middle of the night. However, the tape provoked outrage against Joran in Holland and he no longer considered his homeland to be a safe harbor.

He had already quit the university because of his poor grades. With no reason to stay, he briefly checked himself into a psychiatric hospital before fleeing to Thailand.

TWENTY-ONE

Rangsit University, where Joran again found himself studying international business, is located in Muang Ake, a small suburb about twenty miles north of Bangkok.

Rangsit was a college town, with narrow, congested streets filled equally with mopeds and cars. Lush, tropical vegetation surrounded beautiful town houses painted in pastel shades of pink, yellow, and white. Traditional Buddhist temples were flanked by modern amenities; 7-Eleven stores seemed anchored on every block. The air was hot; the humidity was relieved by brief, welcome sun showers.

The campus of Rangsit University sprawled through town much in the style of a large, American university. Two bustling open-air markets catered to townspeople and students alike. During the day, vendors sold trinkets, clothing, colorful Thai silks, and aromatic treats from pushcarts and small collapsible stands. At night, when the heat had subsided, students shopped for strings of jasmine flowers and inexpensive edibles—sweet corn, grilled seafood, and green papaya salad.

Joran's parents had arranged his enrollment at Rangsit University, a private institution accredited in 1990 that has a reciprocal exchange program with a Dutch university. The situation seemed ideal. Inside the very large student body of 25,000, he would have anonymity; in the subcommunity of Dutch students and compatriots, he would have familiarity.

More than three years after Natalee Holloway's disappearance in Aruba, Joran still generated enormous ratings for American true-crime programs. His notoriety was so desirable to American news programs that he always had a market. Even though he had just been burned by Peter de Vries and his double-crossing friend, Patrick van der Eem, if he needed money, marketing a story was always an option.

When he contacted Fox's Greta Van Susteren in the summer of 2008, he told the cable TV host that he had stunning details, never before revealed.

With titillating clues, he claimed that he had sold poor Natalee into sexual slavery. He had traded her to a man he had met in a casino on Aruba's Palm Beach strip for $10,000. Joran insisted he hadn't hurt the blond beauty, but had merely delivered her to a waiting cigarette boat destined for Venezuela, presumably to work in a brothel.

He claimed to have the paperwork in his possession that would prove it. He had wire transfer records documenting that the slave trader had paid him an additional $10,000 once the case exploded in the news, just to keep him quiet.

Joran said he would include a bonus, a "licensed" tape recording of conversations between his father and him on Skype. He said the calls contained evidence that the elder Van der Sloot knew about Natalee's fate and had paid off two Aruban police officers to cooperate.

Joran's story was dubious, but Greta dispatched field producers Steph Watts and Cory Howard to Thailand to gauge its credibility nonetheless.

After collecting their luggage and cameras at the airport, the two checked into the Mandarin Oriental, a five-star hotel on the banks of the Chao Phraya River. They had flown to this city of more than nine million with one goal in mind—to investigate Joran's pitch. If it looked promising, they had instructions to close the deal for an "exclusive" interview with Van Susteren.

The producers' initial contact with Joran was by e-mail. They had offered to meet the Dutchman in Rangsit, but Joran had not wanted to disclose his address. Instead, he told Steph he would call him at the Mandarin when he arrived in Bangkok.

Steph, a forty-year-old Canadian with silvery-blond hair and piercing blue eyes, had been working as a field producer for Greta Van Susteren's *On the Record* since 2006. This was not his first assignment on the Natalee Holloway case. He had covered the story extensively for the *Nancy Grace* show on CNN's Headline News when it first broke in June 2005. Over the years, he had come to know both Beth Twitty and Dave Holloway personally. But this would be his first time meeting Joran.

Van Susteren, on the other hand, had developed a respectful relationship with Joran since his release from Aruba's KIA prison in September 2005. She had been the first to sit down with Beth Twitty and Joran's parents in Aruba in June 2005, and for a time had broadcast her show from the Caribbean island. In the spring of 2006, she had traveled back to Aruba to conduct a lengthy one-on-one interview with Joran that she touted as "unedited," meaning no content had been taken out. Greta had been tough on Joran, but she was always fair.

Once in Bangkok, Steph was unable to reach Joran and grew worried. After numerous e-mails, he got a response. Still, Joran was cagey and evasive before finally agreeing to meet.

The first conversation between Joran and Steph took place in the Mandarin's luxurious lobby amid breathtaking arrangements of exotic flowers. Steph had been summoned to the lobby by Joran in order to pay his irritated cabdriver. Joran was unable to pay the man himself, he said, because he was broke. That Joran was so desperate for money made Steph uneasy.

Joran was not the character Steph had expected. He was pudgy and unshaven, and was dressed like a tourist in shorts and a baseball cap. In spite of his grungy appearance, Joran was tall, handsome, and charming. His English, coated in a thick Dutch accent, was almost fluent.

Originally, Joran told Steph that he wanted $25,000 for just the documents supporting his story about selling Natalee as a sex slave. He said the price tag was justified because he himself was the provenance of the material. Greta, however, wanted to create interest in the story with an actual interview with Joran, a proposition he heartily resisted. Finally, after backing out several times, he agreed to include an interview. He grew agitated when he learned that Steph had come to Bangkok without any money and he was going to have to wait for a wire transfer from the States in order to provide Joran with $10,000, the first installment of his $25,000 "licensing" fee. Steph explained that $5,000 was the maximum amount allowable per day via wire transfer, and after some discussion, the two set off in a rickshaw, known locally as a *tuk-tuk,* for the Western Union office closest to the Mandarin Hotel to collect it.

Joran paced outside while Steph went inside to sign for the funds. He puffed on a cheap, locally made cigarette, rather than his preferred Marlboro Reds.

When Steph emerged, the two walked back to the hotel. Safely in Steph's room, Joran sat on the edge of the queen-size bed and counted the money bill by bill. When he was satisfied, he stuffed it into his front pocket and made his exit.

Steph and Greta's arrangement of paying Joran in installments assured he would be back. Steph had been in the news business for nearly twenty years. He had begun his career as a print reporter with the *Village Voice* and later worked for *Brill's Content.* In July 1999, he made the switch to TV journalism when he joined Court TV, working as a producer on their daytime trial coverage. He thoroughly enjoyed covering the crime beat. But he had reservations about the Van der Sloot story he was now weighing. The senior producer abominated the idea of paying Joran—a person whom he believed was a killer—to tell more lies.

The following day, Steph and Joran returned to the Western Union office to retrieve the second $5,000 of Joran's $25,000 "licensing" fee. This initial $10,000 was to seal the deal.

Steph and his assistant producer left Thailand with the understanding that they would be returning in two weeks to tape Joran's interview with Greta.

When Steph returned to Thailand that July, he was carrying two TV cameras and cash: some of it Joran's remaining "licensing" fee and $3,000 in expense money. Making contact with Joran again proved difficult, and when he finally showed up at the hotel, he again called Steph down to the lobby to pay for his taxi ride.

Greta would not be arriving in Bangkok for another several days, which meant that Steph needed to keep Joran close until the interview took place. The plan was for Joran to use an additional hotel room reserved exclusively for him. Settling Joran in his room was the next challenge. The Mandarin Oriental was a classy five-star compound, with 358 rooms, thirty-five suites, butler service, nine bars and restaurants, tennis and squash courts, two outdoor pools, and one of the best spas in the world. Rooms were pricey, $500 a night, but travelers were rewarded with great comforts and high security.

Joran wanted to use his accommodation, but he did not want to be a guest registering for the room. The receptionist explained that although Steph could be the responsible party for the bill, Joran still had to register, and that included providing identification, a passport. When the receptionist would not make an exception, Joran reluctantly complied.

He always spoke courteously, rarely using profanity. Whenever women were around, he became gregarious and flirtatious. He liked blondes, he said, but enjoyed checking out girls of all types.

Steph was familiar with the Dutchman's routine after only a couple of days. Joran liked sleeping late, getting out of bed in the early afternoon; he smoked incessantly; he never had money. Not only was he broke, but he seemed to be in debt, perhaps from a gambling or drug obligation.

Joran's behavior caused Steph great concern. Not only was he financially responsible, but he was Joran's host and, in a way, his representative. Joran was lighting up joints in his hotel room in a country with some of the harshest drug laws in the world. As an example, a drug trafficking conviction in Thailand can carry the death penalty. Joran was dismissive, even slightly amused by the producer's fear of being raided by police and hauled off to prison. However, he stopped trying to convince Steph to join him for a smoke.

Joran had other notable habits. He thoroughly enjoyed room service. He ordered from the room menu regularly, but he was courteous about his indulgence and always asked Steph's permission first.

The Dutchman always wore his baseball cap in public. He never left the hotel without it and liked that it protected him from inquiring glances. He often looked over his shoulder and tipped his cap low over his eyes toward his nose, as though he didn't want to be recognized. No one on the streets of Bangkok seemed to be paying him any attention, however, except perhaps to marvel at his exceptional height.

Joran also tended to make his many cell phone calls by first stepping out of earshot. He seemed eagerly involved in some sort of business transaction. These phone calls seemed to make him more anxious than usual.

Part of Steph's duties while in Bangkok was to keep Joran entertained until Greta arrived. Steph knew Joran liked to drink and party, but had no other babysitting activities planned. Luckily Joran had ideas of his own.

The outcast from Holland wanted to show Steph around Bangkok, his new city. Although the heat was oppressive, the two set out on a rickshaw tour.

They sat in the back of the cart while their guide pedaled. Joran knowledgeably pointed out landmarks, and even spoke a little Thai. He was funny, interesting, and engaging. Outside the hotel, he seemed worldly and street smart. He was also manipulative, impatient, and eager to be paid.

Thailand was famous for its hand-tailored suits, and Steph found a well-regarded shop to custom-order one for himself. The Canadian and Dutchman went together for the final fitting. Joran seemed genuinely piqued with excitement as he suggested minor alterations for the seamstress, saying that for his friend he wanted only the best. Steph had to constantly remind himself this was a business arrangement and not a friendship in the usual sense.

One evening, a party of three—Steph, Joran, and an American friend of Joran's—went for cocktails and sushi at the world's highest bar, Distil, in downtown Bangkok. Joran had recommended the outing. The upscale whiskey bar was on the rooftop of the city's second-tallest building, sixty-four floors high, and was frequented by trendsetters and celebrities. Steph nursed a glass of wine while Joran consumed rounds of whiskey and cola.

Joran's indulgence seemed to relax him, and he slowly confided his current plight. He had ended up in Thailand by chance, he said. He had been living in the Netherlands when he decided he wanted to go to Australia for a couple of years and work as a bartender. After the sting orchestrated by Peter de Vries and the scar-faced gangster Patrick van der Eem, he thought Australia would be a place where he would be able to live in anonymity and escape the ostracism his notoriety had created.

His flight to Sydney required a layover in Hong Kong. Authorities there connected him to the Holloway case, flagged him, and announced that Australia was not allowing him entry. He had to decide quickly where to go. He had a friend in Thailand and on a whim chose to go there.

He hoped to travel to Cambodia, where he also had a friend. He was thinking about enrolling in an online business school program.

Steph drew the conclusion that Joran was stuck in a catch-22. Although he seemed to want to shake the stigma of his past, he needed that very stigma to finance his future. Selling variations of his story was his only means of support.

While waiting for Greta Van Susteren's arrival in Bangkok, Steph had been providing Joran with small down payments. But one afternoon, the money Joran had been promised didn't arrive. Joran became edgy, antsy, and demanding. "You have to get the money," he commanded angrily. "Take it out of your personal account!"

Steph persuaded him that the money would be available the next day. As far as his personal account, he simply did not have the funds, and even if he did, he would never fund him with what he viewed as blood money. Joran stormed around in anger. He desperately tried to resolve the issue with impractical solutions, and finally he had no choice but to wait.

Three days later, Greta made her entrance. Steph spent that morning preparing the hotel suite assigned to them for the interview. He set up the two cameras he had brought from New York. He arranged the dark teak furnishings to his liking.

Joran arrived at the suite dressed in a collared shirt and khaki slacks, but without his cap. He had not shaved off a thin scruffy beard. He reluctantly took a seat in a chair across from Greta, his face illuminated by one of the room's table lamps. The pale yellow walls of the expansive suite served as the backdrop.

Joran began the interview by saying that he was going to provide Greta with answers about what had happened to Natalee. He claimed to have three audiotapes, recordings of long-distance phone calls with his father.

But, Joran said, the Natalee portion of his story had to be prefaced with an important related event. Several months before meeting Natalee, he had met a stranger in a casino in Aruba. He had expressed interest in young blond females, and said he would pay Joran $10,000 if he could procure one for him. He then gave him a card with his phone number.

Joran said he contacted the trader the night he met Natalee. "I told him I have a girl with me, and he's, like, okay, come to the Marriott Hotel," Joran told Greta.

Joran said that it had not been his intention to sell Natalee that evening when they first met, although it had been in the back of his mind.

When Greta asked about Deepak and Satish's role, Joran declined to answer. But he eventually told Greta that both men had known of the plan and were paid a cut of the money he had received.

Joran explained that he had called the man while in Deepak's car with Natalee that night, and the two had arranged a meeting. He said he spoke in Dutch so that Natalee wouldn't be able to understand. He said they drove around for nearly an hour before going to the rendezvous site north of the Marriott that night. While he waited, he said he made out with Natalee. "But nothing more."

Joran told Van Susteren that when he arrived, he didn't see anyone at the beach and wondered if the meeting would even happen. "Then I saw a guy, and he came and he just handed me a bag, grabbed the girl by the arm and he went to the boat that he had in the water."

"What did Natalee say?"

"She said nothing, not until she was on the boat," Joran told the Fox News host. "And then she was, like, 'Hey,' you know, 'What's going on? You're not coming with me' . . . She wasn't panicking or anything . . . I think she was pretty drunk."

Joran claimed that the reason Natalee climbed aboard the boat willingly with a complete stranger was because he had reassured her that they were going on a boat ride together. "That's my story, to go to the beach, that we were going to go on a boat," Joran said.

Joran said the bag given to him by the boat driver contained money. While he had been promised $10,000 in cash, Joran lamented that several hundred dollars were missing. He assumed the boat driver had taken a little out for himself.

Next, Joran produced the three promised audiotapes. He said they would provide the evidence that would conclusively implicate his father in the cover-up of Natalee's disappearance.

Joran told Greta he had confessed to three people about selling Natalee to a sex trader: his father, his lawyer, and one of his teachers at the International School of Aruba.

When Greta did not ease up in her questioning, Joran grew contentious.

"You want her alive, right?" Greta probed.

"That would be the best thing in the world," Joran replied. "You're the only one who can help."

"If I had a million dollars, I would look into Natalee's disappearance myself," Joran snapped. With a scoff, he announced he was not going to implicate his father after all. Nor was he going to produce evidence against the two police officers/co-conspirators.

"Why won't you tell us the truth?" Greta pressured.

"Because the truth hurts," Joran growled and ripped the microphone from his collar, threatening to end the interview immediately. The meltdown occurred in the session's first twenty minutes.

Steph, who had been operating both cameras, turned them off to pursue Joran. He found him in the second room of the suite and coaxed him back with the deliverance of a stiff drink.

The interview resumed, beginning with Joran's implications of his father and the two Aruban authorities. After he confessed to his father—that Natalee had been abducted in a boat by his casino contact—his father was compelled to pay $50,000 to two savvy policemen who knew of the event. Joran said he and his father discussed the shakedown soon to be exposed in the secret recordings about to be placed in Greta's care. The recordings would also show Joran's desire to confess to authorities. However, his father would be heard advising him against such a move.

At the end of the interview, Joran took his cash payment and disappeared from the suite, bidding them farewell. Greta and Steph were left with three audiotapes and an envelope. The envelope was promised to contain irrefutable proof that a wire transfer had occurred between the sex trader and Joran for $10,000. This $10,000 was hush money, above and beyond the $10,000 cash he had received for handing over Natalee in the first place.

As Greta and her producer were waiting at Bangkok's Suvarnabhumi Airport to return to the United States, Greta received a text message from the Dutch exile. "Everything I told you was a lie," he wrote. "I did it just for the money. I'm sorry."

Greta turned to Steph to ask him what he thought.

"I think in the text Joran is telling the truth," he answered.

Back in New York, Greta had the materials authenticated. Although a wire transaction for $10,000 had indeed taken place, the document Joran provided left unclear who had sent the money and under what circumstances. Media outlets had admittedly wired Joran $10,000 on various occasions to secure "licensed" interviews and this was potentially one of those transfers.

As for the audiotapes, the experts hired by Fox News were divided. One thought they were authentic, while another believed without a doubt that they were doctored. Either way, fake or real, truth or lies, Joran had been willing to sell out his own father for a fistful of cash.

Fox News dispatched Steph and a legal analyst, Jim Hammer, to Aruba to see if they would be able to get a reaction from Paulus van der Sloot regarding Joran's latest revelations. Hammer was the former head of the homicide unit of the San Francisco district attorney's office and had joined the cable news network in 2005.

In Thailand, Joran had confided to Steph that he was no longer in contact with his father, but he had not elaborated. But that did not preclude a reaction in Aruba from Paulus.

Armed with a transcript of the audiotapes, the two men staked out Paulus's law office in Oranjestad. The elder Van der Sloot had abandoned his dream of becoming a judge after his son's clash with the law and had gone into private practice instead, teaming with Joran's criminal attorney, Antonio Carlo. His office was located in a low-slung, yellow-and-blue cement structure with a red tile roof in downtown Oranjestad.

Jim Hammer managed to catch Paulus's attention as he tried to enter his law office. The newsman barked that Joran had been located in Thailand, and did Paulus have a reaction to his son's latest claims.

Steph operated the camera that captured Paulus's face dropping in the unexpected confrontation. He looked queasy as he ducked into his building. But Hammer was able to thrust a transcript of Greta's interview into his hand.

In spite of Joran's text message that everything he had confessed in his Fox exclusive was a lie, the interview was broadcast four months later anyway. Greta Van Susteren began the piece with a disclaimer and a warning. She enticed viewers with the pledge of a "surprise ending." As promised, the surprise was revealed during the show's wrap up. Joran had sent her a text that everything previously taped and then aired moments ago had all been lies.

Joran's attorney during his civil case in New York in 2006, Joe Tacopina, was critical of the interview and the tactics and the negotiations to procure it in his own interview with Greta.

"You paid him for a tape that he made and wound up getting an hour interview with him," Joe said on air. "And so be it, Greta. Great TV, great ratings."

"Do you have a problem with that?" Greta asked.

"Yes, I do have a problem with it, Greta, because if you offered Joran $10,000 tomorrow and asked him to tell you a fifth story, he would do it. Clearly, he's a sick kid," Tacopina remarked.

He went on to shore up Joran's innocence in Natalee's disappearance. "But I still tell you, I stand by the notion that the investigation into the disappearance of Natalee Holloway has not led to Joran. That's the bottom line. No one expects anyone to believe anything this kid has to say anymore. Quite frankly, he's on the verge of sociopath. . . ."

Not long after Joran's meeting with Greta Van Susteren in July, Peter de Vries, Joran's nemesis, staged another sting captured by hidden cameras.

This time, the video recordings show Joran acting as a recruiter in a sex-trafficking operation. The setting is a guest room in the Landmark Hotel, a five-star high-rise lodging located on Sukhumvit Road in Bangkok.

Casually dressed in a short-sleeved black T-shirt and jeans, Joran promises two young exotic dancers that he can help arrange jobs for them as dancers in the Netherlands. Joran acts crudely. He makes sexual gestures, sometimes gyrating his hips in imitation of a pole dancer. He tells the two Thai women that they can make $15,000 in a ten-hour day in the Netherlands. He pretends to be envious, saying he would happily shake his ass for that amount. Joran uses an alias, "Murphy Jenkins," with the women. He presents them with official-looking business cards imprinted with his phony name and line of business.

In the recording, Joran accepts 1,000 euros, about U.S.$1,300, from the women, promising the money is a down payment for their travel documents. The video ends with vague plans for another meeting soon.

Somehow, Joran learned that the "deal" had been staged by De Vries, and that the Thai women had really been exotic dancer impersonators for the sting. How the recruiting mission may have progressed could only be speculation. Nevertheless, the video was aired on Dutch TV in 2008.

Unlike De Vries's Emmy award–winning documentation of Joran's confession to Van der Eem, this video was coolly received and promptly criticized. Not only was De Vries admonished for his tactics in getting the story; but he was criticized for his "tabloidism," his story airing only two months after Joran's bogus confession to Van Susteren.

The Thai prostitution sting story did not get much play in the mainstream media. But the repercussions in the Rangsit community were substantial. Parents were concerned for the safety of their daughters, replaying their image of the Dutch monster trawling for sex slaves. Joran's fellow students and compatriots were disgusted by his behavior, particularly his cashing in on the Holloways' tragedy.

Parents and students mounted protests and in May 2009,

Joran was officially asked to leave the university. His 1.31 GPA at the time certainly didn't help his case.

Anita van der Sloot must have been devastated when she learned of her son's expulsion. She and her husband had hoped Joran would be able to start on a successful path in Thailand, after his failure in Holland. They blamed De Vries and his obsession with Joran for the latest defeat.

Despite the animosity, Joran was unwilling to abandon Rangsit and Thailand. He used money from his brokered interviews to start a business, opening a coffee shop across the street from the university's athletic center. He named the restaurant the SawadeeCup, *sawadee* being a greeting in Thailand similar to "aloha" in Hawaii.

The storefront was modern and sleek with floor-to-ceiling windows. Outside, several tables occupied the brick sidewalk. Inside, the walls were painted a shiny white and accented with a bold orange stripe in the center. Joran had installed faux hardwood floors, which were impressively polished to a glass-like shine. Black metal chairs, tables and barstools made up the furniture in the front restaurant area. In the rear, a more comfortable lounge area featured a black leather couch with a matching swivel chair and a giant flat-screen TV. A desktop computer had been wired to an elaborate sound system to provide the acoustics. Tall CD racks helped separate the two areas, although the menu of sandwiches, pizza, fruit smoothies, ice cream, coffee drinks, and other light snacks could be enjoyed on either side.

Joran maintained a YouTube page featuring the restaurant. He used the site to upload and share videos as well as market his skills. On the homepage, after introducing himself as a poker player and entrepreneur, he offered poker lessons and an e-mail address for potential students.

"I like to think big and outside the box," he claimed, adding that he was extremely left wing on the political spectrum.

His Web visitors learned that his musical tastes included rap, hip hop and reggaeton, mentioning Lil Wayne, Drake, and Young Money Crew. They also discovered that if he had to choose an animal that described him, it would be a snake. He aspired to be a lion—"I want to be a lion and one day I will be a lion," he predicted. But for the time being, he was a snake.

Joran listed his passions as music, soccer, tennis, poker, nightlife, traveling, movies, and television. His favorite films were *Pulp Fiction* and *City of Ghosts. Californication, Entourage, Breaking Bad, CSI,* and *Law and Order* were his favorite television shows. He admitted that reading was not a passion, but listed *Ace on the River: An Advanced Poker Guide,* by Barry Greenstein, as his favorite book.

He took a moment to reflect on his life's journey. "I think there is a lesson to be learned in every path you decide to take in your life," he wrote. "But one thing I am sure of is that you need to stand up for what you believe in and what you want to do and you will be successful in your life."

By August, Joran was broke. Desperate for money, he decided to sit down with Jaap Amesz, the host of a Dutch reality television show, for an interview. Amesz was known for acting outrageously in public. His antics as a contestant on the popular Dutch TV show *The Golden Cage* had launched his career. In one scene on that show, the grossly overweight showboater allowed himself to be filmed naked and rolling in his own vomit. He went on to create his own reality hit, *Terror Jaap,* a Jerry Springer knockoff filled with tasteless shock-value acts featuring anyone from porn stars to anorexics.

In exchange for an interview, Jaap agreed to bail Joran out of his latest financial bind. Joran's parents had stopped responding to his begging and he had no money. Although the restaurant initially paid for itself, Joran spent any profits recklessly.

Joran made a promise to Jaap, who was dressed in his signature baggy black suit, white collared shirt, and black fedora: Jaap would be receiving the complete story of what happened to Natalee Holloway, the absolute truth.

Joran arrived for the interview sporting a new scraggly beard and mustache. He wore a tidy red-striped polo shirt and nice jeans. His story was graphic: He and Natalee had gone to his friend's house, she snorted cocaine, and then under the influence fell off the balcony to her death. After the unfortunate accident, he dumped her body in a swamp.

To prove he was telling the truth, Joran agreed to take a polygraph test. He was arrogant enough to believe that he would pass. The test and its results were also perfect props for *Terror Jaap*.

Joran appeared confident when he sat down across the table from Jaap to hear the results. He was dapper, dressed in a black-and-white V-neck sweater and black jeans. He listened intently to the results as the camera rolled. He was relaxed when results in his favor were revealed, namely that Natalee had fallen to her death and that his parents, Paulus and Anita van der Sloot, had played no role in her disappearance or subsequent cover-up.

However, he became infuriated at unfavorable findings. His responses to questions about the disposal site, whether or not Natalee's body had been moved, and about his sneaker lost in the swamp, all showed signs of deception.

The TV host announced that Joran had failed the polygraph and Joran's anger exploded. Dramatically, he sprang from his chair and hurled a glass of water he had been given to the floor, then stormed out of the studio.

In the fall of 2009, Joran met a beautiful blonde from southern California. The young woman was in her early twenties, slender and attractive, with long, silky hair and delicate features. Like Natalee Holloway, she looked like an all-American girl.

Joran's new love interest was a graduate of a university in California and had come to Thailand to teach. Her course was a service-learning class combining classroom study and volunteer work. She was also an adviser to foreign students studying abroad.

After a short time together, Joran asked the young woman to move into his three-bedroom house with him. He seemed genuinely happy and in a solid relationship. He spoke fondly of his new girlfriend in conversations with his parents in phone calls over Skype. They rode motorbikes around town, took excursions to the white, sandy beaches of Thailand, and spent evenings at the bars and clubs of Bangkok, only forty-five minutes by cab from Rangsit.

But Joran's gambling addiction worsened. Not only was he frequenting the casinos of Bangkok, he was gambling online with multiple accounts. Big wins were followed up by bigger losses, and Joran was in debt. He was constantly soliciting money from family and friends, concocting outlandish stories to explain his financial difficulty.

Sometimes, he was successful. When his parents had finally stopped funding him, he went to others on his A list before going to his B and C lists if necessary, desperately trawling for cash.

Eventually, Joran's girlfriend grew weary of his lies and left him. By February 2010, he was alone and penniless, his coffee shop now failing miserably. Customers were complaining about the inconsistent hours and the lack of staples such as milk for coffee or bread for sandwiches.

He was no longer able to pay the $1,000 monthly rent on his apartment, and he was evicted. After his eviction, his landlady described his tenancy to a reporter from *People* magazine. She said he was boisterous, he frequently had late-night gatherings with too much booze and marijuana, and he had caused extensive damage to her property. Ultimately, an uncle in the Netherlands paid the cost for her repairs.

With no place to live, Joran moved into his coffee shop, still open but struggling.

That February, he received devastating news from Aruba. His father had died. Paulus had gone into cardiac arrest while playing tennis at Aruba's Tierra del Sol Resort on Palm Beach. He was in the middle of a match when he collapsed on the court. Efforts to resuscitate the fifty-seven-year-old Van der Sloot were futile, and doctors pronounced him dead upon his arrival at the hospital.

Anita was overwhelmed and distraught. She managed to make arrangements to fly Paulus back to Arnhem, where he was cremated. Her three sons flew to Holland to be together and say good-bye to their father. He was remembered in a private memorial service protected from the media glare.

Paulus had died nearly penniless. Joran's legal fees had drained the family's bank account, his suspected involvement in the Holloway case had ravaged Paulus's legal career, and his ruinous lifestyle had created so much stress and strain that Joran may have contributed to his father's demise.

Joran's younger brothers, Valentjin and Sebastian, had already distanced themselves from their notorious brother. They had witnessed their parents' suffering on his behalf. They had watched his repeated, shameless sales of his story. They had seen him squander opportunities, always as the victim, and they disapproved.

In Arnhem for the memorial, Joran appeared to be inconsolable. His mother told a Dutch newspaper that he had cried nonstop for two days, and that he took the blame for his father's sudden death. She described how he had even cried over the coffin.

" 'It's my fault, Dad,' " Anita said Joran had whined, " 'I gave you the heart attack.' "

After his father's death, Joran decided not to return to Thailand. He announced he was moving back to Aruba to be with his mother. He had always been close to her, sometimes parasitically. He telephoned her from all over the world to keep her from worrying, and in a calculated aside, would then ask her to bail him out of a mess.

Anita provided spiritual bailouts as well as financial ones. She was not a practicing Buddhist; however, she had adopted a Zen philosophy of life.

When Joran needed help, she offered uplifting messages about the power of positive thinking. She often suggested that Joran volunteer for those less fortunate to gain perspective about misery.

Although she thought Joran was spiritually wanting, she also strongly believed he was mentally ill and needed treatment. She suspected he suffered from bipolar disorder. She and her late husband had been aware of Joran's gambling addiction, and knew that addiction and depression were frequent dual-diagnosis partners.

She could not commit Joran for treatment without his consent because he was an adult. He needed to take responsibility for his behavior.

Years of rescuing Joran had taken a toll on the family's finances. The Van der Sloots had never been wealthy. But between legal fees and enabling Joran's lifestyle, their full-time jobs were barely adequate. Their two younger children were now attending American universities and the Van der Sloots struggled to pay their household bills. Without Paulus's salary, Anita had to take care of herself.

Joran made arrangements to sell the SawadeeCup for $12,000 and he returned to Aruba and moved back to his apartment behind the main house. To Anita, he seemed extremely depressed.

"He no longer laughs," she told a Dutch reporter. "He even stopped playing poker." Two months into his return, Anita thought he was improving after he managed to paint the family's fence.

But Anita continued to worry. She had researched a mental health facility in the Netherlands and begged Joran to commit himself there. Much to her surprise, he agreed.

While Anita was making arrangements for her son's in-patient treatment, Joran was making a deal of his own. On March 29, 2010, Joran began exchanging e-mails with a New York defense attorney, John Q. Kelly. He had represented Natalee's parents, Beth and Dave, in the wrongful death suit they had filed against Joran in New York in 2006.

Kelly was a former prosecutor who earned a reputation as a star litigator. He had represented the estates of Nicole Brown Simpson, heiress Anne Scripps Douglas, and Kathleen Savio, the third wife of the infamous Drew Peterson, ex–police officer and convicted wife killer.

Although Kelly's civil filing on behalf of the Holloways had been dismissed, he had remained an active spokesperson for the family. Over the years, he had appeared on cable news shows to weigh in on Joran's various "admissions."

Now, he found himself on the receiving end of one of Joran's propositions. According to an FBI indictment filed in Birmingham, Alabama, Joran initiated the e-mail exchange, and during a series of correspondences, offered to share the circumstances of Natalee's death, identify those involved, and show the lawyer her burial site. In exchange, he wanted Beth, now divorced from Jug Twitty, to pay him $250,000.

Joran made it clear that he would only share the information if Beth paid the full sum.

In subsequent e-mails, Joran agreed to an initial payment of $25,000 to show Kelly where Natalee's body had been buried. Upon recovery and confirmation of the remains, Joran would receive the remaining $225,000.

Joran e-mailed the lawyer bank information for an account he held in the Netherlands. He then asked that Kelly draw up a contract between Beth Twitty and him, outlining the terms of the agreement.

On April 15, Beth wired $100 to Joran's account at the SNS Bank in the Netherlands to establish its functionality. She then wired $10,000 from her bank in Birmingham to her lawyer's account in New York for Joran's down payment. The remaining $15,000 was going to be wired to the Netherlands.

On May 10, John Kelly flew to Aruba to meet with Van der Sloot. The meeting took place in Kelly's hotel room. He gave Joran $10,000 in cash, and the signed contract from Beth. Joran and Kelly each signed two copies, documenting the events in photographs.

Next, Joran waited while Kelly phoned Beth Twitty in Alabama. He told her all was going according to plan and to now wire the $15,000 to Joran's account in the Netherlands. Once Joran confirmed that the transfer was complete, he and Kelly exited the hotel and climbed into the lawyer's rented car.

Joran directed Kelly to a single-story house he claimed had been under construction in May 2005 within five miles of the Marriott. He insisted the body would be found within the home's foundation.

Kelly pulled out his camera, and took a few photos of the house. He waited while Joran began his explanation: Joran started by claiming he had taken Natalee to the beach and that he had thrown her down on the ground when she tried to stop him from leaving. When she fell, she hit her head on a rock and died. He hid her body and returned home where he told his father what had happened. Joran claimed that Paulus accompanied him back to the location that night, but said he went back to the car while his father further concealed the remains. A few days later, Joran said that his father buried Natalee under the house. He said he did not actually see his father inter the young woman's remains, but insisted that Paulus showed him the site later.

The unfolding of the extortion plot was an incredible coup, however untrue Joran's narrative. Kelly had managed to capture the admission and the exchange of money on tape. He had contacted the FBI shortly after Joran's first demands, and the agency had agreed to monitor the event. Aruban authorities were alerted and aware of the sting. The hotel room and rental car had been wired for surveillance. The mission was a complete success.

A review of the permit for the house that Joran had selected as the burial spot revealed there had been no foundation or structure at the location at the time of Natalee's disappearance. Although a building permit had been requested for the parcel on May 26, 2005, and an inspection had been conducted on June 15, the permit was not issued until October 18, 2005, more than four months after Natalee vanished.

Furthermore, an interview with the contractor who had built the residence confirmed that the home was not under construction at that time. Aerial photographs of the parcel taken on May 29 and June 5, as part of the search for Natalee Holloway, showed no construction.

Although Beth Twitty had come no closer to finding out what had happened to her daughter, she had participated in a sting operation that she hoped would lead to federal charges of extortion and wire fraud against the man she was sure was responsible for her daughter's death. Kelly flew back to the United States with enough evidence for an indictment. Meanwhile, Joran now had $10,000 in cash and $15,000 in his bank account at his disposal.

Fox News producer Steph Watts had cautioned the Twitty-Kelly team about dealing with the cad, when he learned from them what Joran had proposed. Watts had warned them not to give Joran any real money. Coincidentally, $25,000 was the standard asking rate of Joran's "licensing" fee for an interview. Steph said the probability of Joran fleeing Aruba once he had the down payment was almost certain.

Once back in New York, John Kelly continued his e-mail correspondence with Joran, as the deal had a $225,000 outstanding balance. He underestimated the flight risk that Steph had cautioned them about. As far as he was concerned, the FBI was monitoring the situation, having been involved in the sting. The undercover extortion sting was kept under wraps.

Why the FBI hadn't arrested Joran in the hotel in Aruba was harshly criticized. The FBI responded to the criticism that it should have moved immediately. They explained the extortion case was indeed a criminal event, but they were hoping Joran was going to lead them to a body and murder charges could follow.

Being so hell-bent on the murder conviction may have been short-sighted, but Beth Twitty held that as her ultimate prize, as well. In hindsight, Joran's escape to Peru could have been avoided had an extortion charge been used to detain him. Instead, he managed to flee the country with $25,000 of extorted money, having only led his victims to another dead end of lies. The money, in turn, funded an opportunity for the horrific crime that followed. But nobody could have foreseen such tragedy.

Meanwhile, back in Birmingham, Alabama, the U.S. District Court was in the process of drafting an indictment against Joran for wire fraud and extortion. Aruban officials claimed they notified the FBI of Joran's intention to leave the island, but the tips went unheeded and he fled.

Joran's sudden departure took his mother by complete surprise. Anita had already arranged his flight to Holland, scheduled in two days, where he had agreed to receive inpatient psychiatric treatment. The written note she found on her kitchen table was to the point.

"I've gone, don't worry," Joran had written. "I've been invited to Peru to participate in a poker tournament."

TWENTY-TWO

JUNE 4, 2010
CHILE–PERU BORDER CROSSING

Joran van der Sloot was in handcuffs when he arrived back at the Santa Rosa border crossing that Friday afternoon. Members of the Arica-Parinacota police department had escorted him the final twenty miles from the Arica airstrip to the immigration facility. Security was enormous, both the Chilean and Peruvian authorities providing extra officers for transfer of the high-profile fugitive.

Joran emerged from a Chilean police vehicle wearing the same outfit as the previous afternoon when he had been captured: khaki pants and a black hooded sweatshirt. As usual, hordes of news people were in the parking area to capture the twenty-second event.

Joran appeared calm and in control, flanked by high-ranking law enforcement officials. Interpol agents had outfitted him in a drab military-green bulletproof vest. Inside, he was examined by two doctors, who certified him to be in good health, with no indications of recent scratches, bruises, or traumas. He was lucid and his vital signs were normal.

At 3:00 P.M., he was officially transferred to Peruvian authorities.

"We demand that all the rights that are due Mr. Van der Sloot are honored," the Chilean prosecutor told his Peruvian counterpart.

Joran was read his rights and given a copy of the resolution that had been signed by a judge in Lima on June 2, ordering his preliminary detention for twenty-four hours. He had one request—that someone call his mother in Aruba to let her know that he was being taken into custody in Peru.

Joran was ordered to open his bags so authorities could inventory his personal effects. His backpack contained a pair of blue dress pants, a Von Dutch T-shirt, a black T-shirt with the inscription "Kiss," and several pairs of Bermuda shorts. He was also carrying a beige baseball cap; a red synthetic belt; a notebook with a green cover; a cherry-colored appointment book; one brown business card holder containing several cards; one black HP Pavilion laptop; one HP flash drive; one black external hard drive; two white lighters and a pen from the Atlantic City Casino; one photo album with some photos; one silver chain; one blue lighter with a golden eagle; one bank card from the Caribbean Mercantile Bank N.V. Aruba; a yellow laminated medical insurance card; seven prepaid phone cards; two memory sticks; one small appointment book with the inscription "2001"; one red folder containing various documents numbered through page sixty-one; two white shoelaces; one black string; one skin renewal lotion by Gillette, and one deodorant; and one platinum Egoiste cologne.

Police found two wallets among his belongings, one black and one light brown with the logo "Granny." Both were empty. Joran was also carrying a wad of bills and coins from various countries and in various denominations. There was money from Trinidad and Tobago, Chile, Indonesia, Hong Kong, Malaysia, France, Lebanon, Macau, Venezuela, and the United States. But they turned out to be worth less than twenty dollars.

Peruvian authorities debated how to transport Joran to Lima. Normally, they would have dispatched a national police aircraft. But the planes were predisposed, being used for events sponsored by the Organization of American States Summit (OASS) in Lima.

Peru was the host country for the international conference. Diplomats and dignitaries from thirty countries, including Secretary of State Hillary Clinton from the U.S., were in attendance.

Van der Sloot's sensational capture had overshadowed any news coming out of the summit.

A commercial flight was considered and rejected, in deference to paying passengers. Ultimately, the decision was made to transfer Joran by land. Interpol was in charge of the operation, supported by Peruvian highway patrol officers.

At 4:30 P.M., a convoy of sixteen police vehicles departed Tacna and headed north on the Pan-American Highway. Joran, handcuffed, sat in the backseat of an unmarked SUV between two Interpol agents. Ironically, he was retracing the route of his escape when he had traveled with the naïve cabbies; for this trip he had no need to negotiate a fee.

More than twenty media vehicles shadowed the convoy, recording every second of Joran's eight-hundred-mile voyage back to Lima. The sixteen-hour trip was grueling for the former fugitive. Every time the caravan crossed into a new province, a circus-like frenzy erupted as Joran was physically pulled from one vehicle to be placed in another. Each jurisdiction wanted to be part of the event with each agency receiving its time in the spotlight. The captive was transferred from vehicle to vehicle as the cameras flashed. The depraved celebrity remained unfazed, often seen laughing with his police escorts during the ride.

The caravan arrived in Lima the following morning, June 5. More than one hundred reporters and photographers swarmed the silver unmarked SUV carrying Stephany Flores's alleged killer, pressing their lenses against tinted windows hoping to catch an image of the monster inside. SWAT teams served as a barricade between the media horde and the vehicle before it disappeared into a parking area of the fourteen-story headquarters.

Joran was pale, his usually alert brown eyes half-closed as he emerged with his hands still shackled. He appeared nauseated, but two Interpol agents grabbed him by the elbows, led him to the underground entrance, and shoved him into an elevator. At least ten officers crowded in with him before they rode to the upper-floor auditorium. Joran was pushed to the center of the room packed with reporters, all authorized to be there by police. The public display of his endgame was deliberate. Joran was a trophy.

Burly officers, immaculately dressed in suits and ties, positioned their prisoner with slight adjustments so photographers would be able to gain different angles. Joran scowled and blinked furiously, blinded by the camera flashes.

"Joran, you're on American television, what do you have to say?" one reporter managed to yell over the mayhem.

Joran glared but remained silent.

After two minutes, Joran's exploitative exhibition was halted and he was removed from the auditorium. Interpol, the lead law enforcement agency since Joran's transfer at the border, now delivered him into the custody of Captain Juan Callan and his homicide team.

Five Interpol officers marched him down a brightly lit hallway to the division's third-floor office, painted a drab mustard. Captain Callan's metal desk, one of six in the room, was in front of an expansive window, overlooking a construction site. The Virgin Mary hung in a small frame over his chair.

Captain Callan rose to introduce himself. He and his four-member team were dressed in the department's official black vests, white collared shirts, and dark slacks. Callan's tinted glasses with silver frames distinguished him from the group.

The captain had researched the murder suspect since his escape from the Hotel Tac. He knew about his involvement in the Natalee Holloway case; in fact, Aruban investigators had contacted his office after Stephany Flores's murder. He was aware of the FBI's extortion proceeding against him in Alabama.

At 2:00 P.M., official business began. Callan and a representative from the prosecutor's office faced off against Joran and a small team provided for him. He had a Dutch translator, Maurice Steins, a native from Holland living in Peru who had been dispatched by the Dutch embassy. A defense lawyer, Alberto Paima Luyo, had also been assigned to him.

Joran was advised of his rights. He agreed that he understood the reason for his detention and the charges against him, the murder of Stephany Flores.

His brief interview offered very little information. He relied on the story he had told the Chilean police that either thugs with fake badges, or real police who practiced off-duty thuggery, were waiting for Stephany at the Hotel Tac, demanding his documents and 1,000 nuevos soles.

He did not explain how this was inconsistent with the video images from outside Room 309, where he and Stephany entered the room together but ultimately he alone exited at least twice.

Callan asked what he did for a living.

"At present, I do not have a job," Joran explained. "I am a poker player and I have been traveling around the world since I turned eighteen."

"Where do you live?"

"I have been living with my mother and younger brother for the past four months. Before that, I lived with my girl-friend in Thailand."

Next was a medical examination, standard protocol for suspects in serious crimes. Joran was fingerprinted, and swabbed for gunshot residue, despite no evidence of a gun or gunshot at the crime scene. Blood typing determined Joran was type A, the same as Stephany. A drug test was negative. A tattoo was discovered inked across his left chest. "No Problem," it read in a bold, black Thai script.

In the afternoon, under police scrutiny, Joran was allowed to e-mail his mother in Aruba about his incarceration.

The laptop was then confiscated as evidence and sent for analysis.

That night, shortly before 10:00 P.M., Callan attempted to carry on with the interview, but Joran was not cooperative. He answered only a handful of nonchallenging questions before announcing he was too tired and wanted to postpone the deposition until the morning.

Callan thought that Joran was stalling in order to find an aggressive celebrity lawyer to represent him. In the past, lawyers had offered Joran their services pro bono hoping to elevate their visibility with such a high-profile client.

Before agreeing to end the interrogation, the prosecutor asked, "Mr. Van der Sloot, did you participate in the homicide of Stephany Flores?"

"I am very willing to help you," Joran replied flatly. "But I have not slept in twenty-four hours. I'm tired and I do not wish to continue with this statement."

After the interview, Joran was taken to a ten-by-thirteen-foot holding cell. He was placed in solitary confinement out of fear for his life, so reviled was he in Peru. His meal preparations were monitored to reduce the risk of poisoning. He ate his meals in the company of homicide detectives, his menu the same as theirs.

At 11:30 A.M. the next morning Joran and Callan reconvened in Callan's office. The investigator greeted him with, "Good morning, Señor Van der Sloot. How did you sleep?"

Joran was tired, unshaved, and unbathed.

"Please, have a seat," the captain directed, gesturing to the metal chair across the desk. Captain Callan was the only member of his team who was authorized to speak directly with Joran.

Joran winced as he lowered himself down, the handcuffs cutting into his wrists.

The Dutchman's calm demeanor did not surprise Callan. In his career, he was familiar with the hard eyes of murderers. He had interrogated more than fifty of them. Joran had escaped murder charges before and was savvy to the process.

Callan had already developed his strategy for Joran. He knew he loved gambling, so he was going to approach him like a poker player, showing only one card at a time.

"Are you ready to talk?" the captain asked.

"I'm too tired, I just want to sleep," Joran replied in Spanish.

Callan noted that Joran spoke Spanish very well. He also noticed his collected and observant demeanor.

Callan decided to make his detainee more comfortable. He instructed an officer to remove the handcuffs, which had remained in place for several hours.

Joran stretched his arms vigorously and sank deeper into the metal chair.

"Can I get you a drink? Something to eat? Perhaps a cigarette?"

"Cigarettes! I want a cigarette!" Joran growled.

Callan tossed a pack across the desk. The chain-smoker had not been permitted to light up in his cell, and Callan hoped to put him at ease and gain his confidence with the gesture of kindness.

The captain quietly watched as Joran pulled a cigarette from the pack, lit it up, and took a long, deep drag. Several minutes passed with neither man saying a word. Joran reached for the pack and grabbed a second cigarette.

"So, Joran, what do you do for a living?" the captain asked.

"I have a business in Thailand that sells pizzas, bread, and coffee. I have been doing this for two and a half years."

Callan recalled the previous afternoon's interview, when Joran had told him he made his living playing poker in tournaments around the world, but was currently unemployed. "And how much do you earn from this business?"

"I make about 20,000 euros [U.S.$27,000]," Joran replied.

"Why did you come to Peru? What was your intention?"

"I wanted to play in the international poker tournament," Joran explained, dragging on a cigarette.

"How did you get here?"

"By plane via Bogotá, and then Lima. I arrived on May 14."

"Tell me what you did in Lima from May 14 when you arrived until May 30."

"I went to the Atlantic City Casino many times and to Larco Marco to go shopping," Joran explained, misnaming Larcomar, the tri-level complex of stores and restaurants carved into the cliffs overlooking the ocean. "I also did some shopping downtown, and I gambled at the casino in the Marriott Fiesta Hotel across the street from the Atlantic City in Miraflores."

"Where did you stay? And how much did you pay for your room?"

"I took room number 309 at the Hotel Tac, located across the street from the Wong Supermarket in Miraflores. I paid fifty soles a day for lodging.

"I'm tired," Joran complained. "Can I sleep now?"

"I hear you are an excellent poker player," Callan said, smiling. "I also like to play poker. Let me show you my cards."

Joran perked up at the prospect of a game, completely missing the metaphor.

Callan pulled a large envelope from a desk drawer. One by one, he placed the eight-by-ten color pictures of Stephany Flores's crime scene on his desk.

Joran sucked on a cigarette, but had no reaction as he gazed at the images of his hotel guest, battered and covered in blood.

"Do you recognize this girl?" Callan prodded.

Joran sat slumped, eyes down to avoid Callan's stare.

"Look at me. Do you know this girl?"

Joran watched as more photos were spread out, this time including stills from the surveillance camera, some of Joran and Stephany entering Room 309 together, and others of him exiting alone.

Joran smoked and said nothing. He watched the detective walking around his desk to retrieve a bag of evidence from another drawer.

"Perhaps you recognize this?" Callan asked, pulling out a long-sleeved button-down shirt stained with blood. He held the garment close to Joran's face.

Joran finally reacted, recoiling from the rancid stench. He motioned for the captain to remove the garment.

Callan continued to wave it, the very shirt Stephany Flores had been wearing when discovered by Adeli Marchena, the Hotel Tac's receptionist.

"Take it away!" Joran implored. The stench, not his remorse, was making him nauseated.

"This is my hand," Callan announced, returning to his poker metaphor. "You may be good, but I win! Now I will ask you again, Señor Van der Sloot, did you know Stephany Flores?"

Joran admitted he did, staring down at the red tile floor. The admission was also witnessed by a representative from the public ministry, the Dutch translator, Maurice Steins, and Luz Romero, Joran's third defense attorney in twenty-four hours.

"Now, I ask you again, my friend, to tell me where you were beginning at 6:00 P.M. on May 29 until 5:00 A.M. of May 30."

"On May 29 at 6:00 P.M., I went to the Atlantic City Casino to play blackjack and poker. I drank alcohol, pisco sours and whiskey colas. I believe from 6:00 P.M. until 2:00 A.M., I played blackjack and between 2:00 A.M. and 5:00 A.M. I played poker."

"Do you know a man named Elton García?" Callan asked, referring to the Uruguayan poker player who had tried to contact Joran at the hotel the night Stephany's body was discovered.

"Elton García is a friend of mine," Joran said. "I met him at the Atlantic City Casino two weeks ago."

"And Stephany Flores, how did you know her?"

"I also met Stephany at the Atlantic City. I met her on or around May 27. She is an acquaintance. I haven't known her for that long."

"Tell us in detail how the crime against Stephany Flores occurred inside Room 309 of the Hotel Tac," Callan directed.

"On May 30, 2010, at around 2:00 A.M., I was playing poker at a table with several people when Stephany approached the table and started to play, as well. I played in her presence for about two or three hours and then around 5:00 A.M. she mentioned that she wanted to play on the Internet and asked me to go with her.

"We continued to play a little longer at the casino and then we left for the Hotel Tac, where I was staying. We went to her car, which was a black four-by-four, and we arrived at the hotel around 5:30 A.M. We went to my room and we played poker on my laptop. It was at that moment that I opened my e-mail and I noticed a message saying 'I am going to kill you, *mongolito*,' in reference to the Holloway case.

"So I talked about the case with Stephany, and I indicated that five years ago I had been detained as a suspect in connection with the disappearance of this girl," Joran said. He claimed that Stephany became angered upon learning of his involvement in the case. "After about a half hour of having been in Room 309, during our conversation, Stephany struck me on the left-hand side of my head with her fist. And I impulsively struck her in the face with my right elbow exactly above the nose.

"There was blood everywhere. I thought she was passed out. It affected me so much that I grabbed her by the neck with both hands, and I choked her for about two minutes.

"Then at that moment, I thought about what I was doing. I stood up thinking 'What am I going to do now?' I had blood on my shirt, and there was blood on the bed. So I took my shirt, and I put it on her face, pressing really hard until I killed Stephany. Then I thought, 'What am I going to do?'

"I exited the Hotel Tac, but the girl at the reception told me I had to move the car, so I returned to room number 309 and, at first, I thought about fleeing the hotel. I took my bags and I drove the car but I, I don't remember, I just continued on the street.

"I didn't know where I was going, but I took a right out of the hotel. I drove for about five minutes, then I dumped the car.

"I took a cab to the Jorge Chávez airport. Then I said to myself 'Better not take a plane.' I took a taxi to the bus station. There, I took another taxi, paying the sum of 600 soles toward another city that I don't remember the name of, and then from there, I used the services of another taxi to the city of Nazca with an individual who drove me for two hours to the following city paying the sum of 100 soles.

"Upon arriving, I struck up a conversation with the driver of the taxi about the homicide of Stephany Flores. And I said, 'I have committed a homicide. I have murdered a person and I want to exit Peru.'

"And he responded, 'Wait until we get to the next city.' And then the driver told me my friends are not here now, perhaps it is better that you take a bus. And then I said, 'You told me you were going to take me to Arica. Do it, please.'

"To which he said, 'Just calm down, and let's go to eat something.' We went to eat together and then his friends arrived. And he chatted a bit with them and then he came to me and he said that for $1,500 they would take me. And then I responded, okay, but at that moment I only had $500 in cash, so we left and I told them that I was going to get the rest from an ATM.

"And from there, we got in a white vehicle that was like a minivan. But while on the road, the highway police stopped us, asking for documents. After that, the people who I had hired to take me to Arica recommended that I throw away my luggage, so I threw away my beige sports bag, and after that, they told me they were not going to take me to Arica if I didn't give them the following specific items: one cellular phone, a watch, two bottles of perfume, books, clothing, such as a red T-shirt and a pair of jeans, some designer Lacoste T-shirts, and other regular ones.

"And upon arrival at the border control in Tacna, one of the individuals got out of the vehicle because immigration said that his document, the DNI card, was false, counterfeit. So, he remained there.

"The only ones who crossed the border with me were two Peruvians, the same ones that brought me from Nazca. And so in this manner we arrived in Chile.

"At around 4:00 P.M. on May 31, 2010, I tried to withdraw money from the ATM in the sum of $1,000, but the machine only allowed me to take out $500. So they asked how I was going to pay the rest and in order to avoid problems with them, I told them I had two watches.

"One of them was a Ferrari brand and valued at around $7,000. So I handed the watch to one of them, but the other one put it away, and I promised that I was going to call them on the following day and send via Western Union the $500.

"So I told the taxi driver that the moment the money arrived, I was going to give him the address where he was to send the watch and then after I got the watch, I was going to give him $500. And after agreeing to that, they both left.

"I took a room at a hotel in the city of Arica. It was small, and I don't remember the name. And the following day, that is to say, June 1, I spent all day in the city and that same evening, I went to the bus terminal in Arica, where I took a bus to Antofagasta, where I arrived on June 2.

"In that city, I took a plane of the airline PAL to the city of Santiago. When I arrived at 2:00 P.M., I went to a place called Vasco da Gama, where I took a shower in a hotel and left my things. And I took a taxi to the city of Santiago."

In Santiago, he said he met a stranger who invited him to a "*café con piernas.*" *Cafés con piernas,* literally "coffee with legs," were unique to Santiago. They were half coffee bars, half strip joints, where women wearing no more than thongs served beverages in an atmosphere of pulsating rock 'n' roll and darkness, brightened by flickering neon.

"I stayed the night because I was already very drunk," he explained. "The following day, I left and I was again in Vasco da Gama and while in the cab I saw a picture of myself in a newspaper and how they were looking for a Dutchman who was an assassin.

"So I said to the cabbie, please take me to a police station because I have just seen that the police are looking for me because of a homicide. So we found a police station in Vasco da Gama, and I spoke with the personnel there, and I said I have just seen in the paper that the Peruvian police want me for a homicide. So they looked at me really strangely and they told me to wait a minute and the policewoman said, 'You'd better go to another police station because we know nothing about this.'

"So I started talking with a cabbie and I said I have to surrender and he said, 'I have a cousin that is chief of police in Santiago, if you want I can call him.'

"So I said, 'Okay call him.' And so the cabbie was on the phone for five minutes and then he gave me the phone. With my command of the Spanish language, I spoke with him and I explained that I had seen in the newspaper that I was wanted in Peru. He asked me where I was from and I said, 'I am from Holland.'

"Then he said, 'I will call you back' and he called back. And he told me to go to the central police station in Santiago. During the whole trip, he called on the phone. The taxi driver told me that his cousin, the police chief, told him that he was going to come over for the sake of my security.

"An hour went by, and the police came to the cab in a regular vehicle, not a police car, where I got in and was driven to the immigration office in Santiago, where they told me that I *wasn't* being apprehended, that I could do what I wanted.

"So I used the computer. I ate, and one of the people from immigration told me that Peru has put in an extradition request to which I responded that I didn't agree with that; that I needed to speak with a lawyer.

"They said that it was out of their control; that it was a decision from the government. I asked if there was a possibility that I could be extradited to Holland and they told me they were going to look into it. They kept telling me that I wasn't being detained, that it was above them, and they had to give me back to the country through which I came in, meaning Peru, and that is the way I arrived in Peru."

Callan took in the fantastic story without expression. He

knew some of the pieces were different from the evidence, but he made no challenges. After a pause in the narrative, Callan changed the subject to the murder weapon. "Did you use any type of blunt object to kill Stephany?" he asked.

"No," Joran replied.

"Can you tell me, in which areas of the face and body did you strike her, and how many times?"

"I only struck her above the nose with my right elbow."

"We found a Prince racquet at the scene of the crime," Callan said, showing Joran a photograph of the tennis racquet officers had collected from Room 309. "Is it the same one that was used to victimize Stephany?"

"I did not hit her with the racquet that you are showing."

Callan again pulled the long-sleeved beige shirt that was soiled in blood from the evidence bag. "Please indicate if the garment that we are showing you, name brand One Star Converse, is the same garment that you were wearing on May 30 and the one you used to asphyxiate Stephany."

"Yes, it's the same shirt I had on at the casino, and the one that I used to smother Stephany until she was dead." Joran was unable to maintain eye contact for more than a few seconds.

"Can you look at me, please?" Callan directed. "Tell me what happened."

Joran claimed that he first elbowed Stephany in the nose, hard, and then he climbed on top of her. He struck her head, wrestled her to the ground and smothered her with his shirt.

"Could she have been alive after that?"

Joran said it was conceivable, admitting she may have agonized for a while. He was unable to elaborate, remembering the time after the attack as a blur.

Callan noted that Joran's demeanor had become more relaxed now that he was confessing. Sometimes he smiled, and occasionally he showed remorse. At moments, he was even charming.

Callan next showed Joran a photograph of a white-and-turquoise purse that had been found in Room 309. "Whose pocketbook is this?" he asked.

"The bag belongs to Stephany. She was carrying it on May 30."

"What was inside the bag?"

"Three cards; one was a Visa, another one from a bank and her ID, as well as 850 nuevos soles [about U.S.$300]."

"So what happened to the contents of the bag after Stephany was dead?"

"I realized that Stephany had money, but I didn't know about the credit cards or how much money. But I knew that she had exchanged the chips for cash before leaving the casino. So after killing her, I took the cards and the money."

Joran's response supported Callan's theory: Stephany's murder was motivated by robbery alone. Joran was a consummate gambler, strapped for cash, who opportunely selected Stephany. He knew she had been a winner that evening, and lured her to his hotel room to rob her of her winnings and her credit cards. Her jewelry, a ring, a pair of gold earrings and watch, did not interest him. Joran had no cuts or scratches on his body, yet he claimed that Stephany had, without warning, punched him in the face. He was at a loss to explain the violence that followed, but appeared to be setting up a self-defense scenario.

After the murder, Callan surmised, Joran stole the Jeep hoping to find money in the vehicle. Joran's explanation for abandoning the Jeep was that he did not know the city.

Callan was hoping Joran would reveal his motive in his own words.

"So, what motive did you have when you killed Stephany that morning?"

"I don't know, but the moment that she struck me in the head I just lost control. I didn't know what I was doing. Uh, I remember what I was doing, but not the motive. It was an impulsive act, a reaction to her striking me on the head."

"Why after killing Stephany, did you flee to Chile? And why in that country did you decide to turn yourself in when you could have done it in Peru?"

"I wasn't thinking clearly. I only wanted to the leave the scene of the crime as quickly as possible and leave the country. But when I arrived in Chile, and I saw my picture in the papers, I decided to turn myself in to the authorities in Chile."

Callan reworked the time line back to the murder scene. "Why after killing Stephany on May 30, did you leave the hotel room only to return with two cups of coffee in your hands?"

Joran didn't know the answer.

Callan's investigators had interviewed the barista at Holly's Coffee Shop about Joran's physical appearance the morning of the murder. She had indicated that he had patronized the shop before and seemed no different, calm and relaxed as usual.

"Did you ever think of hiding the body of the victim after killing Stephany in the hotel?"

"Yes, it crossed my mind at one point to hide the body, but I couldn't take the sight anymore, there was too much blood in the room."

"How do you explain the lesions that are on her face and several parts of her body, as well as the cranial fracture that was found during the autopsy?"

Joran shrugged his shoulders. "I don't know because there wasn't much of a struggle."

"Keeping in mind what you previously said, that you took Stephany by the throat using both hands to strangle her, can you tell us where the victim was, and what position you adopted?"

"She was on the bed when I struck her with my right elbow hard, and I think her head went backwards and hit the wall, then she started bleeding so I immediately positioned myself on top of her and with both hands I started to strangle her, keeping her like that for a minute.

"After that, I threw her to the ground because she was still bleeding and it was then that I took my shirt off and put it over her face and kept pressing, I don't know for how long, and in this manner I think I killed her."

"Is it true that after killing Stephany you undressed her? If so, what was your motive in undressing the cadaver?"

"Honestly, I don't remember, but I think so. It was after killing her. It was her pants and her shoes but nothing else. I don't know why I did it."

"As you indicated before, did you think about hiding the body and if so, where would you have hidden it?"

"I have no idea. It just crossed my mind for a second."

"What did you put on, keeping in mind the shirt that you had on was bloody, what did you put on after killing Stephany?"

"I wore a V-neck T-shirt colored red with black and red stripes."

"You said that after killing Stephany, you observed a great deal of blood in the room. Can you indicate if you cleaned the floor and if so, what did you use to clean it?"

"Yes, it's true," Joran affirmed matter-of-factly. "I used a bedspread and the sheets to clean the blood off the floor. And I only wiped the floor."

Next came questions about the flight through Peru to Chile. "Describe the physical characteristics of the people that facilitated your escape to the city of Arica and if they solicited money and goods in exchange for leaving the country after they knew that you had killed Stephany?"

"They were three individuals who took me to Arica. The first person was thin, had a lot of hair, short, he wasn't black, but dark skinned and he took me from Ica up to Nazca.

"The second person was heavy, had dark-colored hair, tall and he took me from Nazca to Arica. And again he was dark skinned but not black. And the third person, he was the first one's brother, and they looked alike but his face was fuller. And he was the owner of the vehicle.

"And these people were the ones who asked me for money and they robbed me, they took my cellular phone, clothing, my $7,000 Ferrari watch, and two bottles of cologne, I don't remember the brand. And they told me that if I didn't give them the money, they were going to report me to the police."

Callan showed Joran a photo lineup that included mug shots of the three Peruvian taxi drivers who had transported him from Nazca to Tacna.

"Do you recognize anyone?" the investigator asked.

Studying the photographs, Joran pointed to the one of Carlos Euribe Pretil. "That's the guy," he remarked.

The questioning returned to incidents in Room 309. "When you left the hotel, Room 309, after killing Stephany, what did you take along with you?"

"I took a backpack with documents, my laptop, some clothing, a beige bag with some clothing, books. The money that I took from her wallet, I put together with my money."

"Did Stephany win any money during the time that you were playing in the Atlantic City Casino?"

"I don't think she did," Joran replied, looking down at the floor.

"Why did you go to room number 309 with Stephany?"

"To keep playing poker on the Internet."

"What did Stephany say when she struck you on the head?"

"I was explaining to her that five years ago I was accused in a case where a girl disappeared because at that moment I had received a message through Facebook. One moment she was listening to me, and the next moment she hit me in the head and I don't know why."

"Why did you kill Stephany?" Callan again demanded.

"After I struck her, I was afraid that she was going to go to the police and I was going to be detained. It was an impulsive act. I think, I wanted to kill her, but I wasn't thinking."

"The autopsy shows the presence of amphetamines in her body. Did you give her anything to drink that contained amphetamines?"

"No," Joran said, shaking his head.

"What kind of alcoholic beverages did you drink during the time that you were playing in the casino?"

"I had Pepsi Cola, pisco sour, and whiskey cola and I think that Stephany was drinking wine. From 6:00 P.M. to 1:00 A.M., I drank about ten glasses."

"How did you obtain the money that you used to leave the country?"

"I arrived in this country with $25,000, but I didn't declare what I had on me. In Chile, I withdrew $500 from the ATM on June 2, from the Banco Santander, I believe. My account is called 'Click to Pay.' It's an organization that makes money online available. I have a card, but it's in Chile with my belongings."

"What is the origin of the money that you brought to Peru, the $25,000, and why didn't you declare the money?"

Joran claimed he had been working with an Israeli mentalist, Uri Geller. For $25,000 he was going to expose an online gambing fraud for Geller's live TV program *The New Uri Geller,* which aired in Holland. He claimed he had been advanced $25,000; $10,000 in cash and $15,000 in a wire transfer to his Holland SNS bank account.

What Joran failed to tell the police were the significant details of the Uri Geller connection. To begin, what a remarkable coincidence that Joran's story had Uri Geller advancing him $10,000 in cash and $15,000 in a wire transfer, the exact transactions as in the extortion of Beth Twitty two weeks earlier.

Saying a deal with Uri Geller was being negotiated was not a total fabrication. Joran *had* been in contact with the TV host, but not until after he had arrived in Peru. They did discuss Joran going undercover to investigate online gambing fraud, but no advancement had been secured. The offer was not for $25,000 but for $600 and a one-way ticket for Joran to travel back to Aruba, and this ticket was available before the brutal attack on Stephany Flores.

Geller had a plan to obtain a confession from Joran. His lure was the Internet gambling fraud story. However, he really was hoping to hypnotize the Dutchman to find out what really happened to Natalee Holloway. He admitted to sending him $600 and a plane ticket, but that was all.

Remarkably, Joran acknowledged that $9,000 of the $25,000 in cash was from Beth Twitty via John Quincy Kelly, although he shortchanged the amount and misrepresented the circumstances.

The final $6,000 cash to bring the total to $25,000 was

ascribed to his winnings in Aruban casinos before his trip to Peru to play in the big tournament. He was annoyed by the concept of declaring cash.

"I fly around the world playing poker for a lot of money," he boasted. "It takes longer to declare it than to make it."

Natalee Holloway was briefly mentioned in a line of questioning about previous involvements in serious crimes.

Before the interrogation ended, Callan offered Joran's defense attorney an opportunity to ask questions.

Joran's current court-appointed attorney, Luz Romero, posed two. "Did you turn yourself in of your own volition or were the Pisconte brothers and Euribe Pretil the ones that suggested you turn yourself in?" was the first.

"I turned myself in voluntarily," Joran claimed. "It was my decision," contradicting any evidence.

Romero's second question was broad. "Do you have anything else to add, change, or modify in this statement?" Romero asked her client.

Here, Joran seized the opportunity to focus on Natalee. "First, I want to have the possibility of talking about Natalee Holloway's case five years ago, and the possibility of requesting that the proceedings are fast so that I can be extradited to Aruba.

"I want to speak of the case, but not right now. It's a case that has gone on several years and I would prefer to speak with the police in Aruba about the possibility of closing the case. I would like to clarify things in the case."

Joran the manipulator was on stage. The idea of a lengthy and dangerous prison sentence in Peru was unpalatable so he was his own plea-bargainer, seeking to have himself extradited to Aruba. He alone knew what happened to Natalee, he offered, and he would tell Aruban authorities the truth, but only on Aruban soil.

His bargain was unsuccessful. The interrogation concluded and a transcript was typed up and signed by all parties present. Callan noticed that Joran's signature had changed overnight, dramatically different from the previous interview's autograph. That signature, identical to his passport, was an illegible inch-long script. Now, he signed his confession with a tiny scribble resembling the letter "P."

Luz Romero later explained that Joran's two signatures were calculatedly different, leaving him the possibility that he could argue one wasn't his. That option was nullified, however. In addition to the signatures, all parties agreed to the veracity of the transcript by providing an impression of their right index fingers.

Joran's confession hadn't ruined his appetite. He and the detectives sat down for a late lunch ordered from the sixth-floor cafeteria. They all indulged in helpings of *lomo saltado,* a classic Peruvian favorite of stir-fried beef and vegetables over rice.

At 7:15 that evening, Joran was permitted to call his mother in Aruba from a pay phone on a third-floor hall. The call, made in the presence of his defense attorney and a public ministry representative, lasted six minutes. Joran informed his mother that he had given a statement regarding his involvement in the murder of Stephany Flores.

TWENTY-THREE

Captain Juan Callan was confident in his evidence, but he worried about the psychological profile Joran might present. He had reached the conclusion that the Dutchman was calculating, manipulative and evil, but was he sane? The idea of him shirking responsibility in a murder with an insanity defense distressed him.

Callan knew Joran had slithered out of accusations and confessions in the Holloway case. He had made a personal vow that the snake would be convicted in Peru.

The following morning, Joran met with Silvia Rojas Regalado, a forensic psychologist from the Peruvian National Police. Regalado had a reputation for getting inside the minds of criminals. When not assisting in criminal investigations, she taught forensic psychology at the Escuela Iberoamericana de Desarrollo Social, the Latin American School of Social Development. The university is home to Peru's premier criminal justice program.

Regalado was already familiar with the Flores case. She had been briefed by Callan's team and had read a detailed report on Van der Sloot's history before sitting down with him that Monday. Nevertheless, she needed to build her own profile of the suspect, one that would hold up in a court of law.

Joran was escorted into the room at 11:25 A.M. amid a tight circle of police. His face had a serene expression that masked his fear; his body was trembling. His posture was stooped but he walked with deliberate coordination.

After he sat, he sustained eye contact with her. In her official report, she remarked that his gaze was fixed and sad.

Speaking in Spanish, Dr. Regalado asked Joran a few questions—his name, his age, did he know where he was and why he was there?

Joran answered all her questions lucidly and cooperatively, without hesitation. He had a thick foreign accent, but spoke Spanish well.

Dr. Regalado leafed slowly through Joran's case file while the accused killer squirmed anxiously in his chair. As a precaution, officers stood guard in case he became enraged. For now, the psychologist was more interested in his actions and mannerisms than his case file. She wanted to observe him speaking as well as in silence, aware that he was an accomplished liar. Her plan was to focus not so much on what he said, but how he said it.

Perusing her notes, Regalado was amused when she arrived at the doctor's notation about Joran's "No Problem" tattoo. It was an unusual sentiment for such a problem-ridden young man. Her own physical observations took in his incredible height, well-manicured nails, and his neatly trimmed hair dyed a reddish blond.

"Why don't you just walk me through what happened to Stephany," Regalado suggested.

Joran became pensive and introspective. His body stiffened. "I met Stephany on May 28 at the Atlantic City Casino at approximately 6:00 P.M.," Joran began.

"She approached me. I was playing poker. She had heard I was a Dutchman and she said to me, 'You're the Dutchman who plays poker.'"

Joran explained that Stephany had told him that she was an amateur player herself and wanted to learn from an expert. He said that after talking for about five minutes he and Stephany exchanged phone numbers and Stephany promised to call him about getting together the following day.

"And the following day, May 29, she called me in the morning and said, 'I am going to have coffee and I am going to play poker.' I said 'I'll see you later,'" Joran explained.

Police learned that Stephany did indeed have Joran's Peruvian cellular phone number programmed into her black Nextel phone. His number was listed as speed dial number 20, but Stephany had misspelled his name as "Johan."

"Around 6:00 P.M. I went to the Atlantic City Casino alone," Joran continued. "From 6:00 P.M. until two in the morning I played blackjack after which I went upstairs to the poker room and Stephany showed up at my table.

"I spoke with her and she asked me if I had a girlfriend. I told her that I was single and she said 'I have a girl, I am a lesbian.'"

"I said, 'It doesn't matter; in Holland I have homosexual friends, lesbians.' Afterwards I said to her let's go to my room to play poker on my laptop."

Joran admitted that he had consumed quite a few cocktails by this point. He said he'd begun with his trademark whiskey and Cokes and later moved on to pisco sours, Peru's signature libation.

"I don't know if she drank a lot, but she did drink wine," Joran explained. "We were there up until five-thirty in the morning. After playing poker the two of us lost $1,000, which is not a lot of money. I had cash on me when I arrived.

"On May 28 I won $1,500," he bragged.

"We went to the room. She went of her own accord, we entered the room and we sat on the bed, I opened my Facebook account and saw that I had received a message that said, 'I'm going to kill you.'

"It was because of the Aruba case," Joran explained. "They insulted me."

Joran told Dr. Regalado that ever since the disappearance

of Natalee Holloway he had frequently received vile and threatening e-mails from strangers. Stephany had apparently seen the message and wanted to know what it meant.

"I was chatting with Stephany, telling her about the Aruba case, that I hadn't done anything wrong," Joran told the psychologist.

He explained that during the uncomfortable discussion with Stephany, he had lost control and struck her on the nose. "I had an impulsive reaction," he said, using psychological terms.

Joran rewound the narrative to make Stephany the instigator. "She struck first with her hand on my head," he described. His next act was in self-defense, he said. He reenacted the gesture he had made that night, forming a fist and drawing back his arm.

The tremble the psychologist had first noticed when he arrived was markedly more pronounced. His legs were also in constant motion, bobbing up and down.

"We then began hitting each other," Joran said. He complimented Stephany as being an admirable opponent. "She was strong," he said.

Joran continued by pantomiming the act of strangling Stephany, and describing his fear when she wouldn't die. "She began breathing heavily and I took her pants off," he said. He then pressed his shirt on her face until all sounds coming from her stopped.

For the first time, the doctor noticed a tone of anger in his words.

He continued his account. He changed his T-shirt, but didn't take a shower. He left the hotel in her car, but not knowing Lima, he abandoned the SUV and hailed a taxi. Before fleeing Lima, he dumped Stephany's car keys in a trash bin at the airport. He confirmed no sex had taken place, nor was sex ever suggested.

Dr. Regalado noted that Joran van der Sloot had recounted the events of the investigation coherently, had responded clearly to the questions asked, and had accepted the blame for the criminal events for which he was now being investigated. Her job was not to suggest innocence or guilt.

When the psychologist turned the conversation to family, Joran became extremely volatile and began to cry. Before Natalee, he sniffled, he had enjoyed a good relationship with his family. He had recently lost his father, with whom he'd had better communication than with his mother. He was most emotional when talking about his youngest brother, Sebastian. As for his own childhood, he had positive memories.

"I was never beaten or abused as a child," Joran told the psychologist. "I lived with my parents until I was seventeen, until I was accused in the death of a young woman in Aruba. After three months, the time it took to process the investigation, of which I was absolved, I traveled to Holland to forget the events, especially the time I spent in prison."

Joran described living in Holland for two years while he studied international business. He claimed the Dutch government had even provided him with a stipend of 800 euros a month while he pursued his studies. "However, I didn't take my studies very seriously," he admitted, confessing obsessions with poker and tennis. "I abandoned Holland because I was filmed in a hidden camera interview by a friend about the death of the girl in Aruba," he explained, never mentioning Natalee by name.

He said he traveled to Thailand, where he had his first real job, running a casual restaurant.

When he learned that his father had died, he returned to Aruba to be with his mother. He rented the SawadeeCup to a friend who promised to send him $1,500 every month.

Besides describing his adventures, he described himself. He said he had been a restless child but a model student, never skipping classes and succeeding academically. He never fought or argued excessively. His life had been close to perfect until "that girl" disappeared. Because he was falsely implicated, he was forced to abandon his dream of a higher education in the United States and now he wandered the world as an outcast.

His sex life was normal, he said. He was not shy. He had masturbated since he was fourteen, usually alone, but sometimes with a group of friends watching Internet porn. One of his first sexual experiences was with a male friend, who had performed oral sex on him. He lost his virginity around that same time and had enjoyed a steady stream of girlfriends. He bragged about experiments with sex toys with a girlfriend in Thailand.

Regarding drugs and alcohol, Joran lied, claiming his first drink was when he was eighteen. He had been drinking a lot since his father's death, he admitted. In Lima, he had been drinking whiskey and Cokes or pisco sours daily.

He smoked pot occasionally, beginning in jail in Aruba. He liked the effects. Smoking pot hardened his sentimental side.

Healthy activities were explored next.

Joran explained that while he did enjoy sports, like soccer and tennis, his passion was poker. He grinned when he said that poker made him a lot of money. Cheating was acceptable behavior, as long as he was the one cheating.

Joran exaggerated his worth as a television personality, saying he was able to charge between $50,000 and $100,000 for interviews.

After the psychological exam, Dr. Regalado sat down to record her findings, making them part of the body of evidence that would be submitted to a judge. Her conclusions were as follows:

> Joran van der Sloot, age twenty-two at the time of this exam, does not exhibit psychopathological disorders, which would impede his ability to evaluate reality. He exhibits an average intellectual level, which potentially could broaden his intellectual efficiency.
>
> The examinee presents an anti-social personality characterized by the ease with which he establishes superficial interpersonal relationships, indifference when it comes to others' well-

being and the capacity to maintain a fraudulent social style; deficient social conscience that shows in the violation of rules and the mixing in events that affect others' rights, looking only to advance his own interests.

He shows social irresponsibility, the enjoyment of superficial activities, in general a libertine and hedonistic lifestyle in search of new sensations in order to be stimulated.

He shows certain dominance over the opposite sex with the devaluation of the feminine figure.

He exhibits a low tolerance to frustration, is unable to stand inconveniences and shows a tendency to generate a vengeful attitude. He is emotionally immature, which prompts sudden changes in his behavior that can go from simple criticism, to out of control emotions, which make him prone to commit acts against the lives of others.

After the psychological exam, authorities next wanted to effect a reenactment of the crime scene. Like in Aruba, reenactments are commonly used in Peru, allowing a perpetrator to demonstrate his version of a crime. The reenactments are visual aids for the police officers establishing the scene. They help uncover inconsistencies in a defendant's statement. They are also important in the sentencing phase after a conviction.

Joran's account suggested that Stephany had not been murdered, but had died as a result of his self-defense. He claimed that a robbery had not been his motive, but an afterthought.

In Peru, the charge of homicide, or second-degree murder, carries a sentence of as little as fifteen years. With good behavior, Joran would be eligible for release in less than seven years. However, if police proved the death was premeditated, the mandatory sentence was thirty-five years. Peru has no death penalty. They believe in inmate reform.

Aggravated robbery, in which a victim is killed during a robbery, was also a consideration. Police had evidence that Stephany had won money at the casino and believed Joran knew about the bonanza.

Not surprisingly, the press, local and international alike, knew about the reenactment in advance and filled the street outside the Hotel Tac on its scheduled Tuesday. The scene reached mob proportions, with reporters using labels of "monster," "psychopath," and the "May 30 killer" when referring to the suspect.

Late Tuesday afternoon, amid security concerns, the reenactment was postponed and by Wednesday was canceled altogether. Officials believed they had ample evidence to present their case without it.

In Peru, police can hold a suspect for twenty-four hours. With a judge's order, they can hold a suspect for an additional seven days while they conduct an investigation. After that, investigators must submit their findings to a judge, who determines if a suspect will be held for trial.

Callan had worked feverishly to put together his case before Friday's hearing in front of a judge. Based on his interviews, he was convinced the Dutchman had charmed Stephany to his hotel room intending to rob her. He chose her specifically because of her winnings. She was a gambler, like him, and he was able to lure her easily with his online gambling accounts accessible from his laptop in Room 309. He knew the two had met before the murder because of the Atlantic City Casino's surveillance photos. He believed he knew that Stephany had won a staggering $10,000 earlier in the week. No money had been deposited in her bank account, confirmed by bank records. When Joran only found a few hundred dollars in her wallet, Callan suspected he stole the Jeep, hoping to find more.

Callan's master file was nearly four hundred pages, and contained sixteen witness statements, descriptions of surveillance videos, crime scene photos, the autopsy report, and of course, Joran's own confession. He listed his twenty-one reasons for believing Joran had murdered and robbed Stephany Flores:

1. Before leaving the Atlantic City Casino with Stephany, Van der Sloot observed Flores exchange poker chips for cash, which made robbery an attractive crime.

2. Van der Sloot admitted in the presence of a public ministry representative, his defense lawyer, and translator of having robbed Flores of 850 soles, her national ID, credit cards, bank card, as well as her Jeep on May 30. When Flores resisted the attack, Van der Sloot physically assaulted her, before he asphyxiated her, thus causing her death.

3. Stephany's empty purse was found at the scene of the crime missing her money, bank cards and ID, which Van der Sloot admitted to having stolen.

4. The cruelty exhibited by Van der Sloot as evidenced by the lesions on the different parts of her body, leaving open the possibility that inside Room 309 Van der Sloot may have tortured Stephany in an attempt to obtain the passwords to the victim's credit and bank cards in order to access the money in her accounts, showing no appreciation for human life.

5. The way in which Van der Sloot attempted to lighten his penal responsibility in this crime by saying that he committed the murder in self-defense, claiming Stephany initially struck him on the head. This is hardly credible given that Stephany sustained severe injuries to the head, face, and neck.

6. The autopsy report established that Stephany's body, in an advanced state of decomposition—presented signs of cranial, encephalic, and cervical trauma; the cause of death being a blunt instrument, namely, Joran's fists.

7. The time of death coincides with the time when the victim was seen alive for the last time entering Van der Sloot's hotel room. A fact corroborated by security videos captured inside the Hotel Tac between 5:30 and 8:13 A.M. on May 30, 2010.

8. Van der Sloot employed physical force, which resulted in concussions to the head, traumatic lesions to the face, cranial fractures, and sub-cranial hemorrhaging in order to subdue his victim. He then strangled her with both hands and lastly asphyxiated her, as was corroborated in the autopsy report.

9. Footage from the security cameras of the Atlantic City Casino show that Stephany Flores arrived at the casino on May 30 at 2:54 A.M. driving her black Jeep and was captured again on video at 5:15 A.M. leaving the casino in the company of Joran.

10. Through a photo lineup Hotel Tac employees Geidy Salazar Santillan, Reynaldo Cruz, and Adeli Marchena recognized the Dutchman as the guest who on May 30 at 5:20 A.M. entered Room 309 in the company of Stephany Flores before driving away alone in the victim's Jeep that same morning at 8:45 A.M.

11. Upon observing the videos of the security cameras inside the Hotel Tac, one can see the nervous attitude of the alleged perpetrator entering and exiting Room 309 after committing the crime,

presumably attempting to come up with a possible alibi.

12. Driver John Williams Pisconte, his brother John Oswaldo, and Carlos Euribe Pretil all identified Van der Sloot as the passenger they had driven to the city of Arica.

13. The contradictions between Van der Sloot's confession while in Peruvian custody and the voluntary deposition given in Chile in which he made up a story about a robbery perpetrated by two subjects that were inside Room 309 armed with a knife and a firearm when he entered the room in the company of Stephany Flores. His first version of events was hardly credible considering that the employees of the Hotel Tac never observed other persons entering Room 309, a fact that is backed up by surveillance footage.

14. The attitude and criminal conduct exhibited by the Dutch citizen in having abandoned the body of Stephany Flores after perpetrating the crime, demonstrating coldness in his acts, and then fleeing for the Chilean border with the only purpose of evading justice.

15. The pre-existence of money was established through the Prize Reports and videos of the Atlantic City showing the victim, Stephany Flores, had won on a $10,000 bet on May 24, 2010, and on April 30 she also obtained winnings in the amount of 676 soles. The money was stolen by Van der Sloot, a fact that is corroborated through records turned over to police by the casino.

16. Video records from the Hotel Tac prove that the striped red shirt Van der Sloot gave the drivers

during his trip from Ica was the same piece of
clothing that he was wearing when he fled the
Hotel Tac.

17. The recovery of clothing among which was the
striped red shirt, this being the piece of clothing
that he wore after victimizing Stephany Flores
before fleeing the crime scene in her SUV. The
shirt was given as partial payment to the cabbies
who transported him to the Chilean border with
the objective of fleeing Peru after committing a
crime.

18. The clothing abandoned at the scene of the crime
after murdering Stephany Flores was clearly recognized as belonging to the suspect.

19. Police established that the "modus operandi" of
Joran Andreas Petrus van der Sloot was selecting
female victims in casinos and through deceit ob-
taining his victim's money, and in this way obtain-
ing easy money.

20. It was scientifically established that fingerprints
obtained from Van der Sloot while in custody in
Lima matched prints lifted from Stephany's Jeep.
The prints corresponded to the pinky and ring
fingers of the detainee's right hand.

21. It was scientifically established that other fingerprints lifted from the scene of the crime gathered
by homicide technicians, from the edge of the
glass ashtray, nightstand, the central part of a
plastic bottle found on the TV table, and a transparent plastic bottle without a lid, were a match
to the middle and ring finger of Van der Sloot's
right hand, as well as the middle finger of his left
hand.

Summing up his report, Captain Callan asserted that the death of Stephany Flores was an act of cold-blooded murder, "committed with premeditation, violence, ferocity and cruelty, using physical force to cause her death." Callan was confident his evidence would lead to a conviction, unlike his predecessors in Aruba five years earlier. He looked forward to presenting his case at trial.

Meanwhile, the threats against Joran and his defense team were formidable. Earlier in the week, the young man had hired a private attorney, Máximo Altez, recommended by his friends. Altez was a former officer with the Peruvian National Police. He had been part of the department's antiterrorism squad, and had once been shot in the line of duty. When the lawyer agreed to represent Stephany's attacker, he received outraged letters, phone calls, and death threats. He and his family were harassed, his office was vandalized, and his wife sought temporary refuge in Miami, where the couple had a second home.

On June 11, Joran joined eleven other detainees in the back of an armored police van for transport to Lima's Palacio de Justicia. He emerged from the DIRINCRI building wearing the black hooded sweatshirt he had on when he was captured. The multicolored towel around his neck had been intended to obscure his face, but had slipped, giving the photographers a coveted headshot. Officers in full riot gear escorted him to the van for the ten-minute ride to the courthouse on Avenida Paseo de la República.

The revivalist structure was home to the Supreme Court of the Republic, the Criminal Chambers of the Superior Court, and several criminal courtrooms. The Sheraton Hotel, the Italian Art Museum, and the city's Civic Center were adjacent to the courthouse. Joran and his eleven van mates were brought to a side door, bypassing the thirty-three steps leading to the building's grand entrance.

As usual, dozens of reporters and photographers lurked. Police in helmets carried Plexiglas shields and batons in case of a disturbance. Ordinary citizens packed the square and held up their cell phones to catch images of "El Monstruo" on their tiny cameras.

Joran was the last to emerge, outfitted in a bulletproof vest. He was immediately bombarded with taunts of "*asesino!*" ("murderer") and pelted with rotting vegetables. He was unable to adjust the towel, now only partially covering his head, because of his handcuffs. He appeared to shrink in terror as officers pulled him by the elbows and led him up some stairs and into the building.

The hearing was short, with the determination that Joran remain in custody. He was reloaded into the van with the same fanfare. This time he traveled alone. He was destined for Peru's infamous Miguel Castro Castro Prison.

The prison was an hour's drive from central Lima, but still within city limits. It occupied a dusty hillside in the desperately poor district of San Juan de Lurigancho. The area was a mesh of unpaved streets lined with single-room cinder block structures, curtains serving as windows and doors. Ramshackle stores mainly serviced the two prisons in town, Castro Castro and San Pedro.

Castro Castro, as Miguel Castro Castro prison was nicknamed, was the smaller of the two prisons, and with 1,400 prisoners, held twice its intended capacity. Prisoners could sleep six to a cell, or in hallways. It was so unsanitary and dangerous that it had been investigated by the Inter-American Commission on Human Rights.

Inmate transports occurred daily, but Joran's arrival in the dusty, squalid barrio was unique. He was heralded by the screeching of sirens atop the twelve security vehicles used in moving Peru's most nefarious inmate. Shopkeepers capitalized on the event selling bottled water, chewing gum, and candy bars to reporters camped at the prison gates. New arrivals already suffering from dysentery chose the bottled water. Stray dogs wandered through the crowd scrounging for food. Freshly washed laundry flapped on wires stretched across rooftops.

Prison guards with modified Russian AK-47 assault rifles provided the first line of security. They stood guard at a series of twelve cement block buildings secured by metal gates and scrolling barbed wire.

The prison was built in the 1980s, originally to house drug-trafficking terrorists with antigovernment agendas. Severe overcrowding in other prisons had changed the population, and now hardened criminals incarcerated for other felonies, such as murder and child molestation, served sentences at Castro Castro. Sanitary conditions were horrific, and tuberculosis and AIDS were endemic.

One of Joran's attorneys referred to the facility as "Dante's Inferno."

Joran complained of a headache as soon as he was inside the gates. A doctor examined him, and determined he was in good health.

Despite the overcrowded conditions, Joran required a private cell for security reasons. He was too high profile and too reviled to be in the general population. The one chosen for him almost adjoined the warden's office.

His cell was a six-by-eleven-foot room with no windows, cement walls painted yellow and green, and a heavy steel door.

In a primitive system of bolt plates and padlocks, the steel door was locked with a key by guards from the outside. Once it was closed, Joran could not see the outside world. A single lightbulb screwed in the ceiling provided light. His cell had a twin mattress on a slab, a sink with running water, and a hole in the concrete floor for a toilet. Rats climbed up through the hole at night and chewed on his clothing.

The only other inmate on the special cell block of ten solitary cells was Hugo Trujillo Ospina, known as "El Payaso," the Clown. The suspected Colombian hitman was accused of strangling a Peruvian businesswoman with an electric cord in 2006. An investigation suggested that the victim's own daughter had ordered the hit. Like the majority of inmates, Trujillo was in a long wait for a trial, a process that often takes five years.

El Monstruo, or the Monster, as he had become known in the Peruvian media, and El Payaso became fast friends, playing cards and watching TV together outside their cells. Joran was adjusting well to prison life, perhaps because of his past experience.

Joran's mother, however, refused to visit. Anita van der Sloot had initially defended her son, telling reporters she believed Joran had been framed. But as more factual evidence emerged, she could not deny he was responsible for Stephany Flores's death.

In an interview with a Dutch reporter for *De Telegraaph,* she maintained her faith in his innocence in the Holloway case in Aruba. "I believed Joran, despite all his lies," she said. "I sensed that he had nothing to do with the disappearance of Natalee Holloway in 2005. He left her behind at the beach. I still believe that's what happened.

"However, I say to you now: he could have killed Stephany. . . . He should have listened to his mother, and none of this would have ever happened."

Fighting back tears, she muttered, "He remains my son, no matter how awful the thing is that he did. I tried to raise my sons right. Two are doing well. One got into trouble.

"It is my wish that he be treated humanely, nonetheless, and that he receive psychiatric help," Anita pleaded. She made it clear that the time had come for her "to let Joran go."

Anita concluded by minimizing Joran's responsibility, saying the press was partly to blame for her son's trouble. She cited Peter de Vries in particular. "If Joran hadn't been so hounded, perhaps that would have kept this from happening," she lamented.

EPILOGUE

As of this writing, Joran van der Sloot remains in a solitary cell at the Castro Castro Prison, awaiting trial. The young jailbird seems to have adjusted well. He claims to be receiving countless letters of support, particularly from female admirers. He is giving English lessons to the guards on his cell block.

Police in Aruba have canceled plans for a trip to Lima for the previously planned reenactment. Because of the number of Joran's false stories, they have decided the trip is not worth the expense or the effort. It would not gain them a break in the Holloway case. The Peruvian authorities seem to have a solid murder case against Joran for the death of Stephany Flores. A conviction for "simple" murder results in a mandatory sentence of fifteen to twenty-five years to be carried out in one of the world's most violent prisons. However, if prosecutors can convince the judge that Stephany's demise was an "aggravated robbery resulting in death," the sentence is much more severe: life in prison.

If Joran is not subjected to jailhouse justice, or the Peruvian court system fails the Flores family, the United States Department of Justice is next in line, ready to try him on fraud and extortion charges. Although their chance to arrest Joran red-handed was an opportunity lost, now the department is prepared.

Joran has received several visitors at Castro Castro, the most newsworthy being Beth Twitty. She came to the prison with a Dutch news crew and Joran's nemesis, Peter de Vries, in mid-September, and she confronted Joran inside the warden's office using hidden cameras. The meeting was emotional, but Beth's attempts to find a compassionate Joran were unsuccessful. He narcissistically responded to her pleas with his own difficulties in talking about the case.

"I hope you can understand also that it is very hard for me to talk to you. It's really not easy. I'm really doing my best," he said in a soft voice. Scanning the room as if hoping to find someone with a pad and pen, he told Natalee's mother to be sure to leave him her address; he would be writing to her soon.

Also since Joran's imprisonment, Captain Juan Callan has been informed that Joran was recanting his confession. Callan was not surprised. Joran had been interviewed by a *De Telegraaph* reporter and told him the confession had been coerced. He described being threatened by the captain, who, he claimed, kept a bucket of water beside his desk, suggesting he would have no problem using it to submerge the young man's head.

When Callan learned of this, he reacted with a chuckle. "I know he said there was a bucket of water next to him, but it's not true," the captain said. "We never wanted to exert any pressure on him. I know from experience that torturing or pressuring a detainee never yields the truth."

Callan also pointed out that with four witnesses in the room during Joran's interrogation, the accusation was baseless.

According to Joran, however, anything he had signed was

now null and void because of police tactics. In fact, Joran bad-mouthed his entire team. His translator, Maurice Steins, was not properly certified; his lawyer, Luz Romero, was a double agent working for the police; Elton Garcia, his poker-playing friend at the Latin American Poker Tour, was an FBI plant used to lure him to Peru, a jurisdiction willing to extra-dite him to the United States. He went so far as to claim that the surveillance cameras at the Hotel Tac had been planted by the feds.

In October 2010, Ricardo Flores broke his own silence. He had dedicated himself to his family's privacy since Steph-any's death. However, his outrage about Joran's pastimes in jail compelled him to speak. He had seen photos and videos of the murderer behind bars, buying marijuana and engaging in good times with other inmates. Ricardo had lost his only daughter, and Joran appeared to be "living like a king" be-hind bars. He told reporters that the Peruvian justice system had betrayed his family.

The worldwide media has not lost interest in the story and a spree that has spanned five years and four continents. As recently as December, a story was leaked about the trea-sure trove of information found on Joran's confiscated black HP laptop.

According to the Peruvian television program *Cuarto Poder,* the laptop's hard drive confirmed that Joran had indeed visited the online European gambling site, Online Poker Stars (www.pokerstars.com), early in the morning of Stephany's death. How much time elapsed between this event and his next Web activity is currently unkown. How-ever, Joran is rumored to have next researched options for routes out of Peru. Stephany would have been dead or dy-ing on the floor of the room while he was Googling on his laptop. The search engine revealed the following queries were made:

- Relationship between the Peruvian and Chilean police

- Chilean border pass
- Buses in Chile
- Countries that do not extradite in Latin America

The poker king had been loose and cold and calculating after his attack on his Peruvian friend. He plotted an escape, he calculated the benefits and risks of various destinations, he fled with a plan, and he expected to avoid justice.

The itinerant gambler still peddles his life story, but his asking price has been raised to $1 million. A ghostwriter on an authorized visit was busted for trying to smuggle in a bottle of vodka. Other than that, Joran isn't left with much to sell.

El Monstruo, still manipulative and greedy, sits in his rat-infested cell. He is still in solitary, but wouldn't mind being in the general prison population. He is not concerned for his safety and doesn't find the isolation for his own protection necessary. He would rather be mainstreamed and partake of the athletic opportunities the other inmates enjoy. The prosecution hopes to begin the trial in the spring of 2011, an incredibly expedited process considering most Castro Castro detainees wait five years. His defense is hoping for an acquittal based on a coerced confession. However, self-defense is an option should the case go to trial.

Natalee Holloway may never be found. But Beth Twitty and Dave Holloway's commitment to discovering her fate is as strong as it is unwavering. Ricardo and Mariaelena Flores have lost their only daughter, but her teddy bears remain to remind them of her. Natalee will never be a doctor. Stephany will never open her own restaurant.

However, El Monstruo is no longer a wanted fugitive. As he awaits his trial, only his future and his personal safety remain in jeopardy.

In March 2011, Joran's lawyer announced that he intended to plead guilty by reason of insanity, thus reducing a possible sentence to three to five years, minus time served. Also in March, U.S. federal agents were in Peru, accessing the Peruvian authorities collected evidence against Joran, including his laptop computer. Hopefully, it holds answers to what happened to Natalee, at least giving peace to the Holloway family.

ACKNOWLEDGMENTS

First, we would like to extend our sympathies to the families of Natalee Holloway and Stephany Flores, whose lives have been irrevocably changed by the unimaginable and senseless loss of their cherished daughters.

To all the friends, family, and associates of the Holloway and Flores families who graciously agreed to speak with us, we extend our heartfelt thanks.

We are grateful to Dave Holloway for permitting us to quietly observe him during his anguished days on Aruba, working with Tim Miller and members of Texas EquuSearch, and for allowing us to shadow him and the family's private investigator, Art Wood, as they worked to piece together clues. Thank you, Veronique Louis, for all your reporting and photographs from this segment. You are a true professional and a good friend.

We would also like to extend a special thank-you to Ricardo "Richie" Flores for introducing us to the Floreses' world.

We could not have written this book without the expert translation services of Cole's wife, Marcela, an Argentine native, and Shannon McKenzie, an American now living in Holland. For months, Marcela and Shannon translated hundreds of pages of police documents and helped us sift through dozens of newspaper articles and television accounts in both Spanish and Dutch.

We also had the luxury of working with linguistic genius Martha Smith, whose objectivity, literary mind, and editorial savvy helped us through many difficult moments.

In Aruba, we would like to acknowledge Mickey John, members of the Mansur family, and attorneys Helen Le Juez and Vinda de Sousa.

In Peru, Peruvian narcotics officer Eduardo Martin Cruz Chavez, Francisco Alberto Pineda Pecart of Platino Tours, and translator Roxana Rolon were invaluable, as were Rosa Deustua Landazuri, Carlos Deustua Landazuri, and Javier Polti Figallo.

Of course, *"¡Muchas Gracias!"* to members of the Peruvian National Police Department. Many portions of this book would not have been possible without the assistance and guidance of Captain Juan Callan Vargas, lead investigator of Homicide Team 2 of the Peruvian National Police Department. Captain Callan took us behind the scenes, made himself available to us over the course of many months, and we thank him for his professionalism, patience, and friendship.

In New York, we would like to thank Steph Watts, Dr. Larry Kobilinsky, Joe Tacopina, and Jean Casarez of CNN. We also extend our gratitude to good friend Teresa Rodriguez of Univision television, whose leads and assistance proved invaluable.

And, a special thank-you to Barbara and Jim Gordon, Jill Fitterling and Tim Hurley. And to Susan Panetta, who tirelessly ran the Pulitzer & Panetta Creative Studio in Lisa's absence.

To our editorial team at St. Martin's Press, Charles Spicer and Yaniv Soha, as well as Heather Florence, John Murphy, John Karle, and Danielle Fiorella, the pleasure was all ours. To our literary agent, Madeleine Morel of 2M Communications, working with you brings out the best in us.

On a personal note, our families always sacrifice so

graciously and we love you for that. To Marcela Rotela Thompson, and Douglas, Francesca, and Juliet Love, hats off!

Authors' Note: While writing this book, we reached out to Joran's Peruvian attorney, Maximo Altez, and attempted to arrange a jailhouse interview with inmate #326390. After conferring with his client, Altez responded. "His mother doesn't think it is a good idea," he told us in a telephone call. "Perhaps after the trial?" he suggested.

INDEX